SPORTS EVENT MANAGEMENT

New Directions in Tourism Analysis

Series Editor: Dimitri Ioannides, E-TOUR, Mid Sweden University, Sweden

Although tourism is becoming increasingly popular as both a taught subject and an area for empirical investigation, the theoretical underpinnings of many approaches have tended to be eclectic and somewhat underdeveloped. However, recent developments indicate that the field of tourism studies is beginning to develop in a more theoretically informed manner, but this has not yet been matched by current publications.

The aim of this series is to fill this gap with high quality monographs or edited collections that seek to develop tourism analysis at both theoretical and substantive levels using approaches which are broadly derived from allied social science disciplines such as Sociology, Social Anthropology, Human and Social Geography, and Cultural Studies. As tourism studies covers a wide range of activities and sub fields, certain areas such as Hospitality Management and Business, which are already well provided for, would be excluded. The series will therefore fill a gap in the current overall pattern of publication.

Suggested themes to be covered by the series, either singly or in combination, include – consumption; cultural change; development; gender; globalisation; political economy; social theory; sustainability.

Sports Event Management
The Caribbean Experience

Edited by

LESLIE-ANN JORDAN

University of the West Indies, Trinidad and Tobago

BEN TYSON
Central Connecticut State University, USA

CAROLYN HAYLE
University of the West Indies, Jamaica

and

DAVID TRULY
Central Connecticut State University, USA

Routledge
Taylor & Francis Group

LONDON AND NEW YORK

First published 2011 by Ashgate Publishing

2 Park Square, Milton Park, Abingdon, Oxon OX14 4RN

711 Third Avenue, New York, NY 10017, USA

Routledge is an imprint of the Taylor & Francis Group, an informa business

First issued in paperback 2016

British Library Cataloguing in Publication Data
Sports event management : the Caribbean experience. -- (New directions in tourism analysis)
1. Hosting of sporting events--Economic aspects--Caribbean Area. 2. Hosting of sporting events--Social aspects--Caribbean Area. 3. World Cup (Cricket) (8th : (2007 : Caribbean Area) 4. Sports and tourism--Caribbean Area.
I. Series II. Jordan, Leslie-Ann.
338.4'791729-dc22

Library of Congress Cataloging-in-Publication Data
Sports event management : the Caribbean experience / by Leslie-Ann Jordan ... [et al.].
p. cm. -- (New directions in tourism analysis)
Includes bibliographical references and index.
ISBN 978-1-4094-1855-9 (hbk) 1. World Cup (Cricket) (2007 : Caribbean Area)
2. Sports and tourism--Caribbean Area. I. Jordan, Leslie-Ann.
GV923.S66 2010
796.06'9--dc22

2010028222

ISBN 978-1-4094-1855-9 (hbk)
ISBN 978-1-138-24591-4 (pbk)

Contents

List of Figures

List of Tables and Appendices

Tables

Appendices

Foreword

This book makes a significant contribution to the understanding of the challenges involved in hosting mega-events like the ICC Cricket World Cup in the West Indies. In 2003, the same World Cup was hosted by South Africa, but matches were played in Zimbabwe and Kenya. There were political ramifications associated with that World Cup which caused some teams to forfeit some matches on the basis of either security or political directives from their home governments. Such problems did not arise in any territory for the 2007 Cricket World Cup. The event marked the entry of the region into the global league of nations that manage and host such events with the legacy items being touted as a major benefit for all—legacy items such as new stadia, high class facilities, introduction of new systems for crowd management, international security management, and the creation of a single regional space for entry to a large portion of the Caribbean.

The book examines many of the economic benefits that may be derived from hosting such events and the challenges of managing anticipated culture clashes between the West Indian way of recreation and entertainment and the demands of the ICC in respect of ambush marketing and security. It appears in hindsight that the West Indian psyche was undervalued in the preparations that were made for the World Cup and that the fear of terrorist insurgents using the World Cup as a forum for their activities weighed quite heavily in the planning.

The fact that India and Pakistan fell out early from the competition meant that a sizeable financial loss was incurred. This had an impact on attendance at games as well as international television interest as Ireland and Bangladesh qualified for the Super Eight stage of the competition at the expense of Pakistan and India. This led to one game at the Kensington Oval in Barbados being played between these two countries as opposed to Pakistan and India. The resultant effect was for the gates to be opened during the course of play to allow spectators to enter the ground for free so that the stands would be filled for the benefit of television viewers.

The issue of hotel room availability was addressed by some regional governments through an incentive programme for accommodating visitors in the homes of residents. The use of tax incentives was unique, but it was an attempt to address possible room shortages, while at the same time allowing the visitors to enjoy local hospitality and a true local experience. Alongside this initiative, were other ones that addressed urban renewal and environmental concerns. The book adequately addresses these issues and provides the reader with a case study approach in respect of Barbados and Jamaica.

The region has learnt many lessons from hosting the 2007 Cricket World Cup. One of the immediate benefits is the fact that the ICC is hosting the Twenty/Twenty

Cricket World Cup in the West Indies during April and May 2010. The facilities and venues to be used are those that were built for the 2007 ICC Cricket World Cup. There is already a virtual template in place for the staging of this event and all of the chapters in this book demonstrate their relevance to the staging of major international sporting events in the region. Indeed, many lessons were learnt in 2007 and mistakes ought not to be repeated.

The book makes a major contribution to the literature on sports management and leisure, in general, and in the Caribbean, in particular. It will be useful for readers in the fields of sports management, hospitality and tourism. Researchers in sustainable tourism and environmental management will find it useful as well. This is buttressed by the fact that it also includes chapters on "Greening of Events" and "Work of the Sports Agronomy Team" which are highly informative. Policy-makers will find this book to be very useful in a general way, but also specifically in the fields of sports, entertainment, hospitality and also in a socio-economic context. There is enough material in the book to satisfy policy-makers for future use and one hopes that regional governments will make this book an essential part of their collection of valuable data and information. The guidance to be obtained is invaluable.

Dr Hamid Ghany
Dean, Faculty of Social Sciences
The University of the West Indies
St. Augustine, Trinidad
West Indies

Preface

Mega sports events such as the Olympic games, the football World Cup or the Cricket World Cup have been highly sought after commodities by countries and cities throughout the world. These events are viewed as powerful tools for both stimulating economic development, as well as gaining international recognition (Hall, 1992; Andranovish et al., 2001; Burbank et al., 2002). Over the past two decades, sports, and the hosting of mega sports events, has assumed a greater role in the economies of developing countries as they attempt to regenerate regional, national and local identities within the globalization process (Holder, 2003; John, 2004). While major sporting events still cater to a core fan base, most organizers realize the market for sporting events has broadened considerably and that many visitors are as interested in the destination as the event itself (Hall, 1992; Emery, 2002).

Most events now borrow from the Olympics event model, incorporating entertainment, culture and other activities that highlight the destination's culture and heritage knowing that today's tourists often use a hallmark or special event as a motivation to visit a new destination. The term "Hallmark Event" now commonly refers to "a recurring event that possesses such significance, in terms of tradition, attractiveness, image, or publicity, that the event provides the host venue, community, or destination with a competitive advantage (Getz, 1997: 5).

Traditionally, the emphasis of these major events has focused on revitalizing urban centers through the creation of new facilities (e.g., stadiums), improvements to the infrastructure (e.g., transportation and hotels), and an increase in tourism revenues (Hall, 1992; Emery, 2002). However, governments and organizers now recognize that these events can have significant impacts on areas outside of the urban center. Many researchers agree that sports tourism can produce significant socio-cultural benefits such as promoting and preserving local culture and identity through the involvement of local communities in the development of events, products and activities (Hall, 1992; Getz, 1997; Andranovish et al., 2001; Burbank et al., 2002; Holder, 2003; Waitt, 2003).

Purpose of the Book

This book originally emerged from a fundamental belief by the editors and many Caribbean nationals, that as often as possible, whenever an opportunity presents itself, the "Caribbean story" must be told. This is especially the case with the topic of this book, the region's hosting of the 2007 Cricket World Cup (CWC).

The lessons learnt from this event need to be heard as they can provide important guidance to those hosting similar hallmark events both within and beyond the region. So, when the Caribbean won the bid to host the CWC, we made a commitment to tell some of these stories. We believe that we have put together a successful collection of regional and international perspectives that highlight some of the strengths and weaknesses of the CWC 2007, including different topics addressing economic, socio-cultural, and environmental impacts. The contributors have made a point of highlighting the event's shortcomings, triumphs, key lessons learnt as well as the best practices, so that our readers, whether they are students, academics, practitioners, planners or sports fans, can use this body of knowledge to enhance and improve future events. It is also our hope that this book will inspire other researchers in the region to tell other Caribbean stories that benefit both our people and people in other regions of the world.

The main aim of this book is to explore sports event management from a Caribbean, small island developing state perspective, using the Cricket World Cup 2007 as a launching pad for identifying best practices and the way forward. The hosting of the event has produced significant lessons that the region and the world can learn from concerning sports event management.

How the Book is Organized

This book is divided into four main parts: Introduction; Event Impacts Assessment; Event Logistics and Marketing and; Conclusion. In Part I, Jordan (Chapter 1), provides the relevant context for the information presented in the following sections by presenting a comprehensive overview of the Cricket World Cup 2007. She highlights some of the major challenges of hosting the event, as well as the potential benefits to the region.

Part II comprises Chapters 2–7. In Chapter 2, Sinclair-Maragh, assesses the socio-economic impacts of CWC 2007 on the hosting Caribbean islands and the region as a whole. Two main objectives of this study were to compare the projected and actual impacts of CWC 2007 and also to assess the future implications of hosting this game in the Caribbean. The findings from this study can be used to provide valuable information to policymakers and event planners regarding the costs and benefits of executing future events of this magnitude.

In Chapter 3, Cumberbatch and Bynoe examine some of the environmental challenges of hosting sports events by evaluating the "Bag Your Own Garbage" (BYOG) programme implemented in Barbados. Given the outcome of this programme, the chapter documents some success factors and a number of measures that could be implemented at sports events in order to minimize negative environmental impacts associated with hosting events.

Chapter 4, by Hayle and Jordan, discusses the issue of utilizing hallmark events as a tool to leverage long-term community, national and regional development. The focus of the chapter is on the micro-enterprise sector with specific reference to community-based tourism enterprises. The authors use primary data collected in 2005 from focus groups conducted in three of the host venues: Barbados, Jamaica and Trinidad and Tobago. The discussion on the impact of sports events on community tourism continues in Chapter 5, as Tyson, Truly, Jordan and Hayle, discuss findings from a follow-up survey conducted in early 2008, to assess what respondents to the 2005 studies perceived did and did not happen regarding recommendations presented in the 2005 report and what factors they thought helped or hindered these actions. This follow-up study addressed ten categories of issues: Research, Legacy Planning, Coordination, Community Tourism/Crafts, Community Tourism/Agro-culinary, Community Tourism/Special events, Community Tourism/Lodging, Standards, Service and Safety, and Environmental Impacts.

Rampersad (Chapter 6) examines issues relating to the socio-cultural impact of hosting sports events. He explores two main factors that might have accounted for the poor local spectatorship during the CWC 2007 in Trinidad and Tobago. First, he discusses what he calls the "McDonalization" of the tournament and secondly, he asserts that the organizers within the region failed to demonstrate a proper comprehension of the historical and contemporary sociology of Caribbean people.

The socio-economic impact of hosting events is the focus of Chapter 7 by McFarlane. Research conducted in Jamaica found that the city's staging of the event can be viewed as shattered hopes—at least in the eyes of residents. The chapter explores a key question: What has the Cricket World Cup done for the city's poorest individuals and communities?

Part III comprises Chapters 8–11. Chapter 8, by Lopez and Chinnery, examines the work of the Sports Agronomy Team (SAT) which was set up to provide consultancy services to the CWC executive on matters relating to pitch and field. The authors critically analyze the programme that was set up to help ensure that cricket grounds selected for play and practice were of the required standards expected for competition at the highest level of the game. The chapter also outlines some of the successes and shortcomings and makes suggestions on possible improvements to be considered in future strategic planning.

Jönsson (Chapter 9) addresses one of the major challenges of hosting sports events: accommodation. The chapter investigates residents' attitudes of the Home Accommodation Programme developed by the government of Barbados to address the accommodation shortage. The study seeks to explore whether differences in attitudes towards the programme exist with respect to various demographic factors such as age, gender, educational level and income. Furthermore, it also seeks to investigate whether frequency of contact with tourists, awareness of the programme, area of employment and perceived obstacles facing the Home Accommodation Programme are related to attitudes towards this initiative. Finally, the chapter identifies factors that are associated with these attitudes, and assesses these outcomes in the context of social exchange and contact theory.

In Chapter 10, White examines the images, signs and symbols surrounding the CWC 2007. the chapter discusses how some of the key organizations involved in staging the mega-event such as the International Cricket Council (ICC), the West Indies Cricket Board (WICB), the Caribbean Community (CARICOM), national governments and their tourist boards, Local Organizing Committees, and the ICC CWC WI 2007 Inc. organized the event and arranged the associated rights to sponsorship, licensing, display of corporate logos, mascots, trademarks and other event branding issues. The national symbolism associated with the 16 teams participating in this key event will be examined.

Turco, Ally and Cox, in Chapter 11, present the findings for research conducted in Guyana, with the aim of developing a profile of international sport tourists to the 2007 Cricket World Cup, in particular, the watching friends and relatives (WFR) market. Little is known about the characteristics of sport event tourists in the West Indies, as this region has not hosted an international event on the scale of the Cricket World Cup and so this research presents some important implications for future planning and development.

In the final part of the book, Part IV, the book closes with a concluding chapter (Chapter 12) by Hayle, Truly, Tyson and Jordan which draws attention to many of the incorrect assumptions that plagued the planning, coordination, organization and management of this event. The authors use examples from this book to illustrate issues at both the macro and micro level that affected the outcome of this regional effort. Most importantly, the chapter underscores the need for long term planning in order to avoid some of the problems experienced from the 2007 World Cup event.

The geographic, socio-cultural and economic diversity of this region make this a unique and important case study. Hallmark events such as this are difficult even under the best of circumstances, but the number of stakeholders and integration issues associated with this regional event offer both researchers and practitioners alike unique insights into the complexities of Hallmark event development and management. This book highlights the need for a more holistic approach to long term planning of similar events.

Acknowledgements

We want to extend our sincere appreciation to all the contributors for their willingness to bear with us on the long journey to getting this book published.

We are especially grateful to the Ashgate Publishing Group for taking on this project. We are also grateful to our families, friends and colleagues for their love, support, tolerance and encouragement.

In the true spirit of Caribbean love and unity, all the royalties of this book will be dedicated to the Haiti earthquake relief fund in an attempt to help relieve the pain and suffering of our fellow brothers and sisters.

Leslie-Ann Jordan*
Trinidad and Tobago, West Indies
Carolyn Hayle
Jamaica, West Indies
David Truly
Connecticut, USA
Ben Tyson
Connecticut, USA

* On a personal note, I (Leslie-Ann Jordan) wish to thank God for his wisdom and enabling power that brought this book project to completion.

PART I
Introduction

Chapter 1
Staging Sports Events:
Challenges and Opportunities

Leslie-Ann Jordan

Introduction

Mega sports events such as the Olympic games, the football World Cup or the Cricket World Cup have been highly sought after commodities by countries and cities throughout the world. These events are viewed as powerful tools for both stimulating economic development, as well as gaining international recognition (Hall, 1992; Andranovish et al., 2001; Burbank et al., 2002). Over the past two decades, sports, and the hosting of mega sports events, has assumed a greater role in the economies of developing countries as they attempt to regenerate regional, national and local identities within the globalization process (Holder, 2003; John, 2004). While major sporting events still cater to a core fan base, most organizers realize the market for sporting events has broadened considerably and that many visitors are as interested in the destination as the event itself (Hall, 1992; Emery, 2002).

Most events now borrow from the Olympics event model, incorporating entertainment, culture and other activities that highlight the destination's culture and heritage knowing that today's tourists often use a hallmark or special event as a motivation to visit a new destination. The term "Hallmark Event" now commonly refers to "a recurring event that possesses such significance, in terms of tradition, attractiveness, image, or publicity, that the event provides the host venue, community, or destination with a competitive advantage (Getz, 1997: 5).

Traditionally, the emphasis of these major events has focused on revitalizing urban centers through the creation of new facilities (e.g., stadiums), improvements to the infrastructure (e.g., transportation and hotels), and an increase in tourism revenues (Hall, 1992; Emery, 2002). However, governments and organizers now recognize that these events can have significant impacts on areas outside of the urban center. Many researchers agree that sports tourism can produce significant socio-cultural benefits such as promoting and preserving local culture and identity through the involvement of local communities in the development of events, products and activities (Hall, 1992; Getz, 1997; Andranovish et al., 2001; Burbank et al., 2002; Holder, 2003; Waitt, 2003).

The main aim of this book is to explore sports event management from a Caribbean, small island developing state perspective, using the Cricket World

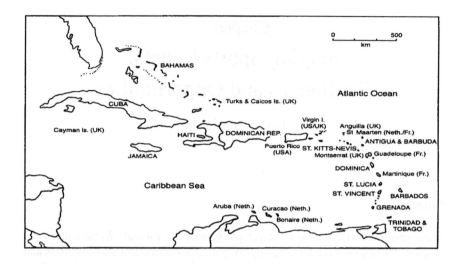

Figure 1.1   Map of the Caribbean Region

Note: Island names in full capitals (e.g., TRINIDAD & TOBAGO) are independent states.
Source: Wilkinson, 1997: 162.

Cup 2007 as a launching pad for identifying best practices and the way forward. The hosting of the event has produced significant lessons that the region and the world can learn from concerning sports event management. In order to provide the relevant context for the information presented in the rest of the chapters in this book, the next section will present some basic analysis of the Cricket World Cup 2007, which was held in the Caribbean from February to April 2007.

Overview of the Cricket World Cup 2007

For the first time in the history of the International Cricket Council World Cup (ICC CWC), the Cricket World Cup (CWC) was hosted by the West Indies (see Figure 1.1). Also, for the first time in any sport, a World Cup was staged in eight independent countries—Antigua and Barbuda, Barbados, Grenada, Guyana, Jamaica, St. Kitts and Nevis, St. Lucia, and the Grenadines, and Trinidad and Tobago—each with its own government, flag and anthem. None of the Caribbean territories hosting a match has a population larger than Jamaica's 3.4 million; most have less than quarter of a million people. Economies are small and infrastructure limited. In order to develop best practices for sports event management in the region, it is first necessary to examine the major challenges and issues faced by these small island developing states (SIDS) as they attempted to host the single biggest sporting event ever in the Caribbean, which was being called a "logistical nightmare" by some. More specifically, some of the key issues to be analyzed include: regional co-ordination and co-operation; challenges with the free movement of people and border control between the islands; the ability of the islands to accommodate and service an estimated 100,000 visitors; safety and security and; strategies to maximize public and private sector involvement. This section will also examine the institutional arrangements and logistical procedures that had been designed to help manage the expected economic, socio-cultural and political impacts of this mega-event. Additionally, it will also document some of the critical success factors that will help determine the overall success of the event.

Cricket World Cup 2007

The ICC CWC West Indies 2007 (ICC CWC WI 2007) comprised a record 16 teams set to contest 51 matches, including 24 first-round games, 24 matches in the Super Eight stage, two Semi-finals and the Final. It officially began on March 13, 2007 in Jamaica and ended on April 28, 2007 at Kensington Oval, Barbados. It was expected that the World Cup was to be seen by over 1.4 billion around the globe, over five continents, by at least 10 international broadcasters.

Whether or not these benefits have been realized depended largely on whether or not the necessary was done in a planned and co-coordinated manner between all the stakeholders involved. According to Donald Lockerbie, the Venue Development Director, "There is no blueprint for putting on a World Cup in eight countries! Nobody has ever done it before!" (Campbell, 2005). Given this background, the main objective of this chapter is to lay the foundation for the rest of the book by providing a brief analysis of some of the major challenges and issues faced by these small island developing states (SIDS) as they attempt to host the single biggest sporting event ever in the Caribbean.

The information for this section was drawn from multiple primary and secondary sources, including: face to face interviews with key stakeholders in Grenada, St. Kitts and Barbados, local government documents, official documents, media reports, national and regional newspapers, Internet resources and other available sources (e.g. speeches, papers, press releases and presentations).

Institutional Arrangements

This mega-event required a regional effort and there were several key stakeholders involved in the event management process: the International Cricket Council (ICC); the West Indies Cricket Board (WICB); the Caribbean Community (CARICOM); National Governments; the ICC CWC WI 2007 Inc.; the eight Local Organizing Committees (LOC); National Tourist Boards and; the general public.

The regional planning and management of the World Cup was conducted by the ICC CWC WI 2007 Inc., which was the company set up by the WICB to manage and deliver the event (*Guyana Chronicle*, 2003a). Headquartered in Jamaica, the ICC CWC WI 2007 Inc. operated as a separate entity and its main responsibility was to "plan and deliver a seamless World Cup that will bring honour and economic benefit to the Caribbean, not only for the World Cup but long after" (Barbados *Nation Newspaper*, 2004). More specifically, their vision statement was:

> To execute the hosting of the ICC Cricket world Cup West Indies 2007 to world class standards in order to achieve the operational requirements and economic and strategic objectives of the WICB and the ICC, in a manner which enhances the international reputation and prestige of the Caribbean and specifically, West Indies Cricket.

The ICC CWC WI 2007 Inc. listed eight key objectives of the event:

1. High Quality Event Management—to demonstrate indisputably to the world the Caribbean's capacity to successfully plan and execute a world class event, specifically world class cricket, and to develop supporting facilities worthy of a global event.
2. Brand Legacy—to ensure an enduring, positive emotional association with the ICC Cricket World Cup 2007 by the international and Caribbean cricketing community.
3. Infrastructure Improvement—to make permanent improvement to the sporting and general country infrastructure in the Caribbean.
4. Widespread Economic Opportunity—to facilitate a widespread, equitable and fair participation in the economic opportunities of the event.
5. Unique Caribbean Promotion—to promote a unified Caribbean as a premier business and tourist destination for all the world's nationalities.
6. Regional Integration—to advance the process of regional integration.
7. High Profitability—to maximize profitability to WICB and member territories so as to secure the foundation for West Indies cricket development, before and after the ICC Cricket World Cup 2007.
8. Enhance the International Popularity of Cricket—to meet the ICC's objective of raising the international profile of the glorious game in the Caribbean, the Hemisphere and the world.

The ICC CWC WI 2007 Inc. had sought to keep the leaders of CARICOM fully informed and involved by partnering with the CARICOM Prime Ministerial Sub-Committee on Cricket, chaired by Grenada's Prime Minister, Dr Keith Mitchell. They recognized that it was principally with CARICOM'S assistance that they would be able to develop world class venues, grounds and practice facilities as well as stage world class opening and closing ceremonies; provide high quality accommodation for participating teams and visitors; put in place appropriate legislation to protect commercial rights; and implement security and anti-terrorism strategies (WICB, 2004a).

At the country level, the planning and management of country-based activities were designated to LOCs, which reported directly to their respective Governments, as well as to the ICC CWC WI 2007.

Venue Selection Process

In order to assist the WICB with assessing venues for the allocation of matches, the ICC CWC WI 2007 Inc. used an Olympic style bidding process to determine the venues. The term "venue" in this case referred to, not just one small geographic area within a country, but to the entire country. In order to select the host venues for the competition, a five-step process was followed:

1. Develop venue development blueprint—the Bid Book.
2. Countries applied or "bid" to host matches.
3. Independent technical assessment by Venue Assessment Team (VAT)
4. Matches awarded.
5. Contracting and monitoring to ensure compliance.

Bid Book

This was the first time in the history of the ICC CWC that a Bid Book had to be developed. The Bid Book was developed to ensure that any Caribbean country could make its bid to be a host venue with the full knowledge of the detailed technical, operational and legal requirements (10). The Bid Book was the culmination of months of collaboration between ICC CWC 2007 Inc., the Venue Assessment Team (VAT), the ICC and Global Cricket Corporation. According to Chris Dehring, Managing Director and Chief Executive Officer (CEO) of the ICC WI CWC 2007 Inc., the 300-page Bid Book was designed to "prepare potential host venues for events of this scale and facilitate selection in a professional, fair and transparent manner" (WICB, 2004b; WICB, 2004c). The Book outlined 24 deliverables, which venues had to be able to achieve to world-class standards. These deliverables included:

1. Cricket stadia.
2. Match day operations.
3. Cricket grounds.
4. Security issues.
5. Medical facilities.
6. Spectator facilities.
7. Finance.

8. Accommodation.
9. Political environment.
10. Local organizing committee.
11. Disaster management.
12. Media facilities.
13. Accreditation.
14. Communications.
15. Marketing support.
16. Immigration and customs operations.
17. Host venue agreement and related legal issues.
18. Transport.
19. WICB Rights/Sponsor Contractual Obligations.
20. Climate and environment.
21. Ambush marketing.
22. Generic event functions.
23. Economic impact assessment.
24. Bid commitment and guarantees (WCSL, 2004; WICB, 2004a).

In an attempt to ensure national support, bid submissions required the endorsement of both the national cricket association, as well as the respective Government, in order to be accepted. As is the case with other international sporting events such as the Commonwealth Games, FIFA World Cup and the Olympics, host venues were required to execute the terms and conditions laid out in a binding host venue agreement, which was a requirement of the ICC.

In total, 12 countries submitted bids: Antigua and Barbuda, Bahamas, Bermuda, Cayman Islands, Guyana, Grenada, Jamaica, Trinidad and Tobago, St. Lucia, St. Vincent and the Grenadines, St. Kitts and Nevis and the United States. These countries were then visited by the Venue Assessment Team (VAT).

Venue Assessment Team (VAT)

The Venue Assessment Team, which is an independent body of international experts who have prior experience in World Championships and Cricket World Cup, assessed each bid. Between May 24 and June 11, 2004, they visited each country that submitted a bid in order to understand first hand the strengths of each ground and examine the challenges that some venues face (*Trinidad Express*, 2004; WICB, 2004d). After this process was completed, the VAT reported the findings and recommendations to the ICC CWC WI 2007 Inc., which then made the allocations of matches that was sent to the ICC for approval.

Finally, eight tournament venues were announced: Antigua and Barbuda, Barbados, Grenada, Guyana, Jamaica, St. Lucia, St. Kitts and Nevis and Trinidad and Tobago. These countries are all considered small island developing states (SIDS) and they are sovereign countries, each with its own government, flag

Table 1.1   Profile of Host Countries

	Area (sq. km)	Population	GDP (US$ million)	Tourist Arrivals (000s)
Antigua & Barbuda	440	71,800	459	236.7
Barbados	431	267,500	2,154	544.7
Grenada	344	101,700	256	128.9
Guyana	216,000	772,200	569	105.0
Jamaica	11,424	2,600,000	6,271	1,322.7
St. Lucia	616	156,000	434	269.9
St. Kitts & Nevis	269	40,400	207	73.1
Trinidad & Tobago	5,128	1,300,000	5,927	398.2

Source: Data compiled from CTO, 2001.

and anthem. None of the Caribbean territories hosting a match has a population larger than Jamaica's 3.4 million; most have less than quarter of a million people. Economies are small and infrastructure limited (see Table 1.1).

Allocation Matrix

During the World Cup, the West Indies, Australia, India and England were placed in four separate groups during the opening stages of the Cup (see Table 1.2). Organizers justified this grouping by stating, "the placement of teams has been designed in an attempt to give a fair breakdown of not just high-quality cricket matches, but give the venues where the matches will be played, a chance to maximize on the fan support of the four countries" (WICB, 2004e). According to Dehring, "We want to spread the ICC World Cup Windies 2007 to as wide a constituent as possible because it is our obligation to this region to make sure that the economic benefits of this is felt by everybody in the region …" (WICB, 2004e).

Teams, matches and events for the Cup were categorized in a multi-coloured allocation matrix. As Table 1.2 shows, there were eight packages awarded:

Table 1.2   Allocation Matrix for CWC 2007

Country	Package	Cricket Team	Venue
Jamaica	*Yellow package* – The Opening ceremony, the Opening Game, the Semi-final and six first round matches	West Indies base	*Sabina Park* Capacity: 16,000 CWC: 30,000 After event: 20,000
St. Lucia	*Blue package* – The other Semi-final and six first round matches	England's base	*Beausejour Stadium* Capacity: 12,000 CWC: 21,000

Table 1.2   *Continued*

Country	Package	Cricket Team	Venue
St. Kitts & Nevis	*Orange package* – Six first round matches	Australia's base	*Warner Park Stadium* Capacity: 4,000 CWC: 10,000
Trinidad & Tobago	*Brown package* – Six first round matches (12)	India's base	*Queen's Park Oval* Capacity: 25,000
Barbados	*Black package* – Six Super Eight/quarter-final matches including three of the biggest Super Eight matches, Final		*Kensington Oval* Capacity: 32,000
Antigua & Barbuda	*Red package* – Six Super Eight/quarter-final matches including three of the biggest Super Eight matches		*Sir Vivian Richards Stadium* – new venue Capacity: 20,000 of which 10,000 will be permanent
Grenada	*Green One* – Six Super Eight/quarter-final matches		*Queen's Park* Capacity: 13,000 CWC: 20,000
Guyana	*Green Two* – Six Super Eight/quarter-final matches (21)(37)(38)		*Providence Stadium* – new venue Capacity: 20,000

Sources: WICB, 2004e; ICC, n.d.

Table 1.3 shows the timeline for the entire venue selection process:

Table 1.3   Timeline for Venue Selection Process

Date	Activity
February 19, 2004	Bid books handed over to representatives of the 13 registered Bid Committee
March 10, 2004	Letters of intent submitted to ICC CWC Windies 2007 Inc.
May 6, 2004	Bids submitted to ICC CWC WI 2007 Inc.
May 24 to June 13, 2004	VAT visits each country that submitted a bid
July 4, 2004	Venues/countries announced
July 13, 2004	Awarding of matches

Infrastructure Developments

It was estimated that a total of US$250 million was to be spent to build eight new stadiums across the Caribbean in preparation for the matches (Hines, 2004; WICB, 2005d) (see Table 1.4). Of this, regional governments were expected to spend a total of US$180 million. Generally, the cricket stadiums in the

Caribbean were in poor shape (WICB, 2002c). They averaged around 15,000 in minimal quality seating capacity against an average of 30,000 high quality seating that was required for 2007. The region had learnt from other countries that have been left with unused mega-structures after hosting mega-events and so additional seating capacity was to be constructed in such a way so that the region was not left with the proverbial "white elephants" when the 2007 World Cup was over (WICB, 2002c). Individual host countries had to invest in their airports, seaports, roadways, hotels, power plants (electricity) and internet (broadband) connection speeds, which had to be on par with the developed world (Pestano, 2003).

However, some of these developments have come with social costs. For example, in Barbados, in order to facilitate the massive restructuring of the Kensington Oval, the government had to acquire houses and relocate local residents surrounding the Oval. Space around the Oval was also acquired to

Table 1.4   Samples of Infrastructure Costs of the Cricket World Cup 2007

Country	Infrastructure Developments	Estimated Costs
Jamaica		US$28 million
St. Kitts	• Upgrade Warner Park	US$15 million
Barbados	• Upgrade Kensington Oval • Modernize highway system	US$90 million
Guyana	• Construct 500 houses that can hold about eight persons each • Contruct a second road to the Cheddi Jagan International Airport (CJIA) • Upgrade CJIA • Construct international hotels at Liliendaal • Beautify landscape in capital city (51)	US$20 million
Grenada	• Upgrade Queen's Park	US$15 million
Trinidad & Tobago	• Upgrade Queen's Park Oval • Security • Upgrade of roads • Entertainment	US$22 million
St. Lucia		EC$35 million

Sources: CaribbeanCricket.com, 2004; *Trinidad Express*, 2004.

facilitate improved car parking, practice pitches and the relocation of some stands that had to be demolished and upgraded (WICB, 2003b).

Challenges of Hosting the Cricket World Cup 2007

It was predicted that the 2007 World Cup would attract an unprecedented number of visitors to the Caribbean, spending more money and time than the current tourist. More than 100,000 visitors, not counting returning Caribbean residents from the United States, Britain and Canada, were expected in the region for a six-week period. They were expected to spend about US$250 million on accommodation, transportation, entertainment, food and beverages and souvenirs. Given these predictions, there were several challenges to hosting this event such as:

- Accommodation.
- Transportation.
- Customs and Immigration.
- Security and Safety.
- Public awareness and public participation.
- Ambush marketing and other legal issues.
- Ticketing and hospitality package logistics.
- Managing event impacts.

This chapter, while addressing all of these challenges, will discuss transportation and accommodation in greater detail as they were considered the two biggest challenges that would affect the smooth running of the CWC 2007.

Table 1.5   Accommodation Supply in Host Venues—CWC 2007

Countries	Number of Rooms
Antigua & Barbuda	3,185
Barbados	6,456
Grenada	1,822
Guyana	730
Jamaica	23,640
St. Lucia	4,525
St. Kitts & Nevis	2,029
Trinidad & Tobago	4,532
TOTAL	46,919

Source: Data compiled from CTO, 2001.

Table 1.6   Accommodation Supply for Host Venues by Room Type—CWC 2007

	Antigua & Barbuda	Barbados	Grenada	Guyana	Jamaica	St. Lucia	St. Kitts & Nevis	Trinidad & Tobago	TOTAL ROOMS
Hotels	2,963	1,942	1,197	—	16,110	2,801	1,503	2,672	—
Apartment Hotels	—	2,309	—	—	—	—	—	—	—
Apartment/Cottages	—	2,019	393	—	—	—	275	—	—
Apartments	168	—	—	—	1,381	1,201	—	—	—
Guest Houses	54	186	232	—	2,417	523	251	945	—
Resort Lodge	—	—	—	86	—	—	—	—	—
Hotel/Guest House	—	—	—	644	—	—	—	—	—
Resort Cottages	—	—	—	—	3,732	—	—	—	—
Condos	—	—	—	—	—	—	—	471	—
Other	—	—	—	—	—	—	—	444	—
TOTAL ROOMS	3,185	6,456	1,822	730	23,640	4,525	2,029	4,532	46,919

Source: Data compiled from CTO, 2001.

Accommodation

At the time, there are approximately 46,000 hotel rooms in the entire English speaking Caribbean (WICB, 2002) and the CWC was expected to draw about 100,000 visitors to the region (see Tables 1.5 and 1.6). The seriousness of the accommodation challenge can be understood by examining the following scenario —if you were to take all the hotel rooms in the entire Caribbean and put them in Barbados, Barbados would still be stretched to host a hypothetical match between England and India.

For example, in St. Lucia they acknowledged that there was a need to increase the island's hotel room capacity from 4,500 to about 7,500. In order to accomplish this, the St. Lucian government announced a special package of incentives for new developments or expansions of properties completed before December 31, 2006 (*Guyana Chronicle*, 2004a). Other host venues had also employed similar strategies to help address the huge deficit between accommodation demand and supply.

There were several solutions offered to try to accommodate the thousands expected for the Competition (CTO, 2005; WICB, 2005f). Some of these included:

- Housing visitors in private homes—this would allow visitors to experience Caribbean culture and culinary skills up close and personal. However, stringent standards must be developed and implemented before private homes can be deemed suitable for international travelers.
- Designating official team hotels.
- Using Cruise ships as "floating hotels".
- Using bed and breakfast homes.
- Using off island accommodation—yachts.
- Accommodating people in one country and transporting them to another on a daily basis for games of their choice.

Ticketing and Hospitality

Cricket Logistics 2007 was chosen as the Official Tour Operator for the event. They were a consortium made up of Gullivers Sports Travel, UK and Hospitality in Partnership UK. Gullivers handled all aspects of travel while Hospitality in Partnership dealt with all facets of match-day hospitality. They were the sole source of commercial tickets that were sold as part of a tour and travel or hospitality package for the event. They manged all travel and accommodation arrangements for participating teams, official and event sponsors, as well as provided for media (WICB, 2005a; WICB, 2005b). As Official Tour operator, they were mandated to appoint a worldwide network of Official Travel Agents (OTA), through public tender process, in consultation with ICC CWC WI 2007 Inc. These OTAs were responsible for the sale of official supporters' packages, consisting of travel, accommodation and match tickets for overseas supporters (WICB, 2005b).

However, there was some discontent amongst accommodation providers in the region concerning the monopoly that Cricket Logistics had. In addition to booking lodging, attractions and transportation, Cricket Logistics was also reserving large blocks of airline tickets and event tickets for these packages. They had also requested that hotels reserve a large percentage of their rooms for their packages but there was some resistance among members of the Hotels Associations in the region, due in large part to the lack of information concerning how these arrangements were to be governed. Hoteliers argued that they were not prepared to turn down their regular guests—and in the case of Trinidad and Tobago, their Carnival bookings—until they are assured by Cricket Logistics that they would be adequately compensated. Some hoteliers also voiced their concern about the fact that if they did not work through Cricket Logistics, they risked not being able to obtain event tickets for their guests.

Freedom of Movement—Transportation, Customs and Immigration

Freedom of movement within each country, as well as between islands was a critical success factor for the event. Sixteen teams had to be housed and moved from match to match over a five week period. So too, did the attendant media and the tens of thousands of disparate supporters. According to one sports journalist, "for anyone who has to endure the long lines, perennial delays and incidents of lost luggage every season when there is just one visiting team in the Caribbean, the consequences of thousands of fun-loving but impatient fans traveling through the region are almost frightening" (Mohammed, 2005: 53).

Given this situation, the burning question had been—How will all these visitors move through the Caribbean and within the venue, given the fact that it is often difficult for regional media workers to travel hassle free through airports while covering regional competitions? (Devers, 2003). Given the expected capacity and the fact that most of the inter-island aircrafts could only carry 50 passengers at one time, it would have been necessary to conduct flights throughout the night for some games, as well as to wet lease some aircrafts, charter others and even use international flights. However, the existing aviation laws in the Caribbean did not allow an aircraft registered in the United States or Europe to fly between Caribbean countries. Therefore, hosting a successful event would necessitate a relaxing of those laws in order to allow foreign pilots to come into the region and fly for that period. It also required that all facilities at designated airports (such as air traffic control, immigration, customs, baggage handling and security) be open all night (Hosein, 2005; Street, 2005). The ICC CWC WI 2007 Inc. had attempted to alleviate some of the inter-island traffic by scheduling games three to four days apart and keeping the "Super Eight" games relatively within the Eastern Caribbean countries. Compounding this issue was the fact that inter-island ferry services barely existed and the three main regional airlines at the time, BWIA, LIAT and Air Jamaica had been experiencing major financial and operational difficulties (Cozier, 2004; Wilkinson, 2004).

Another major related challenge was customs and immigration. Those who travelled through the region for the World Cup had to deal with different immigration and customs procedures in each territory and make at least five currency changes at contrasting exchange rates (e.g. Barbadian dollar, Eastern Currency, Guyanese dollar, Jamaican dollar and the Trinidad and Tobago dollar) (Cozier, 2004; Vice, 2005). The members of CARICOM, along with the ICC CWC WI 2007 Inc., committed themselves to issuing one World Cup "passport" to media and fans throughout the tournament to loosen possible ties of red tape. Other plans included:

- Special system for processing for Teams and Officials.
- Once only immigration processing—machine readable cards.
- Electronic processing: World Cup passport.
- Visa fee waived.
- Departure tax waived.

Additionally, sunset legislation was drafted in consultation with CARICOM and the Attorney Generals of the host countries and was expected to address the movement of people and equipment for the duration of the event.

Security and Safety Issues

In the global climate of terrorists' attacks, the issue of security is of enormous importance, as well as health care and emergency services. Some authors have noted that in the Caribbean, there is a general indifference to safety and security issues and so the greatest challenge was perhaps trying to educate the general public concerning the new "rules" that would be put in place for the event. For example, it was a bit of a culture shock when the World Cup came around and fans who have been accustomed to parking close to the venue or taking in their ice coolers filled with drinks were told that they could no longer do so (Mohammed, 2005). Although people were more aware of their personal safety, it took a special effort on the part of the LOCs' to get them to accept repeated searches at various points entering the venues, as well as again upon entering.

The security and safety of visiting Teams and Officials was also paramount. In the past, teams such as Australia, Sri Lanka and even the West Indies, had complained about missing items from their bags as they passed through the Caribbean ports, as well as the late arrival of luggage and gear (Devers, 2003; WICB, 2003a). In order to ensure the readiness of the region, senior representatives from the police force of all eight participating countries received training on the role and function of security in the execution of an international mega event

(ICC, 2005a). A Security Directorate Seminar held in May 2005 covered issues including emergency evacuation, stadium access, crowd control and anti-social behaviour (*Stabroek News*, 2004).

Opportunities for Hosting Cricket World Cup 2007

Major sports events have the potential to offer significant benefits to any city or destination and the CWC 2007 was no different. In order to garner public support and participation, much was published about the potential benefits of hosting the CWC 2007 in the Caribbean, including:

- Generation of new industries and a stimulus for infrastructural development.
- Creation of employment.
- Creation of government revenue form regulatory fees and taxation.
- Increased sports and recreation facilities for local communities leading to improved social interaction.
- Creation of other economic benefits as visitors arrive and spend money across the society (WICB, 2002a; Holder, 2003; Pestano, 2003).

Economic Benefits

In terms of the economic impacts, there were several estimates of the potential positive economic impact of the World Cup on the region. Some reports claimed that the event would gross an estimated US$300 million over the six-week period, generating an estimated US $500 million in direct revenue as a result of the various activities associated with the game and US$750 million in economic activity (*Trinidad Express*, 2004; WICB, 2002a). Other estimates stated that Caribbean countries stood to earn about US$600 million over the next three years (2004–2007) (Hines, 2004). In the ICC CWC 2007's Master Plan, the measurable goals to achieve economic benefits from the event, included:

- The creation of about 2,000 jobs in each match-playing country;
- The value creation of US$500 million in gross economic impact; and
- External cash inflows of US$300 million (CTO, 2005).

The WICB also stood to earn a hefty sum for staging the event. Andrew Eade, the new International Cricket Council (ICC) Global Development Officer, had disclosed that over a seven-year period, the WICB would earn about US$103 million in television money alone for the month long competition (Davidson, 2002; Spooner, 2003).

In the midst of all these predictions, there were doubts and questions about how much money would actually remain in the periphery. In response to this concern, the ICC CWC WI 2007 inc. developed the Caribbean Economic Enterprise (CEE) Initiative. The main objective of the CEE was to ensure that the people of the Caribbean benefited from the World Cup, not only economically, but also in terms of knowledge, skills and infrastructure (WICB, 2005a). Under this policy, even if contracts were awarded to non-Caribbean entities through the competitive process, they in turn must develop programmes that would benefit Caribbean companies or nationals and show how nationals would benefit both economically and developmentally. As part of the CEE, the only companies that Cricket Logistics 2007 would deal with in the Caribbean would be of Caribbean origin. As a result, it was predicted that many hotels, bed and breakfasts, ground handlers, guides, bus companies, boast and ships in the region would benefit from CWC 2007. The key to this arrangement working efficiently greatly depended on the strength of the partnerships that Cricket Logistics 2007 was able to build with regional and local Tourist Boards in the Caribbean (WICB, 2005b). Such engagements or partnerships would facilitate the objectives of empowering persons within the region and leaving a legacy of local persons with the knowledge, understanding and experience of hosting a world-class mega event.

Socio-cultural and Political Benefits

The CWC was advertised as more than just a mega-event for the Caribbean. It was to be a platform on which small island developing states with the lingering colonial stigma of 'underdeveloped, third world status' could finally prove to the world that they had the expertise, managerial capacity, resources and wherewithal to plan and deliver a 'first world, world class' event. The event was being used as a platform to promote the destination and gain positive publicity for the region; elevate national and regional pride and morale; bring together various elements of the society, public and private sector, to work for the common good of the society; and catapult the calls for greater regional integration (Stabroek, 2002; Holder, 2003). According to Edwin Carrington, CARICOM Secretary General, the CWC 2007 can be used as "… an instrument for grasping opportunities in the globalized world as well as a platform from which to launch the effective integration of the region's economies into the global economy as efficient and competitive players" (*Stabroek News*, 2002: n.p.).

Tourism Opportunities

The CWC 2007 was viewed by the region as a major tourism opportunity. The ICC CWC WI 2007 Inc. had also entered into a partnership with the Caribbean

Tourism Organization (CTO) and had established a Tourism Task Force on the ICC Cricket World Cup 2007. The hotel and tourism sector were admonished to position itself to take advantage of the benefits and linkages that would be created as a result of hosting the games. These linkages included: construction/ renovation of facilities and overall state infrastructure (accommodation, venues, roads, etc.); strengthening the auxiliary and other services; development and promotion of the cultural expressions of the region; marketing of the Caribbean at a global level; strengthening intra-regional linkages at the political and local levels; and increased competitiveness of the Caribbean tourism industry (CTO, 2005).

However, there were concerns that continued negative reports on the Caribbean region would result in the region not being able to fully maximize tourism opportunities. In addition to the service related problems, visitors had also complained about the increase in crime in Guyana, Trinidad and Jamaica and this was another problem that had to be dealt with by the regional governments if the WICB hoped to encourage massive support for the staging of a World Cup in the region.

Private Sector Involvement

Private sector involvement and support was another critical success factor. The region's financial institutions had been challenged to raise the capital needed for Caribbean businesses to exploit the substantial opportunities being offered by the CWC 2007 (*Stabroek News*, 2003). Business opportunities to be created by hosting the event could facilitate much more than internal growth for Caribbean businesses by internationally exposing the best of the region's products and services. However, as Dehring emphasized during his presentation to Caribbean bankers in Montego Bay, Jamaica, "This can only happen if the region's financial institutions consciously develop an understanding of the economics of hosting such a global sports event, and mobilize the debt and equity capital needed to expand their clients' businesses to meet the challenge" (*Stabroek News*, 2003, n.p.).

During his presentation, Dehring also noted that not only larger entrepreneurs would need capital but he also argued that, "We must facilitate the small businesses as well and unleash the creative entrepreneurial energy of the region. There will be a need for an increase in virtually every service area from more taxis to increased and varied food supply and Caribbean banks have a responsibility to grow their customers' businesses to take advantage of the opportunities, while at the same time expanding and strengthening their own portfolios" (*Stabroek News*, 2003: n.p.). Businessmen in the region were challenged to get together with their Caribbean partners within the new CSME to provide on a regional basis, the services, equipment, facilities, accommodation, transportation and other requirements which the organizers would need (*Stabroek News*, 2002).

Community Participation and Involvement

The CEO of the ICC CWC WI 2007 Inc. had said that one of the most challenging tasks ahead was to make the people of the Caribbean understand that "what we are talking about is the ICC World Cup ... this is not the West Indies' World Cup to do what we want and to any standards we choose" (WICB, 2002b). Many authors also noted that the more difficult task to accomplish was the education of the public over sponsors' rights and ambush marketing (Cozier, 2004). For example, it was feared that many West Indians felt it was their right to swig their Mount Gay Rum, Carib Beer or Red Strip Beer in the venue, but in 2007, it would have to be the booze of the sponsor who had spent millions to have its brand associated with the event. If the general public was not fully educated about these issues and if they did not accept the terms of engagement, then the potential for multi-million dollar lawsuits increased, particularly if one country let down the rest of the region (*Guyana Chronicle*, 2003b).

In order to address this issue, the *ICC World Cup Cricket West Indies 2007 Act*, which was the legislation to govern the event was to be drafted and enacted by the middle of 2005 and become fully operational across the region by the end of 2006. as an example, this Act dictated that Kensington Oval in Barbados and its environs would have to be absolutely "clean" of all signage in order for it to be usable as an official stadium (WICB, 2002b). The Act also addressed a range of issues including security, customs and immigration matters, ambush marketing, taxation, events management and other operational aspects of the World Cup. Additionally, the ICC CWC WI 2007 Inc. managed to secure US$100 million of insurance for the event from the international insurance market (WICB, 2005c).

Critical Success Factors

There were a number of critical success factors that would determine the overall success the CWC 2007, including: executive management; collaboration and communication; community participation and involvement; and the creation of BEST practices based on this event. The documentation of these critical success factors was merely a first step in the process of assuring their implementation and making them a permanent part of the event management process. There was also the issue of assuring their effectiveness and use by the appropriate stakeholders who had a vested interest in the success of the CWC 2007.

Critical Success Factor—Executive Management (ICC CWC WI 2007 Inc.)

- Clear prioritization of tasks.
- Use accurate data to support actions at all levels of decision-making.
- Create accountability for all Committees.

- Clarify expectations, roles and responsibilities of all Committees and their members.
- Conduct regular reviews to assure and verify progress.
- Provide timely information to decision-makers.
- Management of critical resources.
- Not allowing politicking to interfere with the accomplishment of event goals and objectives.

Critical Success Factor—Collaboration and Communication

- At the executive level, collaboration between ICC, CARICOM, WICB and ICC CWC WI 2007 Inc.
- Inter-island collaboration between relevant Ministries and organizations
- Public and Private Sector Partnerships between Government Ministries such as Sports, Tourism, Finance, Culture, Planning and Community Development and private organizations such as financial organizations, Chambers of Commerce and community groups.
- Communication of pertinent facts about CWC to the general public on a regular consistent basis.
- Development and dissemination of information.

Critical Success Factor—Community participation and involvement

- Ensure the involvement of communities in the decision-making process.
- Determine the key role of community tourism.
- Public awareness and education—the public's ability to understand and accept the rules of engagement—e.g. ambush marketing.

Critical Success Factor—Best Practices: Learning from past mistakes

- Research best practices from other destinations that have successfully and unsuccessfully hosted mega-events.
- Conduct impact assessments (economic, environmental and socio-cultural) before, during and after the event.
- Facilities must be designed with the relevant expert advice.
- Awareness of the recurrent operational costs.
- Clear and innovative ideas about profit maximization to ensure cost recovery.
- Avoid "white elephants".

Conclusion

This chapter attempted to document the essential preliminaries on the way to fully understanding what was happening in the Caribbean in the lead-up to CWC

2007. It explored some of the major challenges facing the eight host countries as they attempted to put on the greatest Cricket World Cup the world has ever seen. Although the CWC 2007 promised significant socio-cultural and political benefits, the region as a whole needed to find creative solutions to issues related to accommodation, the free movement of people between the islands, customs and immigration, event ticketing and security. Additionally, it quickly became apparent that hosting a successful event depended largely on the support of local communities across the region. Consequently, there needed to be an unprecedented network of information sharing and co-ordination that had largely eluded the region thus far.

It is hoped that this chapter, along with the other chapters in this book, would be used as a launching pad for future research. In particular, there is a need to explore mega-event management in small island developing states on a more comprehensive scale, from both a macro and micro perspective. Further research is needed on topics such as the political economy of hosting the event; core-periphery relationships related to the governance in world sport; power relationships between nation states in the Caribbean; the role of the media; the actual costs and benefits of hosting these events; longitudinal surveys of resident perceptions and; community participation strategies.

This Book

This book is divided into three main sections: Event Impact Assessment; Event Logistics; and The Visitor Experience. In Chapter 2, Cumberbatch and Bynoe examine some of the environmental challenges of hosting sports events by evaluating the "Bag Your Own Garbage" (BYOG) programme implemented in Barbados. Given the outcome of this programme, the chapter documents some success factors and a number of measures that could be implemented at sports events in order to minimize negative environmental impacts associated with hosting events.

Chapter 3, by Hayle and Jordan, discusses the issue of utilizing hallmark events as a tool to leverage long-term community, national and regional development. The focus of the chapter is on the micro-enterprise sector with specific reference to community-based tourism enterprises. The authors use primary data collected in 2005 from focus groups conducted in three of the host venues: Barbados, Jamaica and Trinidad and Tobago. The discussion on the impact of sports events on community tourism continues in Chapter 4, as Tyson, Truly, Jordan and Hayle, discuss findings from a follow-up survey conducted in early 2008, to assess what respondents to the 2005 studies perceived did and did not happen regarding recommendations presented in the 2005 report and what factors they thought helped or hindered these actions. This follow-up study addressed ten categories of issues: Research, Legacy Planning, Coordination, Community Tourism/ Crafts, Community Tourism/Agro-culinary, Community Tourism/Special events,

Community Tourism/Lodging, Standards, Service and Safety, and Environmental Impacts.

Rampersad (Chapter 5) examines issues relating to the socio-cultural impact of hosting sports events. He explores two main factors that might have accounted for the poor local spectatorship during the CWC 2007 in Trinidad and Tobago. First, he discusses what he calls the "McDonalization" of the tournament and secondly, he asserts that the organizers within the region failed to demonstrate a proper comprehension of the historical and contemporary sociology of Caribbean people.

In Chapter 6, Sinclair-Maragh, assesses the socio-economic impacts of CWC 2007 on the hosting Caribbean islands and the region as a whole. Two main objectives of this study were to compare the projected and actual impacts of CWC 2007 and also to assess the future implications of hosting this game in the Caribbean. The findings from this study can be used to provide valuable information to policymakers and event planners regarding the costs and benefits of executing future events of this magnitude.

The socio-economic impact of hosting events is the focus of Chapter 7 by McFarlane. Research conducted in Jamaica found that the city's staging of the event can be viewed as shattered hopes—at least in the eyes of residents. The chapter explores a key question: What has the Cricket World Cup done for the city's poorest individuals and communities?

Chapter 8, by Lopez and Chinnery, examines the work of the Sports Agronomy Team (SAT) which was set up to provide consultancy services to the CWC executive on matters relating to pitch and field. The authors critically analyze the programme that was set up to help ensure that cricket grounds selected for play and practice were of the required standards expected for competition at the highest level of the game. The chapter also outlines some of the successes and shortcomings and makes suggestions on possible improvements to be considered in future strategic planning.

Jönsson (Chapter 9) addresses one of the major challenges of hosting sports events: accommodation. The chapter investigates residents' attitudes of the Home Accommodation Programme developed by the government of Barbados to address the accommodation shortage. The study seeks to explore whether differences in attitudes towards the programme exist with respect to various demographic factors such as age, gender, educational level and income. Furthermore, it also seeks to investigate whether frequency of contact with tourists, awareness of the programme, area of employment and perceived obstacles facing the Home Accommodation Programme are related to attitudes towards this initiative. Finally, the chapter identifies factors that are associated with these attitudes, and assesses these outcomes in the context of social exchange and contact theory.

In Chapter 10, White examines the images, signs and symbols surrounding the CWC 2007. the chapter discusses how some of the key organizations involved in staging the mega-event such as the International Cricket Council (ICC), the West Indies Cricket Board (WICB), the Caribbean Community (CARICOM), national governments and their tourist boards, Local Organizing Committees, and the ICC CWC WI 2007 Inc. organized the event and arranged the associated rights to sponsorship, licensing, display of corporate logos, mascots, trademarks and other event branding issues. The national symbolism associated with the 16 teams participating in this key event will be examined.

Turco, Ally and Cox, in Chapter 11, present the findings for research conducted in Guyana, with the aim of developing a profile of international sport tourists to the 2007 Cricket World Cup, in particular, the watching friends and relatives (WFR) market. Little is known about the characteristics of sport event tourists in the West Indies, as this region has not hosted an international event on the scale of the Cricket World Cup and so this research presents some important implications for future planning and development.

The book closes with a concluding chapter (Chapter 12) by Hayle and Truly which draws attention to many of the incorrect assumptions that plagued the planning, coordination, organization and management of this event. The authors use examples from this book to illustrate issues at both the macro and micro level that affected the outcome of this regional effort. Most importantly, the chapter underscores the need for long term planning in order to avoid some of the problems experienced from the 2007 World Cup event.

The geographic, socio-cultural and economic diversity of this region make this a unique and important case study. Hallmark events such as this are difficult even under the best of circumstances, but the number of stakeholders and integration issues associated with this regional event offer both researchers and practitioners alike unique insights into the complexities of Hallmark event development and management. This book highlights the need for a more holistic approach to long term planning of similar events.

Acknowledgements

The author wishes to acknowledge and thank the Campus Research and Publication Fund Committee, University of the West Indies, St. Augustine, Trinidad, for a research grant that made it possible to conduct primary research in Barbados, Grenada, St. Kitts and Nevis and Trinidad and Tobago. The author is also greatly indebted to all the respondents in those countries who took time out from their busy schedules to share their knowledge and experience with her.

PART II
Event Impacts Assessment

Chapter 2

A Critical Socio-Economic Assessment of the ICC World Cup Cricket on the Hosting Caribbean Territories

Gaunette Sinclair-Maragh

Introduction

The ICC CWC is one of the world's largest events, which attracts millions of persons, not only from the actual attendance to the games but also through the media (www.cricketworldcup.com, 2006). It was indeed an honour for the Caribbean as a region to host this prestigious mega event which was even vied for by the United States of America.

The world's third largest event was hosted in eight Caribbean countries between March 11 and April 28, 2007 (*Sunday Gleaner*, 2007a). *See Appendix 2.1.* The opening ceremony was held at the newly built multi-purpose stadium in Trelawny, Jamaica on March 11, 2007.

Hosting CWC 2007 in the Caribbean was a very unique arrangement especially since the territories are separated by the sea. A lot of planning and investment had to be done in terms of infrastructure and superstructure developments within each of the territories, proper scheduling of matches and transportation, implementation of various policies among other logistic arrangements, all of which were at a high cost.

Likewise, there were many expectations among the residents and the private sectors. It was promised that tens of thousands of persons would be coming to the Caribbean territories to spend millions of dollars and this would positively impact tourism in the region (*Sunday Gleaner*, 2007a). The major concern therefore, had to do with the benefits gained from this event in each of the hosting territory and the Caribbean as a whole.

The main purpose of this chapter was to assess the socio-economic impacts of the ICC CWC 2007 on the Caribbean countries that hosted the event and also the region as a whole. The study aimed at comparing the projected impacts with the actual ones and also assessed any future costs to bear or benefits to be derived. These impacts were assessed in terms of what was proposed, what was actually achieved and the projections for the future.

In order to fully assess the impact of this event on the Caribbean region, the social and economic environmental impacts were critically reviewed. The findings from this study will be used to provide valuable information to policymakers and event planners for the planning and execution of future sporting events in the region.

Many events are termed special events as they enlighten, celebrate, entertain or challenge the experience of a group of people. Sporting events is only one such category of special events. This can be traced back to the ancient Olympic Games which were first held in 776BC in Greece as a religious festival of Zeus, the chief Greek God. These games continued for about 1,200 years and were ended in 393 BC by the Roman Emperor Theodosius. The modern Olympic Games which began in Athens in 1896 and then held in Paris in 1900 are held every four years thereafter in other places (Shone and Parry, 2004). The most recent one was held in Beijing, China in August 2008.

According to McMahon-Beattie and Yeoman (2004), the sporting and leisure industries have shown substantial growth and diversity over the past ten years and are now accepted as a subject on its own. Although the nature of sporting events has not changed significantly, modern games are now a major economic activity. Shone and Parry (2004) noted that the nature of the Greek Olympic Games was basically similar to modern times as they offered social events and a parade of champions after the final day.

There are several ways in which sporting events can impact a destination or community. However for the purpose of this research, only two will be analyzed: social impacts and economic impacts.

Social Impacts of Sporting Events

A sporting event can impact a community or destination through the integration and involvement of the hosting community, especially in terms of planning, organizing and coordinating. Cultural impacts of sports are really not new developments as these activities have been facilitating the interaction of various cultures and subcultures (Shone and Parry, 2004).

Holder (2003) pointed to the role of sports in the social development of all communities. He made reference to the 776 BC Olympic Games in Greece which he noted, created harmony among all and facilitated a treaty where participants to the event could travel unmolested. Apart from technology, communication and tourism, there is probably no other activity that has brought countries and continents together, irrespective of distance, culture and language. Sport not only provides the stimuli for local entrepreneurs, civic leaders and the community but it also brings various levels of the society together such as the organizers, volunteers and entrepreneurs to work towards a common goal (Holder, 2003).

Sporting events should not be imposed upon a community as a means of solving social and economic problems. Shone and Parry (2004) warned that although a sporting event can be seen as a potential for strengthening weak community structures and improving relationships among different ethnic groups, it must not be viewed as a panacea for local social and economic problems.

Economic Impacts of Sporting Events

Mega sporting events are known to stimulate economic growth and development. For example, the Olympics in Sydney (Australia) and Atlanta (Georgia, USA) were linked with the macro-economic development plan of those countries and they proved to have positively impacted business development, trade and investments (JAMPRO, 2006). *See Appendix 2.2 for specific economic impacts on selected countries.*

In addition, Business Clubs are now partnering with mega sporting events so as to benefit from the promotional activities and future business. In the case of the Sydney Olympic Games, Business Club Australia provided networking opportunities and attracted 16,000 visitors by linking to the Commonwealth's Trade Visitors Business Programme. Business Clubs were also successfully linked to the Winter Olympics in Salt Lake City and the Athens Olympic Games (JAMPRO, 2006).

Sporting events can also provide economic benefits to the host country through tourism. In an address to the Caribbean Tourism Organization (CTO) Teachers Forum held in July 2003 in Grenada, Holder (2003), the then Secretary General of CTO asserted that there is a huge synergy between sports and tourism which presents economic benefits, as tourism includes areas such as transportation, the construction and renovation of facilities, tours and use of resorts, and also creates various forms of employment. He supported his argument by referring to the *Sports Travel Magazine* which in 1999 estimated that the sports-related travel and tourism market had an approximate value of US$118.3 billion.

Sporting events are major reasons for infrastructural development which consecutively stimulates economic development. For instance, the 1991 Sheffield Student Games led to the development of Sheffield. Facilities such as the Ponds Forge Pool, the Don Valley Athletic Stadium and the Sheffield Arena were built to facilitate this event. Other developments such as a tram system, the Meadowhall Shopping Centre, a multiplex cinema and other businesses facilitated the economic development of Sheffield. Although the Sheffield Student Games resulted in financial loss, in the long term it has contributed immensely to the development of Sheffield (Shone and Parry, 2004).

In Canada, sporting events are deemed as viable economic activities. However, before a decision is made concerning the hosting of any games, an Economic Impact Assessment (EIA) is conducted to approximate the level of economic activity that will result from the event. This is done by the Canadian Sport Tourism Alliance (CSTA) whose mission is to increase Canadian capacity as well as competitiveness in the hosting of both national and international sporting events. In order to standardize the outputs of the EIA, the following techniques are implemented:

- Using standardized visitor expenditure profiles which include primary data collected by the CSTA from athletes, coaches, referees and spectators and secondary data from Statistics Canada.
- Utilizing a model which was developed and modified by the Canadian Tourism Research Institute to generate estimates of the economic impact realized from the expenditure inputs.

The use of Statistics Canada's "Canadian Travel Survey" data showed on average the daily amount visitors spend at sporting events. As a result of this data, the key measurements used to differentiate visitors' expenditure can be ascertained. These indicators include the individual's role at the event, that is, whether the person was a spectator, participant or media personnel; the distance they traveled; age and length of stay (www.sportandtechnology.com, 2004).

- Governments using money to plan for international sporting events which is otherwise needed for the social wellbeing of the residents in terms of health care and education.
- Benefits not widespread as the SMEs or residents did not benefit economically.
- High Balance of Payments by both governments and business operators.
- SME's losing assets as a result of not being able to service loans used to improve facilities and products.
- Governments may increase taxes to realize funds to pay for money borrowed.

The ICC CWC 2007 games in the Caribbean have been described as a very unique agreement. Dehring (2007a) noted that there have never been any other arrangements like this in other World Cups. Caribbean Leaders were themselves enthusiastic about this arrangement and also perceived it to be the pilot test for the Caribbean Single Market and Economy (CSME). With all of this in mind, the proposed socio-economic impacts of this mega sporting event in the Caribbean will be explored in terms of the following.

Proposed Social Impacts

The United Nations (UN) perceived sport to be very important in improving public health. This notion, however, goes beyond the direct benefits of physical activities as sport is deemed to be a tool to support HIV/AIDS programmes. With these two perspectives in mind, this organization has untaken several initiatives to include the establishment of the International Working Group on Sport for Development and Peace at the 2004 Athens Olympic Games; the signing of a Memorandum of Understanding with the International Olympic Committee (IOC) in 2005 to actively involve sport in the response to HIV (IOC Factsheet, 2008) and the declaration of the year 2005 as the "Year of Sports and Physical Education" (UN News Centre, 2008).

It is therefore not a surprise that the UN Programme on HIV/AIDS (UNAIDS) along with the United Nation Children's Fund (UNICEF) and the Caribbean Broadcast Media (CMB) collaborated with the ICC in designing a promotional programme that focused on children and young people living with and are affected with HIV in the Caribbean. This situation was considered a chronic issue, as in 2006, 250,000 persons in this region were living with this disease, of which a significant amount was among children and young people. It was also reported that 27,000 were newly infected. *See Appendix 2.3* (Unicef, 2007).

In an effort to promote the *Spirit of Cricket and its Positive Impact on Society*, Piot noted that (2007: 1 and 2):

> Sport is a force for change that can break down barriers, build self esteem and teach life skills and social behaviour. By highlighting HIV/AIDS issues, the ICC Cricket World Cup and its cricketing stars are showing exactly the kind of exceptional response needed for the exceptional challenge of AIDS.

With an estimated two billion and more television audience, the activities at ICC CWC in the Caribbean was intended to provide information on the stigma and discrimination surrounding HIV/AIDS as well as information pertaining to the protection against this disease. The four key areas suggested were the prevention of mother to child transmission, increased access to antiretroviral therapy for children and young people who need treatment, education programmes to help prevent HIV transmission and increased support for children who are orphaned and left vulnerable by AIDS (Unicef, 2007).

Piot (2007) also stressed the importance of using this cricket event to inform young people as he believed that they have never known a world that's free from AIDS. This is in sync with an earlier declaration which pointed to the correlation between sport and young people, noting that of the 40,000,000 people living with HIV around the world, a third of them are below age 25 and they either fall in the category of participants or spectators (IOC Factsheet, 2008).

This *Unite for Children, Unite Against Aids Campaign*, as proposed in the HIV/AIDS Caribbean promotional programme, was publicized through public service announcements and the wearing of red and blue ribbons by players and officials from each team during their first and last games (Unicef, 2007). The red ribbon is symbolically used internationally to denote the awareness of HIV/AIDS (Avert, 2008). The blue ribbon usually signifies care, concern and support.

Another intention of the CWC games was to create synergy among the Caribbean countries. In view of this objective, Dehring (2007a) pointed to its legacy in terms of it forging lasting relationships among the eight Caribbean countries. In fact, this unique project could be the most important initiative within the Caribbean region that will strengthen the Caribbean Community (CARICOM) in terms of the following:

- Rejuvenate the objectives of the West Indies Federation which was established in 1958 with a purpose of establishing political union and providing central planning for the development of its member states (CARICOM Secretariat, 2008a).
- Drive the CSME which is an integrated development strategy intended to create one large market among member states so as to benefit the people of the region. This initiative will encourage free movement of labour, capital, goods and services around the region and establish common trade policy and external tariff among other objectives (CARICOM Secretariat, 2008b).
- Further encourage the establishment of the Caribbean Court of Justice (CCJ) which is a regional judicial tribunal court that is proposed as more than a Court of last resort for the member states (CARICOM Secretariat, 2008c).

International relations were also expected to strengthen, for example, the Indian partnerships in Guyana and Trinidad and Tobago were intended to facilitate a cultural connection as many of the descendants from both countries are from India. There are even plans to build Indian Cultural Centres so as to sustain this culture (Caribbean Business Club, 2006a). The assistance provided by the Republic of China in terms of the new stadia was not merely for increasing capacity and providing employment but was also deemed as a means of building the China-Caribbean relationship and stimulate the growth of cricket in China (*Nation Newspaper*, 2006).

Proposed Economic Impact

Although 100,000 persons were expected to visit the Caribbean for the CWC games, the actual flow of money through the region's economies was not known. Estimated revenue from ticket sales, merchandising, television rights, concession and sponsorship stands at US$250 million and visitor spending on accommodation, transportation, entertainment, food and beverage and souvenirs is approximated to be US$250 million (Collis, 2006).

The profit to ICC is estimated to be US$239 million of which US$1 million would be given to each member of the ICC. The rest would be shared among associate members and also to be used for the development of cricket among affiliate members (Murgatroyd, 2007).

It's predicted that the West Indies Cricket Board (WICB) would have made approximately US$20 million through television rights, sponsorships and as hosts of the games. As agreed by the WICB and the territorial boards, 80 percent of the profits will remain with the WICB and the remaining 20 percent will be shared among the six territorial boards, to assist with their development programmes. The WICB is hoping to use the profits to provide direct returns to the host countries (*Jamaica Observer*, 2007a).

Several theories of economic growth and development were proposed for this event. Holder (2003) alluded to Sports/Cricket-Tourism; Marcelle (2004) suggested Cricket and Technology while the Jamaica Promotions Corporation (JAMPRO) then renamed the Jamaica Trade Invests (JTI) proposed Cricket and Partnership.

Holder (2003) believed that there is an economic spin-off from sports. In his effort to explain this benefit, he postulated that the Caribbean is poised for Sports Tourism which is one of the fastest growing niche markets. He indicated that if the Caribbean is to be competitive, it has to diversify its traditional tourism product of sun, sea and sand so as to enhance the product offerings and meet the changing consumer preferences. He also noted that the 2007 CWC games will provide the opportunity for the rest of the world to see the beauty of this region in terms of its people and food, among its other unique assets and this will entice them to return after the games, thereby increasing tourism arrivals to the region. Likewise, Neirotti (2006) (Professor of Sports, Event and Tourism Management at George Washington University School of Business) urged the Caribbean to use CWC to promote Tourism.

At the Special Caribbean Development Bank Discussion Forum, Marcelle (2004) proclaimed that although the Caribbean region is challenged by the many small and open economies which are being impacted by the changes in other societies, the region is to move beyond this status by planning for the ICC CWC with a view of using it for further development.

Marcelle (2004) suggested that the coupling of cricket and technology will allow for greater efficiency and income generation. She pointed to the use of Information Communication Technology (ICT) in providing goods and services to a potential market. She also encouraged the region to ensure both excellence on the pitch and in its use of ICT to advance entrepreneurship through the production and sales of memorabilia to include books, videos, DVDs and digital archives, which could become a sustainable venture for publishers.

In support of the economic benefits that can be derived from the ICC CWC 2007, JAMPRO/JTI also forecasted marketing, trade and investment opportunities for the Caribbean region. In relation to its general mandate in promoting and facilitating investment and export development, this agency initiated the Caribbean Business Club (CBC) which was launched in April 2006. This conception stemmed from the 2005 Legacy Strategy which is intended to accelerate trade and investment opportunities resulting from the hosting of mega sports events such as the ICC CWC 2007 (JAMPRO, 2006).

One of the major aims of the CBC was to enable its members to benefit from business matching services and networking opportunities in the international market. With this in mind, JAMPRO/JTI partnered with CricketWorld.com which was launched in 1996 and is perceived to be the number one independent cricket website in the world, The intention of this partnership was to increase the marketing efforts of the CBC in countries such as the UK, India, Australia and South Africa as these countries are deemed not only to have a love for cricket but also to have strong economies (JAMPRO, 2006).

As a result of this partnership, representatives from the regional private sector, the Local Organizing Committees for CWC and other regional bodies participated in a two day workshop to assess the benefits to be derived from this event. These benefits included new international businesses and employment opportunities. Both the operations of the CBC and the Caribbean Business Opportunity Service (CBOS) were analyzed. The objectives of the CBOS were to identify markets for goods and services for major projects and events in the region, promote trade and partnerships among regional and international businesses and establish high level contacts with the top 100 companies across the region and the top 200 executives from targeted countries outside the region.

The success of Business Clubs linked to the Sydney Olympic Games, the Winter Olympics in Salt Lake City and the Athens Olympic Games were also examined. Feedback from the workshop showed that there was a need for businesses to benefit from the hosting of this mega event in the Caribbean and also to connect with key international business personnel who will be in attendance at the games (JAMPRO, 2006).

CWC 2007 was also perceived by other stakeholders to be highly beneficial to the economic growth of the Caribbean. Whatley (2006) declared that it presented a great opportunity for businesses and the region to promote themselves globally in terms of investment, services and tourism. Bennett-Templer (2006) referred to the extensive reach of CricketWorld.com and its potential in enabling the CBC to market to new and emerging markets. Likewise, Lyn (2006) noted that it will provide an avenue for influential business personnel who are avid cricketers to be able to mix business with pleasure (*Jamaica Gleaner*, 2006).

The organizing committee in the Caribbean also had great expectations. Gordon (2006), (then WICB President), postulated that the economy of some Caribbean countries is poised to benefit by more than US$2 million from the CWC as there is an expected expenditure of US$200 per day by each visitor in the areas of accommodation, travel, food, entertainment and souvenirs.

Likewise, Dehring (2007a) promised that this World Cup would have been the best ever. He believed that there would be lots of visitors spending a lot of money. In fact, he specifically noted that "the CWC will sell Jamaica as it has never been sold before". Gordon (2007) also noted that the profits to be realized from this event would help to reduce the debt burden of the WICB. Rousseau (2007), (former president of the WICB) also cited that it would be good for the region's tourist industry and economy (*Sunday Gleaner*, 2007b).

The economic impacts of the CWC in the Caribbean were also debated. A debating session hosted by the CBC and the Mona School of Business mooted whether or not developing countries benefit from hosting major events. Several panelists believed that that CWC can be beneficial in the long term; it can promote brand Jamaica as well as provide economic linkages with the food and beverage and entertainment sectors (Caribbean Business Club, 2006b).

The Local Organizing Committee in both Barbados and St. Lucia had similar thoughts. It was believed that Barbados will be branded as the 'number one place to visit, live and invest' (Nation News, 2007). The period during the games was also expected to bring full hotel rooms, shopping and other forms of visitor expenditure in Barbados (Barbados Democrats, 2007).

It is estimated that there will be a demand for property in Barbados, either for rental or sales (*Trinidad News Chronicles*, 2007). The executives in St. Lucia had also promised that this would be the best Cricket World Cup (Caribbean Net News, 2007).

Small business operators were also expected to benefit from this sporting activity. For example, the Bed and Breakfast Programme in Jamaica was rejuvenated and expanded as more than 500 rooms were made available for the games and the owners were trained in areas of hospitality by the Tourism Product Development Company (TPDCo). A list of these facilities were posted on the Unique Jamaica website which was linked to the CWC website (*Jamaica Gleaner*, 2007a).

Antigua and Barbuda had a similar accommodation arrangement called the Homestay Programme, which aimed at providing visitors with a local cultural experience. An expected spin off from this arrangement is that persons would return in the future and they would also recommend the destination to friends and families (Caribbean Net News, 2006a).

Full occupancy rate for hotels were also projected. In 2006, the Hilton hotels of the Caribbean (Barbados, Jamaica, St. Lucia and Trinidad and Tobago) had e-marked a considerable amount of their rooms (Haynes, 2006). Likewise, two months prior the games, some hotels were reporting an occupancy rate of 95 percent and this indicator pointed to an expected full occupancy rate by the date of the opening ceremony (*Jamaica Gleaner*, 2007b).

Several craft villages were established in the Caribbean territories. In Jamaica, the "One Love Village" was to be set up at the Cable and Wireless Golf Academy and the National Housing Trust (NHT) car park in New Kingston for the period March 12 to 24. This area was expected to accommodate over 100 craft and food vendors offering diverse Jamaican cuisine and craft respectively (Jamaica Information Service/JIS, 2007).

The airlines had also anticipated an increase in flights. For instance, Caribbean Airlines, the Trinidadian airline company had increased its number of flights by 100 and this resulted in an additional 2,500 seats (Caribbean Airlines News Articles, 2007).

In addition to all of the above projections, Scotiabank in Canada anticipated economic expansion and long-term benefits for the region. This was as a result of an Economic Assessment (2007) conducted which provided more detailed empirical data regarding CWC 2007 games in the Caribbean region. The assessment noted the following indicators as economic benefits to be realized:

- Employment opportunities for more than 10,000 persons.
- Foreign Direct Investments (FDI) valuing US$500–US$700 million.
- Increased visitor spending due to an estimated 100,000 event visitors.
- Positive long term non-traditional tourist markets to include India (Scotia Economic Reports, 2007).

In contrast to the above forecasts, the Scotia Economics Assessment also anticipated that the economic growth rate of the Caribbean region in 2007 will be lower than that of 2006 due to the cost of preparing for the event. A projection of 5.5 percent in 2007 was made, in comparison with the more than 8 percent growth rate in 2006. The costs of preparation included resorts and facility construction; approximately US$500 million was expended for the upgrading of airports, roads, power generation and ICT; about US$300 million on stadium development and another US$40 million on temporary facilities. Scotia Economics also noted that the excess demand for goods and services may result in the increase in prices for transportation, accommodations, food and other services (Scotia Economic Reports, 2007).

The assessment was, however, able to identify a balance of both impacts, as it was suggested that the Caribbean currencies can remain relatively stable over the spring of 2007 due to strong foreign currency inflows and an encouraging macro-economic condition and this will balance the cost of imports for preparing for the games (Scotia Economic Reports, 2007).

The Scotia Economic Reports (2007) also projected the economic impact of CWC 2007 on specific Caribbean territories, namely Jamaica, Trinidad and Tobago and Barbados. *See Appendix 2.4.*

Results

It has been almost three years since the staging of CWC 2007 and many persons had anticipated a rewarding event that would contribute immensely to the growth and development of the hosting Caribbean territories. However, several factors challenged its success. These include:

- High entrance prices (US$25–US$90).
- Poor performance of several teams.
- Death of Bob Wolmer (Pakistan's Coach) in Jamaica.

- High occupancy rates.
- Low hotel occupancy (Barbados Democrats, 2007).

One of the major challenges experienced in this research was the unavailability of current data concerning the impact of hosting ICC CWC 2007 in the Caribbean. Nonetheless the following impacts were ascertained.

Actual Social Impacts

The CWC 2007 games have encouraged communication, coordination and cooperation from the people and governments of the Caribbean. Dehring (2007b) reported that planning for the ICC CWC 2007 games encouraged a spirit of togetherness and unity within the Caribbean in terms of cooperation and getting things done in a timely manner.

The UNICEF-sponsored AIDS projects which facilitated the visit of many of the cricketers and ICC officials to meet affected children in St. Kitts, St. Lucia, Trinidad and Tobago, Antigua and Barbuda, Jamaica, Guyana and Barbados have impacted the lives of both children and adults. This also motivated the media to give much attention to the impact of HIV and AIDS (McClean-Trotman and Dabney, 2007).

AIDS awareness was not only communicated via the electronic media but also in creative ways as was done in Grenada where dance and poetry were performed by children and young people and in St. Lucia where a carnival band comprising of hundreds of children wore shirts with the message "HIV Prevention Begins with You" (Unicef, 2007).

The Indian Government's assistance is viewed as providing multiple benefits. Not only was infrastructure improved and developed and economic partnership established but the local workers were exposed to technical training which they can use to market themselves.

Actual Economic Impacts

The low number of visitors in the Caribbean was disappointing and this impacted some aspects of the plan. For instance, after one week, the 'One Love Village' established in New Kingston, Jamaica was closed down as no one was going there to shop or watch the games (*Jamaica Observer*, 2007b).

However, according to an audited report prepared by KPMG for the ICC CWC 2007 Inc., the tournaments held in the Caribbean had an overall net profit of US$53.9 million and this amount is believed to be the highest in the history of CWC (Caribbean Press Releases, 2008). The sufficiency of this amount now becomes a fundamental factor to consider as the intention was to share the expected US$239 million among members, associates and affiliates of the ICC.

Of the net surplus, US$31.4 million was ascertained from the audited ticket sales; again perceived to be the highest ever recorded in the history of CWC (Caribbean Press Releases, 2008), when compared to the US$22 million realized in England in 1999 and the US$9.7 million achieved in South Africa in 2003 (WICB, 2007). This revenue from ticket sales (672,000 tickets) is an imperative outcome to examine, as the entrance fee of approximately US$90 was criticized as being very expensive, thereby discriminating against the average Caribbean national from attending. Further analysis of this actual amount in relation to the expected US$250 million which was quoted earlier as expected revenue from ticket sales, merchandising, TV rights, commercials and sponsorship shows that ticket sales stands at 12.56 percent of the budgeted income. In order to make a more accurate and pronounced assessment of the worth of the ticket sales in comparison to the other variables, their respective income would be required.

Of the total surplus earned from CWC 2007, the Local Organizing Committees were paid US$29.3 million on behalf of the Caribbean Governments to be shared among hosting countries (Caribbean Press Releases, 2008). The other fundamental question to ask is; can this amount cover the cost associated with preparing for the games?

The remaining US$24.6 million was paid to the West Indies Cricket Board (WICB) of which 25 percent will be given to the territorial cricket boards (Caribbean Press Releases, 2008). Trinidad and Tobago has received US$1.05 million from the WICB as their share of the proceeds (Caribbean Media Corporation, 2008).

Some territories were disgruntled about the payment received. Both Barbados and Guyana challenged the audited reports on the ticket sales. At the time of this research, the Guyanese Government was still owed approximately US$1 million dollar as the sum of ticket sales in that territory was US$2.372 million and only US$1.3 million was paid. Guyana is also claiming US$825,000 for services provided to the WICB and WICB in turn is claiming US$467,000 from Guyana for services provided during the tournament (*Stabroek News*, 2008).

Despite this pending legal issue, the WICB was satisfied with the results of CWC 2007 and was appreciative of the success of the tournament. Gordon (2008: 1) [Chairman of CWC] in the Caribbean Press Releases alluded that:

> We have received an unqualified audit report which shows a very respectful
> financial performance and the maintenance of financial integrity in our operations.
> We have completed our task and look forward to the legacy of our efforts.

In terms of Jamaica, the government invested over US$100 million (J$9 billion) in this event; US$46 million on the reconstruction of Sabina Park, US$35 million on the construction of the Greenfield Trelawny Stadium and US$20 million on "off the pitch" expenses. Despite this high level of investment, the Jamaica Cricket 2007 Organizing Committee sought cabinet's approval in writing off loans of J\$375 million which was secured for administrative purposes. The government was advised by the senate to appoint a commission of enquiry to determine whether or not hosting the ICC CWC 2007 games was beneficial to Jamaica (Order of Business of the Senate of Jamaica, 2009).

Long-term Benefits

Several long term benefits that will encourage economic growth are being proposed. These include the following:

Investment Opportunities

The JTI stated that Jamaica is now positioned to capitalize on the benefits of hosting the CWC (*Sunday Gleaner*, 2007b). With the projected revenue of US\$9 million and a cost of US\$105 million (J\$7 billion), the best option is to depend on long term opportunities.

It is believed that this event will allow Jamaica to attract more than US\$400 million in FDI within the next five years, that is, by the year 2012, in the areas of agriculture, tourism, information technology and filming. In fact, it was also reported that non-traditional markets have already been tapped into, for example India and Canada (*Sunday Gleaner*, 2007b).

India has an interest in investing in the ICT, coffee production and film sectors in Jamaica. The ICT investment will be of a value of US\$120 million. It was noted that the coffee production company will be established in Mavis Bank, St. Andrew (*Sunday Gleaner*, 2007b).

According to the JTI, a Canadian bee-keeping company is thinking of moving its operations to Jamaica and there are 12 overseas companies that are in negotiations with Jamaica producers. In addition, one Jamaican packaging company is negotiating to provide the United States' market with its products and nine other companies have already shipped off goods to overseas markets. On the contrary, sectors such as sports tourism and entertainment are yet to be explored (*Sunday Gleaner*, 2007b).

Income Generation for Small Businesses

It was noted that the ICC CWC did not change the lives of many who had prepared for this promising event. In fact, some persons were left in debt, as they had borrowed money to invest in this venture and vendors had reported a reduction in sales as other persons ventured into the same business with the expectation of earning from the event. It was perceived that this prestigious event was not for the "small man" (*Sunday Gleaner*, 2007a).

Tourism

To date, the ICC CWC seems to have had little or no impact on tourism in the Caribbean. In fact, the Jamaica Tourist Board statistics showed a decrease in stop-over visitor arrival for the months of March and April 2007 to that country. *See Appendix 2.5.* Although there was an increase in the number of visitors from countries involved in the event, it was still not certain if these persons came for the CWC (*Sunday Gleaner*, 2007a). *See Appendix 2.6.*

Even though the 2006–2007 Barbados Tourism season was very successful, it cannot be linked entirely to CWC as the World Golf Championship was also held there in December 2006 (www.totallybarbados.com, 2007).

Economic Diversification

The eight Caribbean countries had invested heavily in infrastructure and superstructure developments. Some new stadia were built and existing ones were renovated (*Nation Newspaper*, 2006). Although this cost could have exceeded US$300 million, it is believed that the opportunities from doing so will be much greater (Gordon, 2006). *See Appendix 2.6 for Cricket Playing Facilities.*

All eight Caribbean territories have benefited from improved infrastructure and sporting facilities which propelled the construction sector, making it the main driver of economic growth. This was evident especially in the Eastern Caribbean States such as St.Vincent and the Grenadines, St. Kitts and Grenada (Caribbean Development Bank, 2006).

It is envisaged that the actual facilities will continue to encourage economic growth. The stadia are proposed to be useful venues for local events and they can also be marketed for international games. Noel (2008) has proposed that the Queen's Park in Grenada be used as a venue to facilitate not only Sports Tourism but also Faith Tourism where religious groups can conduct their activities. This could provide sustainable income for the facility from persons who had visited the island for CWC 2007.

Airports were also renovated. In the case of Antigua and Barbuda they had received assistance from the Venezuelan Government in the sum of US$7.5 million to upgrade the VC Bird International Airport (Caribbean Net News, 2006b).

St. Lucia is not to be left out of this preparation for the CWC games. Among its infrastructural development were the Beausejour Cricket Ground, the Beauejour road network and emergency medical responses (Barbados Advocate, 2007). Traffic lights were also implemented in Guyana.

Despite all the difficulties, the ICC CWC 2007 is professed to provide long-term benefits to the Caribbean. Arthur (2007) noted that although it costs a lot to host the games, the money was well spent and the benefits will be reaped in due course. He also mentioned that the cricket oval in Barbados could not have made back the money in this single event as it was an enormous capital outlay.

Similarly, the Local Organizing Committee in Jamaica predicted that Jamaica will also benefit in the long term. Visitor arrivals in Kingston are expected to increase from 17 percent in 2006 to 35 percent by 2009 (*Trinidad News Chronicles*, 2007).

The sponsors for the event were also optimistic about the long-term benefits to be realized. Scotia Bank which sponsored the Kiddy Cricket across the Caribbean reported success although a quantitative analysis was not provided. Pepsi which sponsored the Television Jamaica (TVJ) CWC Coverage in Jamaica and also raised funds via a road show for the SOS Children's Village noted that the sponsorship was "well worth the effort". Cable and Wireless thought it was too early to ascertain the benefits (*Jamaica Observer*, 2007b).

Although there are expected benefits to be gained, the CWC 2007 games were perceived by others as a high cost for which the opportunity cost may not be able to replace. An assessment by the International Monetary Fund (IMF) revealed that preparations for the CWC have stimulated economic activity in the Caribbean region but at a high cost. The report stated that the building of and refurbishing of stadia and expenditure on other infrastructure has resulted in a debt in excess of 100 percent of GDP at the end of 2006 in the host countries. The IMF pointed out that the high tax concession given to the private sector construction to increase tourism capacity will erode the tax base and advised that the region is not to expect a high gain from this event (Caribbean Comment Wordpress, 2007).

The IMF was, however, not certain about the long term impact. It referred to similar events such as the FIFA World Cup held in Korea/Japan in 2002 and the CWC held in South Africa in 2003, both of which realized a small net positive effect. The IMF was, nevertheless, doubtful as to the economic benefits to be had from CWC 2007. Several factors such as the multiple venues across the region and the time of the games which happened to be during the peak winter tourist season characterized by high occupancy rates were cited as major deterrents to the economic benefits. It is believed that if the region is to benefit from CWC2007, it has to continue its tourism marketing efforts and address the macro-economic issues such as the high levels of public debt (Caribbean Comment Wordpress, 2007).

Methodology

The relevant information for this chapter was accessed through desktop research. This involved the review of published resources, speeches/presentations and statistical data. Additional information was garnered from textbooks, newspaper and various Internet websites.

The Way Forward

Sporting events are major contributors to the economic growth and development of the host country. However, the Caribbean should have done a thorough assessment so as to maximize its benefits. The decision to host any sporting event should be based on empirical data and not assumptions.

The following strategies are suggested for the planning and execution of future sporting events within the Caribbean:

- Conduct a thorough cost/benefit analysis to assess both the quantitative and qualitative implications of hosting a sporting event.
- Do a macro-environmental assessment of the possible impacts of the sporting event on the economic; socio-cultural; political; technological; and the physical and natural.
- environments to ensure sustainable use of resources and lasting and substantial benefits.
- Include the Caribbean residents in the target market and keep the price at an affordable rate by carrying out proper and sound negotiations with the Client.
- Conduct careful negotiations on all other variables with the Client so as to realize full benefit for each hosting territory and the region as a whole.
- Develop a feasible marketing plan for the stadia and other facilities so that they can be marketed internationally.
- Use the ICC CWC 2007 event as a benchmark for other sporting events.
- Establish an agency for Sports Management in the Caribbean, with offices in the territories which will facilitate communication and establish synergy between the sport and tourism sectors; set standards in terms of bidding and negotiating practices and processes; conduct research both locally, regionally and internationally; ensure the high quality delivery of sports event management services; create investment opportunities for all sectors (public and private) and establish targets for the future development of the industry.
- Develop an Economic Assessment Model similar to the STEAM used in Canada. Initially it may be expensive and time consuming but the research has shown that in the long term it is a reliable instrument used to measure the likely success of a sporting event.

Appendix 2.1 CWC 2007 Cricket Playing Facilities in the Caribbean Territories

Caribbean Territory	Name of Facility	New Structure	Renovated Structure	Capacity (Seats)	Cost (US$)
Antigua & Barbuda	Sir Vivian Richards Stadium	Partnered with the People's Republic of China		20,000	
Barbados	i) Kensington Oval	State of the Art	Upgraded with more seating capacity, media and sponsor facilities	28,000	
	ii) 3Ws Oval			3,000 to 4,000	
Grenada	Queen's Park	Partnered with the People's Republic of China		17,000	
Guyana	Providence Cricket Stadium	Partnered with the Government of India		15,000	6 million (Grant) 19 million (Concessional Credit)
Jamaica	i) Sabina Park		Upgraded with more seating capacity and better facilities	21,000	30 million
	ii) Greenfield Multi-Purpose Stadium, Trelawny	Partnered with the People's Republic of China			
St. Kitts	Warner Park Stadium		Upgraded facilities	8,000 Permanent 2,144 Temporary	
St. Lucia	Beausejour Cricket Ground		Upgraded with more seating capacity (8,000 more) and better facilities	20,000	
St. Vincent & the Grenadines	Arnos Vale Stadium (St. Vincent)		Upgraded facilities	12,000	
Trinidad & Tobago	i) Queens Park Oval		Upgraded facilities	17,000	
	ii) Brian Lara Stadium	New Structure		15,000	

Source: www.cricketworldcup.com.

Appendix 2.2   Economic Impacts of Sporting Events on Selected Countries

Country	Sporting Event	Year	Economic Impacts

Georgia, USA	Atlanta Summer Olympics	1996	i. Direct Expenditure (1991–1997): US$1.2 billion
			ii. Indirect Expenditure (out of state visitors): US$1.3 billion
			iii. Employment opportunities
			iv. Multiplier Effect
			v. Infrastructure Development:
			  − Olympic Stadium: US$189 million
			  − Wolf Creek Shooting Range Complex: US$17 million
			  − Lake Lenier Rowing Centre: US$10 million
			  − Centennial Olympic Park: US$57 million

Utah, USA	Olympic Winter Games	2002	i. Economic Output: US$2.8 billion ii. 23,000 full-time jobs for a year iii. Income to workers and business owners: US$972 million iv. New Revenue after Expenses: US$140 million
Hamilton, Canada	Road World Cycling Championships	2003	i. Province estimated economic activity: C$48.3 million (inclusive of C$31.1m for the Hamilton region) ii. Additional economic activity for other regions in Ontario: C$17.2 million iii. These totals are derived from C$19.7 million in combined operations, capital and visitors spending iv. Contribution to the provincial GDP: C$20.3 million 9 (approximately) v. Wages and salaries paid in the province: C$13.9 million (more than 527 jobs). The City of Hamilton, alone totaled C$9.4 million in wages (nearly 410 jobs)

Sources: Humphreys, J.M. and Plummer, M.K., 1995; Holder, J. 2003; www.sportandtechnology.com.

Appendix 2.3   HIV/AIDS 2006 Statistics

HIV/AIDS 2006 Profile	Age Group (Years)	Number of Persons Infected	%
Children	0–14	15,000	6.0
Young Women	15–24	2,750	1.1
Young Men	15–24	1,250	0.5
Others	25 and Above	231,000	92.4
TOTAL		250,000	100

Appendix 2.4   The Scotia Economics Study of Projected CWC 2007 Economic Impacts on Selected Caribbean Territories

Caribbean Territories	Economic Impacts
Jamaica	i. Expenditure of US$100 million (J$8 billion) on Sabina Park and the Greenfield Stadium ii. Expected revenue of US$9 million from ticket sales iii. 20,000 visitors with an expected expenditure of US$26 million FDI of US$400 million (2007–2012) iv. Continued tourism growth v. Reduction in Inflation vi. Economic Growth of 3% (2007–2008) supported by tourism and mining
Trinidad & Tobago	i. Continued economic growth at about 7% for 2007–2008 ii. Expansion in the Tourism Construction and Oil sectors iii. Infrastructure and superstructure developments (hotels and stadium) iv. Expansion of Caribbean Airlines v. Estimated 27,000 visitors
Barbados	i. Total Government Expenditure on preparing for the games: US$150 million to include refurbishing of the Kensington Oval (US$40 million) and the Grantley Adams International Airport ii. Reduced Inflation for 2007–2008 with an expected economic growth rate of 4% iii. Reduction in the Current Account Deficit due to increase tourism revenue

Source: Scotia Economic Reports, 2007.

Appendix 2.5   A Comparison of Stop-Over Visitor Arrivals in March and April 2006/07 for Jamaica

Months	2006	2007	% Decrease
March	167,439	164,547	1.7
April	163,273	150,561	7.8

Source: *Sunday Gleaner*, 2007a.

Sports Event Management

Appendix 2.6   Number of Persons Visiting Jamaica from Selected Countries

Countries	2006	2007	% Increase
Australia	171	835	80
Indians	48	398	88
Ireland		263	69
New Zealand	36	136	74
Pakistan	3	37	92

Source: *Sunday Gleaner*, 2007b.

Chapter 3

Greening of Events: An Assessment of the Bag Your Own Garbage (BYOG) Program

Janice Cumberbatch and Kisandra Bynoe

Introduction

Major events can harm the environment by, among other negative effects:

- Changes in land-use and the destruction of natural environments through building construction, transportation, and other forms of physical development;
- The consumption of non-renewable resources;
- Emissions to soil, air, and water, and the generation of large amounts of waste;
- Contributing to ozone depletion, global warming, and air pollution; and diminishing biodiversity (Roper, 2006: 1).

With growing recognition of this, event managers have responded by incorporating sustainable development best practices into the operations and logistics of the event management process (Katzel, 2007). This has been occurring with increasing regularity since the 1990s, with perhaps the most notable example being the 2002 United Nations World Summit on Sustainable Development, during which the South African Government initiated the "Greening the WSSD" project which aimed to plan, organise, manage and implement the WSSD in a manner that reflected environmental and social best practice (Katzel, 2007). Coming out of this experience the World Conservation Union (IUCN), the United Nations Commission on Sustainable Development, and several partner organizations put together a publication entitled *Leaving a Greening Legacy: Guidelines for Event Greening*, which offers generic guidelines for "greening" major events, complemented by many practical tips and numerous examples.

According to the guidelines, the basic principles of "greening" major events that should be incorporated by the host organization include:

- Environmental best practices—reduce negative environmental effects by employing technologies and behavioural practices that minimize waste, energy usage, and air and water pollution, by utilizing resources sustainably and conserving biological diversity;

- Social and economic development—select options that raise public awareness of environmental issues, involve communities in all levels of decision-making, create local jobs, and stimulate urban economies;
- Education and awareness—communicate and explain greening plans and their benefits with the aim of changing public attitudes and future actions;
- Monitoring, evaluation, and reporting—assess the effectiveness of greening activities before, during, and after the major event;
- Leave a positive legacy—ensure that both the short and long-term impacts of decisions and actions in producing a major event lead to a substantial improvement in environmental sustainability (Roper, 2006).

The report also emphasizes six basic sectoral strategies to be incorporated into the planning and implementation of major events:

1. Waste minimization;
2. Water efficiency and conservation;
3. Energy efficiency;
4. Air, land, and water pollution reduction;
5. Biodiversity conservation; and
6. Social and economic development measures (Roper, 2006).

The global debate which has surrounded the issue of greening events is whether it is a genuine effort at implementing sustainability principles or merely marketing through green washing. In response to this various bench marking tools have been designed to assess the sustainability of these greening efforts. Clearly some efforts at greening events will be more laudable and successful than others, depending on the underlying philosophy and values of the implementing agencies and the resources that are made available to the event. In this case study, Barbados focuses on one aspect of greening an event—the waste management component.

Bag Your Own Garbage

In April 2007, Barbados hosted one of the biggest international sporting events, the ICC Cricket World Cup Final. One of the major concerns at such an event is the garbage that is produced; not only the rubbish that is placed in garbage receptacles, but the litter that is strewn across the venue during the event, and which needs to be cleaned up afterwards. When this garbage is not removed, the venue becomes unsightly, and worse, it eventually gets into and blocks drainage systems and some of it can eventually wash into near-shore waters, where it contributes to the destruction of marine life.

The current population of Barbados is 268,000 people and the amount of garbage generated by Barbadians is increasing annually. In a recent solid waste characterization study prepared by L.H. Consulting Limited for the Sewerage and

Solid Waste Project Unit, it was estimated that in 2005 Barbadians produced just under 35,000 tonnes of garbage. It is forecasted that by 2025, Barbadians will be producing more than 450,000 tonnes of garbage per annum. Contributing to this is the transient population of visitors and cruise ship passengers (L.H. Consulting Limited, 2006).

Not only is the quantity of waste to be disposed an issue, but littering has been a persistent problem that has plagued Barbados for many years. Numerous articles in the local newspapers make reference to increasing quantities of garbage being generated by Barbadians who are also not using the waste receptacles that are provided (Lynch-Foster, 2005; Ejimofor, 2002). In several of the articles there has been an outcry for better anti-litter legislation as well as improved enforcement measures for this legislation (Ejimofor, 2002; Ejimofor, 2007; Bacchus, 2005). One article which featured interviews with several waste management officials highlighted that the problem with enforcing legislation was the inability to identify the culprits after they had littered (Lynch Foster, 2005: 7). There have also been several references to the increased amounts of litter generated during the Crop Over Festival, the failure of patrons to utilise waste receptacles provided at these events and the high cost associated with cleaning up after these mass events (Jordan, 2002; Ejimofor, 2004, Atwell, 2006a; Atwell, 2006b; Wickham, 2006).

Therefore, it was clear that as Barbados prepared to expose itself to worldwide scrutiny during the Cricket World Cup 2007 series, that a plan would be required to address the large volume of garbage that would be generated during the events. This plan would serve to diminish the potential negative aesthetic, social and environmental impacts of excessive garbage. In response to this concern, the Environmental Advisory Team (ENVAT) of the Local Organizing Committee (LOC) for Cricket World Cup (CWC) decided to implement the Bag Your Own Garbage (BYOG) programme. The goal of the BYOG programme was to develop and test a system that would make the patrons of large public events acknowledge and take responsibility for the waste they produce on these occasions. This BYOG required that each patron be given a bag when they enter the venue. The patrons are encouraged to put all of their garbage into these bags and place the filled bags into the waste receptacles provided.

The BYOG programme was pilot tested during five Crop Over Festival events to familiarise the local public with the programme (see Table 3.1):

Table 3.1   Events

Event	Date
The Crop Over Opening Gala	July 8, 2006
Pan Pon De Sand	July 23, 2006
Kiddies Kadooment	July 29, 2006
Pic O De Crop Finals	August 4, 2006
Bridgetown Market	August 7, 2006

The Crop Over Festival is a month-long series of art and cultural shows and exhibitions held during summer each year. Its central focus is calypso, and the festival culminates with the selection of an annual Calypso monarch and a carnival in the streets. The BYOG programme was then implemented at all 11 Cricket World Cup matches held on the island. It was hoped that if this BYOG programme could eventually be replicated at all large events that it could become a norm in stadia cross the island where sports and various forms of entertainment are held.

Dealing with Littering—Individual Change versus Collective Action

Littering is a social dilemma, which, according to Van Vugt (1998) is a situation in which there is a conflict between what an individual *wants to do* and what *should be done* for the good of society. Van Vugt (1998) identified two broad categories of solutions to social dilemmas. There are solutions which are the result of individual changes in behaviour and there are solutions which arise from organized collective actions of groups of individuals (Van Vugt, 1998: 290).

At the level of the individual Van Vugt (1998) suggests that attempts can be made to increase the individual's awareness of the social dilemma since people may not be aware of the damage that results from their actions. Van Vugt (1998) also suggested that strengthening the norms in the social dilemma can impact at the individual level. Anti-social behaviour such as littering is done with a certain level of anonymity; it is difficult to identify the source of the litter thus people feel less accountable for their actions. Van Vugt (1998) argues that if the pro-social behaviour is made salient by members of society then this dictates the action of the individual and yields cooperation (Van Vugt, 1998).

The effectiveness of increased awareness at the individual level is supported by an earlier study conducted by John Schnelle and Associates which showed that appropriate newspaper publicity can effectively control litter (Schnelle et al., 1980). However, this is only short term and in order for there to be continuous control of litter there needs to be constant publicity. Evidence of the strength of social norms is supported by the studies of Reno, Kalgreen and Cialdini (1993) who observed that individuals were less likely to litter if they saw someone else pick a piece of litter off the ground than if they did not (Reno et al., 1993). Forgas and Williams also reiterate this point when they state that "influencing and being influenced by others is the very essence of interpersonal behaviour, and the key mechanism that makes coordinated social life possible" (Forgas and Williams, 2001).

The BYOG programme straddles both the individual change and collective action approaches. By announcing the BYOG programme from the main public address system during the event, and handing each individual a bag for their garbage, the programme sought to make each patron aware that garbage management is a shared responsibility between them who create the waste, and the agency that would eventually remove it from the venue. It was intended to make each patron more conscious of his or her actions while attending the event. Simultaneously, as the group of patrons begin to bag their garbage, each individual who is tempted not to use a bag, but instead to litter, would be going against the requested norm of the event, and would hopefully feel some obligation to conform.

Dealing with Littering—Conformity

Another point in favour of strengthening the social norm is the individual's desire to be accepted by his/her peers. To be socially accepted, people usually have to conform to the social norms of the group or society they need to infiltrate. Conformity is a facet of social influence which causes people to change their attitude or behaviour in order to comply with existing social norms (Baron and Byrne, 2000). The work of Reno, Cialdini and Kallgren (1993) demonstrates the power of the social norm for yielding conformity on the part of the individual.

Reno et al. identified two types of social norms, descriptive norms and injunctive norms (Reno et al., 1993). Descriptive norms describe what is done in a particular setting, e.g., the Crop Over or Cricket World Cup event, and stimulate action by informing people of the effective or adaptive behaviour for the situation, i.e., "place your garbage in the bag provided and put it under your seat for collection". Conversely, injunctive norms specify what is culturally acceptable and stimulate action by the promise of social sanctions (Reno et al., 1993).

This group of researchers found that injunctive norms when made salient were more likely to deter individuals from antisocial acts such as littering. Furthermore, the individuals exposed to an injunctive norm in one setting were less inclined to litter in other similar or different environments (Reno et al., 1993). Descriptive norms on the other hand only functioned in the setting where they were evident. Thus, from these studies, it was concluded that the individuals perception of how others would sanction their behaviour is the more powerful deterrent in gaining acquiescence for pro-social behaviour.

Hansmann and Scholz (2003) in their work which focused on reducing littering behaviour in cinemas also identified the injunctive norm as being a good deterrent to littering. However, these researchers also noted that politely appealing for assistance from the public to keep a venue clean can also be effective in reducing littering (Hansmann and Scholz, 2003). Thus, the BYOG programme was essentially a descriptive norm, designed to stimulate conformity of the patrons assembled in the venues for the Crop Over Festival and the Cricket World Cup series. Research suggests that the extent to which such a programme could extend beyond the venue and impact on daily attitudes and behaviours towards littering is limited.

Pilot Testing the BYOG at the Crop Over Festival

As stated before, the BYOG programme was pilot tested at five Crop Over Festival events:

1. The Crop Over Opening Gala—held in historic Queens Park, it is an open air event at which vendors sell arts, craft and food and there are live performances on stage.
2. The Pan Pun De Sand—a beach side event at which local and regional steel pan orchestras perform. Vendors are present selling food.
3. The Kiddies Kadooment—the children's carnival which commences at a local school and the children parade through the streets to the National Stadium where their costumes are judged. This is followed by the Junior Calypso Competition.
4. The Pic O De Crop Finals—this is the adult calypso competition. It is a night time event held at the National Stadium.
5. The Bridgetown Market—a street fair held on the Spring Garden Highway where arts, craft and food are on sale and there are live performances.

Co-author, Kisandra Bynoe, at that time a post graduate student with the University of the West Indies, was assigned to coordinate the pilot test of the BYOG programme. Prior to the start of the pilot test, meetings were held with all the relevant stakeholders including the Environmental Advisory Team for CWC; the events manager of the National Cultural Foundation (NCF), the agency responsible for Coordination of the Crop Over Festival Events; and the Deputy Operations Manager of the Sanitation Services Authority (SSA), the national agency responsible for waste management. During these meetings, critical elements of the programme were identified and confirmed.

It was decided that the BYOG programme would be implemented by volunteers who would hand out the bags to the public. Since the Local Organizing Committee for Cricket World Cup had a functioning volunteer programme, they took responsibility for providing these individuals.

Discussions with the NCF gave an indication of the quantity of patrons expected at each event, and therefore the numbers of bags that would be required. The bags for the Crop Over Opening Gala were provided by the Local Organizing Committee for Cricket World Cup 2007. Bags for all subsequent events were donated by a local supermarket. The bags donated by this company were the 18x22 bio-degradable shopping bags.

It was agreed that a questionnaire survey would be undertaken to gather information from patrons at each event to learn more about:

- Their participation in the event in progress;
- Their garbage disposal habits at the event;
- Their opinions on the BYOG programme and its components;

- The possibility for their future participation in the BYOG programme; and
- To identify any shortcomings of the programme.

With a total expected crowd of 38,000 persons across the five events, it was decided that a sample of 200 patrons per event, 1,000 in total would be the target for the survey. Unfortunately, due to limited human resources a much lower sample of 474 was achieved. While the sample is too low to be representative of the population attending the events, it still provides an indication of how some of the patrons felt about the BYOG programme.

A number of methods was utilised to increase public awareness about the programme and to gain the public's cooperation. The media was utilised; members of the Environmental Advisory Team appeared on the television programme "Morning Barbados" where they discussed the BYOG programme and its implementation at Crop Over events. There was also an article in the August 4 edition of the *Nation Newspaper* which highlighted the use of the programme at the Pic O De Crop Calypso Finals. Volunteers also shared information on the programme with the patrons as they distributed bags and conducted the surveys.

The Process

At each Crop Over event the following process was undertaken:

- Prior to each event, the venue management was contacted and given information about the BYOG and instructions about the placement of garbage receptacles and the need to empty these bins throughout the event.
- On the day of the event, the site was inspected and photographed prior to the start of the event.
- The site was assessed for placement of garbage receptacles.
- Bags and volunteers for the event were organized and provided by the Barbados Local Organizing Committee for Cricket World Cup 2007.
- Volunteers distributed bags to patrons as they entered the venue and other volunteers roved the grounds of the venue distributing bags to those persons who did not receive a bag at the door or persons who required an additional bag. As bags were distributed, the volunteers briefly explained the programme and what was required of the patrons at the event.
- Two to three hours after the bags were distributed a sample of the patrons was surveyed.
- At the end of the event, the venue was inspected and photographs were taken once again.

This process varied according to the uniqueness of the events' venue, venue management, and the type of people in attendance. For example, the Opening Gala was confined to an enclosed venue. Conversely, Kiddies Kadooment involved more than one venue. The bands assembled at the Lawrence T. Gay Memorial School and travelled to the stadium. Thus the bags were distributed at several points along the route, and the pre-site inspection included both venues as well as the route which would be traversed by participants in the parade of bands.

Achievements of the Pilot Test

There were varied responses to the BYOG programme by patrons at the events. At the Opening Gala, Bridgetown Market, Pic O De Crop Finals and Kiddies Kadooment, persons who were approached by volunteers distributing bags were generally receptive and took the bags. Volunteers observed that persons with children were keen on the idea and requested more than one bag. At Pan Pun De Sand, the patrons were less enthusiastic about the programme and the initial response at the event was low. However, as the event progressed and waste was generated patrons became more receptive with some individuals seeking volunteers to obtain bags. People were generally seen to be utilising the bag for discarding waste, however, there were some persons who chose to use the bag for purposes other than was intended such as placing them on the ground to protect their clothing while they were seated.

Of the 474 patrons who were interviewed at the events, 55 percent had participated in the BYOG programme. However, very few of the remaining 45 percent, only 8 percent, said that they thought that the bag and the programme was an inconvenience. Instead, 20 percent failed to participate mainly because they had not received a bag, and another 13 percent claimed that that they had no garbage to dispose of during the event.

Ninety-six percent of all the individuals interviewed who had used the bags provided, reported that they were comfortable using the bags that they had been given. For the other 4 percent their discomfort was mainly caused by their embarrassment at being seen with garbage; others complained that bag ripped during the event, or that it was perceived to be additional garbage and that it was not attractive.

Table 3.2   Reasons for Not Participating

Reasons for Not Participating	Number of Individuals	% of Total (474)
I did not receive a bag	97	20.4
I did not have garbage	64	13.5
It was an inconvenience	38	8.0
I kept it as a souvenir	12	2.5
I brought my own bag	0	0.0
Embarrassed to take bag	2	0.4

Table 3.3   Sources of Discomfort

Source of Discomfort When Using the Bag	Number of Individuals	% of Total (474)
The bag ripped during the event	2	12.5
I did not want to be seen with garbage	7	43.7
The bag was additional garbage	3	18.7
I did not appreciate being given bag	1	6.2
The bag was not attractive enough	1	6.2
No response	2	12.5
Total	16	100

Ultimately, a reduction in litter was the primary goal and the most obvious benefit of the BYOG programme. Instead of cleaning up scattered food scraps, bits of paper and other miscellaneous matter after the event, the cleaners only had to remove pre-bagged material. This meant that the area was left cleaner than if the bags had not been used. When interviewed the patrons confirmed these benefits, in fact 86 percent of all the respondents were able to identify some benefits to bagging their own waste. For example, 45 percent of the respondents said that one of the advantages to participating in the BYOG was that it led to cleaner public sites. Twenty-five percent of the patrons interviewed also acknowledged that there would be a reduction in public health threats and that there could be reduced environmental risks. Five percent pointed out that there would be less work for the cleaners. In addition to this, some of the patrons who were interviewed said that they found the bags to be convenient; this was a view especially stated by persons who were accompanied by children. There was also the suggestion that the programme could lead to better habits by making persons more environmentally conscious, thus it had some public awareness and education impact.

Table 3.4   Advantages of Participating

Advantages of Participating	Number of Individuals	% of Total (474)
Less litter	216	45.5
Cleaner public sites	216	45.5
Reduced public health threats	123	25.9
Reduced environmental risks	107	22.5
Less work for cleaners	27	5.6
Convenient	10	2.1
Better habits	1	0.2
People are more environmentally conscious	1	0.2
Reduced labour costs	1	0.2
Education and public awareness	3	0.6

A measure of the success of the programme was the number of persons who bagged their garbage at more than one event and the percentage who indicated that they would be prepared to participate in the future. Thirty-three percent of the individuals interviewed were repeat baggers and 86 percent of the entire sample expressed a willingness to participate in the BYOG programme at future events. Thus the BYOG pilot enjoyed some success.

Challenges Experienced During the Pilot Test

The BYOG faced a number of challenges. Many of these occurred because of constraints with the planning and coordination, the volunteer system, site management and public attitudes and behaviour.

Limited Planning and Coordination

To be effective, the BYOG programme required the cooperation of a number of agencies. Although meetings were held with key stakeholders, and verbal agreement was given to the programme, this did not always translate into the commitment of required resources. For example, at the management level the event coordinators agreed that the BYOG could be implemented. However, during the Gala Opening, one of the volunteers who had been stationed at the entrance designated for use by VIPs and performers had to be relocated, because representatives from the event coordinators, considered it an insult to present VIPs with a garbage bag.

Another example of this was experienced with the cleaning staff. The management of the cleaning agency agreed to assist with the programme. However, some of the cleaning staff members were unwilling to periodically empty the garbage bins, a component considered essential to the success of the programme. Indeed, this was only done at the Opening Gala; at all other events this task was ignored.

The Volunteer System

The BYOG programme relied entirely on volunteers. Unfortunately, securing the time and services of dedicated and well informed volunteers proved to be a challenge. Some of the volunteers were only available for a limited time and unable to stay for the full duration of the events. Others were unwilling to perform the duties expected of them because they disliked the tasks. This restricted the amount of bags distributed and the amount of surveys that were eventually completed. As indicated, the sample fell short of its targeted 200 interviews per event, and of those interviewed, 20 percent said that they had not participated in the event because they had not received a bag. This implies that had bags been more accessible more persons would have participated.

It would also have been advantageous if the volunteers for each event had been the same people, since they would have been familiar with the project and how it was being implemented. However, new people were used each time because the programme had to utilise the services of those who made themselves available.

Site Management

Research confirms that the presence of litter will encourage further littering, and at all of the venues there was already some litter present at the sites prior to the start of the event. The cleanest venues were the small area on Spring Garden Highway designated for use by Bridgetown Market and the path chosen for use by the Kiddies Kadooment Bands. By contrast, the National Stadium had a significant amount of litter and other garbage prior to the start of the Pic O De Crop Calypso Finals.

A key component of the BYOG programme was the placement of bins for the collection of BYOG garbage and other refuse. At the Opening Gala there were few bins in the vicinity of the activity areas and some of these bins already contained garbage by the start of the event.

Pan Pun de Sand presented a dilemma because it was held at an open venue and was attended by a massive crowd. To address this, the SSA provided additional bins the majority of which were placed in close proximity to food stalls, benches and picnic areas. However, bins at this event were often obscured by the large number of people surrounding them. Moreover, the SSA did not facilitate the periodic emptying of bins. The Operations Manager stated that with such large numbers of patrons it would have been difficult to drag garbage through the crowds to the skip where bins would be emptied.

At Kiddies Kadooment, a number of the garbage cans were either partially or totally full by the start of the event. Also, there were not enough public cans distributed along the route to the point that some patrons resorted to using cans belonging to private residences or attempted to make their own waste receptacles using empty boxes found along the route.

In the case of the Pic O de Crop Finals, the BYOG team prepared a waste management plan detailing the required number of bins and where they were to be distributed. A copy of the plan was given to the stadium manager during a site visit prior to the event. The LOC consulted with both the National Cultural Foundation and the management of the stadium and it was agreed that the bins on site would be redistributed as outlined in the waste management plan. The stadium manager also agreed that the bins would be periodically emptied by staff under the employ of the stadium.

However, on the evening of the Pic O De Crop Calypso Finals it was observed that bins on site were not distributed as designated in the waste management plan. Moreover, several unused bins were left at the waste storage site for the entire duration of the event. In addition, many of the bins that were distributed on site contained garbage prior to the start of the event. There were also several areas where bin coverage was inadequate. For example, on the grounds by the food tents bins were overflowing with garbage at the end of the event. Bins were also absent in the areas in front of the stage where the crowd was concentrated. In addition to the unused bins by the storage facility there were some bins distributed on site which were being under utilised.

Therefore, despite the implementation of the BYOG programme, most of the venues were still heavily littered by the end of the event. Not surprisingly the stadium after the Pic O De Crop Finals was the most heavily littered of all the venues while the Bridgetown Market area was the cleanest of the venues. It should be noted that these two venues were the dirtiest and cleanest respectively at the commencement of the event.

Public Attitudes, Behaviour and Awareness

Responses to the questionnaire indicate that across the five events, 63 percent of the respondents reported that they had used the waste bins provided at the events for disposing of their garbage. Of the remaining respondents, 25 percent stated that they could not find a bin, or they left the garbage where they had been seated. As many as a third of the sample admitted to throwing their garbage on the ground but no one suggested that they were prepared to take it home with them if they could not locate a bin.

The fact that 86 percent of the people interviewed were able to identify some benefits to bagging their own waste at mass events and that specific examples of these benefits could be suggested, indicates that the Barbadian public is aware that littering is a bad habit with negative consequences. However, despite this awareness, littering is still tolerated and those Barbadians who disapprove of the act do not publicly display their disapproval. Thus, due to the perceived social acceptance of the habit, some individuals continue to litter despite being given the resources to properly discard of their waste, and so the current social norm continues to encourage littering. Indeed, being seen with a bag of garbage is more embarrassing than dropping it on the ground and in some circles it would be socially unacceptable to be seen with a bag of garbage if you are a VIP.

Non-application of Lesson Learnt

Unfortunately, in anticipation of the implementation at CWC, there was no post mortem or planning session at which the lessons learnt could be analysed and these challenges addressed. Part of the reason was the fact that the principal researcher who might have taken the initiative was no longer on the island. Although she left a detailed analytical report, frequently these efforts require a champion who would take the lead in ensuring that they occur.

Implementation at the Cricket World Cup 2007

Following the implementation of the pilot, the BYOG programme was nevertheless implemented at all 11 CWC 2007 events in Barbados:

1. The four warm up matches which were held at the 3Ws Oval at the University of the West Indies, Cave Hill Campus.
2. The six Super Eight matches held at the newly renovated Kensington Oval.
3. The final match also held at Kensington Oval.

The implementation of the BYOG during CWC did not undergo the same level of planning that the pilot was subjected to, because the researcher who had been assigned to coordinate the programme had left for studies abroad. The coordination of the component largely became the responsibility of the Spectator Experience Manager (SEM) of the LOC. The following account of the implementation of the BYOG at the CWC is based on an interview that was conducted with the SEM.

The franchise for waste management for the CWC 2007 was won by Clean Events, an international agency which then sub-contracted a local company in each of the Caribbean nations to undertake the waste management of the stadiums. For each match a simple process obtained:

- Clean Events provided the bags for the BYOG to the LOC.
- The LOC made volunteers available to distribute the bags.

The BYOG met with varied success at the CWC matches. It was actually quite successful at the 3Ws Oval but not so at the Kensington Oval.

Achievements of the BYOG at CWC 2007

The BYOG enjoyed great success during the four warm up matches that were held at the 3Ws Oval at the University of the West Indies Cave Hill Campus. There was little or no litter at the 3Ws Oval. This could be attributed to the small size of the venue which holds up to 2,000 spectators compared to the mega stadia such as the Kensington Oval with a total capacity of 13,300, increased with temporary seating to 27,000 for the purpose of the World Cup, and the low attendance of spectators. The temporary stands comprised about 25 rows of seats, thus the volunteers were able to easily traverse the area and distribute bags. In addition, on many of the match days school children were in attendance and they proved to be very cooperative in using the bags. While the patrons had been asked to place the bags under their seats, they were also quite willing to place them directly in the bins, negating the need for cleaning up after the matches.

Challenges Faced by the BYOG at CWC 2007

Once again the same factors of planning, volunteers, site management and public attitudes and behaviour came into play.

Limited Planning and Coordination

When approached by the LOC, Clean Events readily bought into the idea of the BYOG programme. However, the company did not send a representative to attend any of the planning sessions prior to the start of the games. As a result, the LOC was uncertain about whether they were actually going to implement the BYOG programme. Therefore, when Clean Events produced bags for the BYOG on the morning of the first warm up game, there was somewhat of a scramble to put the volunteers in place to manage the programme. There was also the additional challenge of placing an announcement on the PA system at that first event so that the patrons would be aware that the BYOG was in place. Although the event started at 10:00 a.m., it took until noon for the text of the announcement to be approved and to start being broadcast.

Volunteers

On day one of the first match, some of the volunteers were not accredited and could not be admitted to the venue. This limited the numbers that were available to distribute the bags. Since the LOC had not made provision for use of the volunteers for the BYOG, individuals who had been assigned the responsibilities for seating patrons and assisting in the food areas were given the additional task of distributing bags. Additional bags were placed at the information point of the venue.

At Kensington Oval the amount of volunteers available for bag distribution was further restricted because the majority of them were required at the gates to assist with security. Changes in plans also complicated matters. Initially, patrons were not to be allowed to leave and re-enter the Kensington Oval without the purchase of a new ticket. This meant that once the crowd had levelled off, the volunteers that were no longer required to assist at the gates could have come inside the Oval and assist with other tasks such as the BYOG bag distribution. However, when the decision was taken that patrons would be allowed to leave the stadium at lunch time, the volunteers could no longer be released from the gates. Thus the BYOG operated at Kensington Oval with limited volunteers.

Public Attitudes and Behaviour

Unlike the small and cooperative crowd at the 3Ws Oval, the picture was very different at the Kensington Oval. Here there was a much larger crowd in much bigger stands. For example, the Kensington Stand with thousands of patrons took a very long time to traverse to distribute bags, especially with limited volunteers.

The party stand where people were dancing and drinking was filled to capacity with patrons who had no interest whatsoever in bagging garbage, and bag distribution was not even attempted.

As a result of the pilot test during Crop Over, volunteers learnt that they could not approach just anyone and offer them a bag. For example, they learnt to target people who were already eating because they were looking for a way to get rid of their garbage. However, once the cricket matches were ongoing persons did not want to be interrupted and in some cases were verbally abusive, so the volunteers were reluctant to distribute bags. One volunteer described the crowd as hostile.

The foreign patrons were more amenable to taking the bags, but some did not speak English as a first language and communicating the purpose of the bag and the programme to them was a challenge. On days when school children were present they were targeted as with the 3Ws Oval and they were once again amenable to taking bags and using them for their garbage.

Site Management

Bins were not well placed in Kensington Oval and people left litter everywhere, which made cleaning after each event horrendous. It might have been easier had there been some continuous cleaning during the event, but the cleaning staff who were present tended to watch the games and then clean after the match was finished. The litter and overflowing bin situation was so dire that garbage from one day would still be present at the Oval the next day.

By this time, the Clean Events representatives started attending the de-briefing sessions at the end of each day to defend the efforts of the cleaning crews and to plead for more assistance from the BYOG programme. However, there was little that could be done at that stage.

Recommendations

Research has shown that persons will litter because it is socially acceptable. In places where litter is already present, persons lack a sense of ownership for the litter, i.e., once garbage leaves their hands it is no longer their responsibility. Littering is also considered to be more convenient than finding a waste receptacle and in some cases there is a genuine lack of knowledge of the negative consequences of this action. The absence of adequate numbers of waste receptacles or poorly placed waste receptacles may also contribute to people littering (Eco Recycle, 2005).

As a result of the experience of implementing the BYOG at the Crop Over Festival and the Cricket World Cup events in Barbados in 2007, the following are some recommendations that should be considered to address the significant problem of littering at major sports and cultural events in the Caribbean.

Planning and Coordination

Planning for a programme like the BYOG should occur well in advance of the event at which it is to be implemented. All organizations and agencies whose services will be required should be part of the planning process. This can be achieved through inter-agency meetings or the formation of a committee that comprises all the key players. The roles and responsibilities of each agency should be clarified, consented to and confirmed at these meetings. These responsibilities should be compiled into an intra agency plan which should also contain and account for, the complete list of human and material resources that are required for each event. The required tasks must be communicated clearly to the employees who will work at the event, and it should be understood that full completion of these responsibilities is part of their contracted services.

Monitoring should be ongoing before, during and after the events to ensure that each agency that has been contracted fulfils its obligations.

Volunteers

If the programme is to be implemented by volunteers, then the services of a dedicated number of volunteers who do not have additional responsibilities should be enlisted. The time span of the event should be noted and volunteers commissioned for the entire length of time with the possibility of early relief of their duties, once all their designated tasks have been completed. The volunteers chosen should be well informed about the programme. They should be committed to the programme, its objectives and the completion of their required duties to ensure the successful implementation of the programme.

Site Management

A detailed site plan should be designed indicating how the venue will be laid out and utilised on the day of the event. A critical component of this is the estimation of the number of individuals expected to be in attendance.

Site visits should be conducted at the site(s) of the event, to adequately determine the locations for the bins. This will facilitate the placement of bins in areas where there is expected to be a heavy flow of persons.

An adequate number of bins should be provided for the anticipated number of patrons. Based on the proposed use of the site, the bins can be distributed so that they are in accessible points. Bins should be placed at accessible points which coincide with the movement of people (Eco Recycle, 2005).

The bins used should catch the attention of patrons, i.e., size and colour. Consideration should also be given to the time span of the event; for an event which starts in the day and continues into the night when visibility is low, bins should be brightly coloured or fluorescent to increase visibility under these conditions.

People are less inclined to litter when a site is clean. Therefore, the grounds of the venue should be cleaned prior to the event. All litter should be removed, and all bins and garbage holding facilities emptied. Staff should be instructed to empty bins periodically during large events. To facilitate this there should be a skip on site into which the garbage from the bins can be emptied. Waste management companies should identify and obtain garbage receptacles that can be closed and their contents securely contained so that they can be moved through crowds without causing any discomfort to the patrons or staff.

A reliable supervisor from the waste management agency should be present at the event to coordinate the staff and their activities, as well as monitor the patrons and their disposal practices. Should a need arise the supervisor should be authorised to make changes to the original waste management plan to facilitate the particular needs of the event in progress.

Publicity and Public Awareness

Marketing of programmes like BYOG is needed ahead of the events at which they will be implemented so that the public would know and understand what is expected of them. Publicity for the programme can be incorporated into the advertisements for the events where it will be implemented. This would introduce patrons to the concept prior to their arrival at an event, inform them of their role in the programme and possibly increase participation. It should indicate the important role the public can play in preserving the environment which supports the culture and sports. These public awareness programmes should also focus on educating the public about all the negative implications of littering and on increasing their pride in their environment such that there is no tolerance where litter is concerned.

On the day of the event there should be regular reminders via the public address system of the requirement to bag garbage at the event. Anti-litter signage should be erected to remind patrons that littering is not acceptable. These signs should be placed at strategic points across the venue. These could include entrances and exits, by food selling areas and bathrooms.

National Campaign

It was hoped that the CWC BYOG would become an example for subsequent events. However, there has been no evidence up to the time of preparing this article one year later that it has happened. Greening events in Barbados will require consistent and ongoing effort on the part of the critical agencies to ensure that it becomes part of the planning mechanism for any large public gathering. It was been suggested by members of the ENVAT that a system be put in place whereby persons applying for police permission or any other license to stage an event be required to meet specified garbage management stipulations. Until such a mechanism is in place it will be difficult to make responsible waste management a norm with event patrons. This would have to be bolstered by a well produced advertising campaign using television, radio and newspapers. In this regard, well known celebrities—VIPs, should perform in the campaign to make all Barbadian aware that regardless of social status, sound waste management is critical to individual and public health and that taking environmentally and socially responsible actions is a requirement for all citizens.

Conclusion

The implementation of the BYOG programme during five events at the Crop Over Festival 2006 and the 11 CWC 2007 matches experienced gaps in the planning and coordination, which were then reflected in the inability to secure volunteers and efficiently manage the sites. Nonetheless there was some reduction in litter as well as public acknowledgement of the importance of the programme in raising awareness of environmental and public health concerns. With proper planning and coordination the programme should be continued and implemented at sports and entertainment events across the region. This would reinforce the concept, and familiarise the public with the programme, consequently, encouraging their participation and reducing the litter at mass events.

Chapter 4

Leveraging Community Tourism using Sports Events

Carolyn Hayle and Leslie-Ann Jordan

Opportunity for Change

Countries and cities throughout the world have always viewed traditional hallmark events such as World Cup Cricket as powerful tools for both stimulating economic development and international recognition. Most hallmark events borrow from the Olympic event model, incorporating entertainment, culture and other activities that highlight the destination's culture and heritage. The term *hallmark event* commonly refers to "a recurring event that possesses such significance, in terms of tradition, attractiveness, image, or publicity, that the event provides the host venue, community, or destination with a competitive advantage" (Getz, 1997).

While most observers would agree that local communities have much to offer, they also believe that larger size corporations that have historically controlled most of the tourism industry and government policy makers who have had longstanding relationships with these corporations tend to heavily influence funding allocations for hallmark events. Policies and mechanisms necessary to ensure local community involvement in these events have not been formalized in most areas of the world, including the Caribbean. This provides opportunities for local and regional entrepreneurs along with non-governmental agencies and local communities to develop new strategies to encourage development of community-based tourism activities that will enhance the overall success of hallmark events like World Cup Cricket 2007 and future events.

Chalip (2004: 226) provides some useful information regarding the approach to be taken when entering into negotiations for events of this magnitude:

> The processes through which the benefits of investments are maximized are called "leveraging". In the case of events, leveraging divides into those activities that need to be undertaken around the event itself, and those which seek to maximize the long-term benefits from events. Immediate event leveraging includes activities designed to maximize visitor spending, utilize local supply chains and build new markets. Long-term leveraging seeks to use events to build the host destination's image in order to enhance the quality of its brand or market position.

Given the situation in which the Caribbean finds itself, it seems that leveraging for the long term could have been a useful outcome of World Cup Cricket, had the design, negotiations and implementation been carried out by those who had national strategic planning as their portfolios.

Using Cricket to Leverage Community Development

In attempting to analyse the issues relating to mega events, contentious terms like sustainable development, sustainable tourism, development, modernity and post-modernity are encountered. The associated debates, however, have relevance for any discussion on possible new approaches needed for Caribbean development and more particularly, development resulting from Caribbean tourism. For the Governments of the Caribbean, World Cup Cricket 2007 presented an opportunity for educating all stakeholders about tourism, community-based tourism and the need for a comprehensive policy approache for negotiating and hosting Hallmark events on a continuous basis.

Community tourism, community-based tourism, eco-tourism and rural tourism are all used interchangeably throughout the Caribbean. For the purpose of this chapter, community tourism means community-based tourism. That is, tourism based businesses conducted at the community level. A cursory review of the Caribbean's varied tourism products will provide a deeper understanding of the possibilities for economic development using micro-enterprise based tourism products as the vehicle. The *Caribbean Tourism Organization* (CTO) has identified *eight* sectors that comprise the tourism sector. As Table 4.1 illustrates, any one or combination of these sectors can form (a) community-based tourism product(s).

Within each of these sectors there are opportunities for small and medium enterprise development. The overarching benefit from including these sectors is that the wealth from tourism would be more widely spread. Development of these sectors could lead to the strategic creation of series of growth clusters. All of which could possibly be poised to supply goods and services to the foreign direct investment and other elements within the tourism sector. In turn, this would lead to simultaneous strengthening of several industries, the possible spawning new industries and containment of leakage.

Linking Community Development with International Trade

Community-based tourism, therefore, is one of a combination of tourism products offered at a community-level to domestic or international visitors. In the Caribbean context, *community-based tourism* usually refers to visitor interaction with local people in the rural areas outside of the traditional resort areas. *Community-based tourism* does not mean that the rules that apply to traditional tourism sectors are to be ignored. The principles of health and safety for visitors drive tourism regardless

Table 4.1   Tourism Sectors

Tourism Sectors	Description
Accommodation	Within the accommodation sector there are large, medium and small hotels, as well as non-hotel accommodation such as villas, bed and breakfast establishments, and campsites.
Food and Beverage	This sub-sector can be viewed either as a support sector or as a major attraction. In the category of food and beverage there are restaurants, coffee shops, dining rooms, fast food outlets, pubs, lounges, nightclubs, cabarets, catering establishments and specialty shops.
Adventure Tourism	This category includes air carriers, golf/tennis facilities, parks, fishing facilities, cruise lines, hunting facilities, car rentals, adventure tourism, recreational vehicles, marine facilities and taxis.
Transportation	CTO identified air carriers, bus and tour companies, cruise lines, car rentals, recreational vehicles, taxis, and gas stations as a part of this sub-sector.
Attractions	This sub-sector holds the key to raising self-esteem and national pride for every destination. This sub-sector comprises museums, galleries, heritage/historical sites and parks, gardens, amusement/recreation parks, interpretive centres and native/cultural/industrial/eco-tourism.
Travel Trade	This includes travel agencies, tour wholesalers, tour operators and tour guides.
Events and Conferences	Included in this sector are special events/carnival/cricket, meetings/conferences/conventions, festivals, trade shows/ marketplaces, fairs and exhibitions. This is the sector into which Hallmark events fall.
Tourism Services	This sub-sector includes Government Tourism Departments, Information Centres, Research Services, Reservation Services, Advertising Agencies, Trade Press, Marketing, Professional Associations, Consultants, Tourism Educators, Tourism Suppliers and Retail Operations.

Source: Adapted from CTO, 1999: 20.

of the setting in which the product is offered. The issue of the standards of tourism product development was raised several times during this research.

Community-based tourism, however, seems to offer a unique opportunity for the Caribbean. The process of community-based tourism development, if managed effectively, has the potential to alleviate poverty and illiteracy. Community-based tourism also has the potential to develop the natural creative energy of Caribbean people by transforming average citizens into entrepreneurs, developing strong partnerships by twinning existing traditional tourism entrepreneurs with aspiring non-traditional tourism entrepreneurs and by combining with the existing tourism product offerings to create a uniquely Caribbean experience. Community-based tourism can be a stand-alone venture or a partnership of the traditional and the non-traditional products blended with natural Caribbean charm, culture and heritage to create a community tourism spirit that culminates in a truly Caribbean experience. In fact, it provides the platform to positively address poverty reduction, economic growth, and biodiversity conservation, as well as to meet the objectives of the UN Millennium Development Goals (MDGs) (WTO, 2004).

The need to make the link between community-based tourism products (micro-enterprise development), the tourism system and the general health of Caribbean nations does not appear to have been effectively established nor was it being actively pursued during the initial World Cup Cricket 2007 negotiations.

Research Methodology

In 2005, qualitative research was conducted by the University of the West Indies and the Central Connecticut State University in Barbados, Jamaica and Trinidad and Tobago in an effort to determine the likely long-term opportunities for the region as a consequence of hosting the World Cup Cricket 2007. The focus of the research was on the micro-enterprise sector, more particularly community-based tourism enterprises.

This chapter uses qualitative and exploratory approaches in the form of focus groups, personal interviews and desk analyses to determine the many and varied issues associated with hallmark events in the Caribbean, in this case World Cup Cricket 2007. It then seeks to link these issues with Caribbean development for the purpose of highlighting possible opportunities, beyond cricket, for creating strategic approaches to international trade based on the natural environment and talents of Caribbean people. In other words, identifying the potential role to be played by Hallmark Events in leveraging for long term development in the Caribbean.

The following data gathering techniques were used in Barbados, Jamaica and Trinidad and Tobago:

a. Two-hour interviews with:
    *   Two chief administrators of World Cup Barbados, Inc. (the country's organizing association);
    *   The Marketing Manager of Windies Cricket (headquarters for West Indies World Cup Cricket); and
    *   Three chief administrators of the Trinidad and Tobago Local Organizing Committee (for World Cup Cricket 2007).
b. Three two-hour interviews with tour/attraction operators and with owner operators of three retail enterprises (restaurants and art gallery).
c. Three two-hour focus groups with:
    *   Community development NGOs, community tourism specialists, small business associations;
    *   Accommodations representatives;

- Retail enterprises;
- Tour/attraction operators;
- Food and beverage and other retail enterprises;
- Government tourism specialists, small business development company.

The following issues were addressed in the interviews and focus groups:

- Opportunities for developing new community tourism offerings or enhancing existing offerings.
- Facilitating factors.
- Barriers.

The research findings led to areas that were not contemplated at the outset but are significant for the Caribbean. For example, it became evident that World Cup Cricket, for the Caribbean, was more about leveraging long term trade negotiations than about sports. Though not deliberate, Trinidad's approach supports this idea. This is a significant finding given the fact that most if not all contracts for World Cup Cricket were entered into on the premise of increasing tourism numbers than about long-term trade benefits. The opportunity for leveraging does not appear to have been considered when World Cup Cricket 2007 was approved.

Background

Music, sport and a free spirit are the defining characteristics of a blue blooded West Indian. Add to that, good food and free flowing liquid spirits and the ingredients are ideal for a good sporting event. Every year in early spring, anticipation runs high in the Caribbean as test match, after test match is played, analyzed and debated. That is a product of a former British colony. The West Indies cricket team is comprised of players from the English-speaking Caribbean and Guyana on the South American mainland. In recent years, however, cricket like several other sports has moved from simply being a reason for relaxation and debate to what is known in tourism circles as a hallmark event.

Traditionally, the benefits derived from these events were channeled into revitalizing urban centres through the creation of new facilities, improvements to the infrastructure, and an increase in tourism revenues. Governments and organizers now recognize that many of today's visitors view these events as a means to explore the destination and to experience local culture and heritage. Consequently, most tourism specialists now agree that sports tourism can also strengthen a country's national and cultural identity by involving local communities in the development of events and activities that are of interest to today's travelers. However, this goal can only be achieved by strategic design.

World Cup Cricket, organized by the International Cricket Council, was started in 1975 and is held every four years. After a competitive venue selection process, the Caribbean was selected to host the ninth championship tournament in 2007. There were 16 qualifying teams for the 2007 tournament, the largest number in the history of the World Cup. Team members and fans travelled from Australia, South Africa, New Zealand, India, Bangladesh, Sri Lanka, England, Kenya, Pakistan, West Indies, Zimbabwe, and Bermuda, Canada, Ireland, the Netherlands and Scotland. The exact number of visitors that were expected to attend the event region wide was large. However, figures quoted in the newspapers and in conversation ranged from 65,000–100,000. The potential for a significant economic impact was real.

The 16 teams were split into four groups of four. The top two teams from each group advanced to the quarter finals. Four teams from this group of eight then advanced to the semi finals. Eight countries hosted the various matches— Antigua, Barbados, Grenada, Guyana, Jamaica, St. Kitts, St. Lucia, and Trinidad and Tobago. The opening ceremonies will be in Jamaica. Preliminary matches will be held in Jamaica, St. Lucia, Trinidad and Tobago and St. Kitts. The semi finals were in Jamaica and St. Lucia. The final match was played in Barbados. Hence, the potential economic impacts were region-wide. Extensive facilities and infrastructure upgrades costing approximately US$150 million had to take place throughout the region.

In addition to these brick and mortar-type investments, assistance would also be provided to communities so that they could develop local tourist enterprises and share in the economic growth spawned by World Cup Cricket. The multi-nation English speaking West Indies has a long and vibrant cricket culture (having won the first two World Cups in 1975 and 1979) and as summed up by the CEO of ICC Cricket World Cup 2007 (Dehring), the region was determined to make World Cup Cricket 2007 a fundamental event in its history—"this is the biggest collaborative undertaking by the region in history and is a once in a lifetime chance to show the world what we can do … it is a springboard for economic investment" (www.icc-cricket.com/db/archive/cricket_news/2005/feb/184570_ icc-me). The Cricket World Cup called for a team effort. However, Holder intimated that this would not be an easy undertaking for the Caribbean. There is very little history of successful cooperation among and between the island outside of cricket and the operation of the University of the West Indies. This lead to many questions: Are individual nations ready? Are they ready to work together as one region? Have the parameters for success been defined? Are they all seeing the same sides of the coin?

Findings

In each country, a wide cross section of individuals from within and external to the tourism sector were interviewed. These interviews included individual entrepreneurs, companies and policy makers. They were interviewed either as part of a focus group or as an individual. Their views are expressed in the following paragraphs.

Barbados

There was general consensus in the focus groups that the local coordinating group, World Cup Barbados, Inc., was correct in assuming that World Cup Cricket 2007 could be a catalyst for developing or enhancing community tourism ventures (e.g., small scale accommodations, attractions, food, and crafts). At least two of the 17 World Cup Barbados, Inc. subcommittees, i.e., Culture Advisory Committee and Accommodations Advisory Committee, advised on issues relating to community tourism. However, the link between the Culture Advisory Committee and the Ministry of Tourism was unclear. The World Cup Barbados, Inc. had an ongoing campaign to energize the public about World Cup Cricket by providing basic knowledge about the event and encouraging the public to get involved, this was accepted as a good start. Yet, it was thought that many attractions had not begun to consider the potential impacts of the event on their enterprises. It was found during the focus group that, notwithstanding World Cup Barbados Inc.'s efforts, insufficient information had been provided to entrepreneurs about the rules of engagement.

There was also a general consensus that World Cup Cricket was an opportunity to showcase Barbados to visitors from the region and abroad. It was an opportunity for visitors to become aware of the beauty and interesting culture of Barbados and to stimulate positive public relations for the country when visitors return to their homes. It could serve to raise standards of service in Barbados and impact positively on national pride.

Hallmark events such as World Cup Cricket 2007, act as catalysts for improving local coordination within and between communities, government agencies and between neighboring islands. An evident omission with respect to Barbados was the absence of a mechanism which fostered inter-agency collaboration and cooperation. For example, while World Cup Cricket Barbados, Inc. was focused on micro-enterprise development which it felt was important for long-term development, but which was outside if its mandate, the Ministry of Tourism was firmly focused on ensuring that the accommodation sector adhere to international standards. Their focus was on destination image. This response was very similar to the other three national tourism entities in this research but there was very little link between "community enterprise" and the tourism industry.

As in the rest of the Caribbean, some community members were outright resentful of the way tourism seemed to polarize the haves and the have-nots. Yet, anecdotal evidence from the Barbados Tourism authorities suggests that most money circulating in a community in Barbados can be traced back to the tourism industry. In fact, reference to community-based tourism throughout the interviews did not focus on their potential as small businesses but rather focused on the community as an "attraction". This supports the point made by World Cup

Barbados Inc. that community tourism, as a series of micro-enterprise activities, required special attention and may even require the creation of a special agency to nurture these entities. This is an opportunity to build local enterprise as a part of a leveraging strategy.

Another major area of concern that emerged from both the interviews and focus groups was the fear that some islands might benefit more from the event than others. This is a reflection of old rivalries between islands. This is likely a legacy from the past. However, it represents the single most destructive factor in the Caribbean. This divisiveness is not confined to inter-nation rivalry; it also operates at an intra-island level. For example, while the concern about other islands gaining an edge on others was not expressed by Trinidad, it was expressed about Tobago, and *vice versa*, notwithstanding that both islands comprise one nation state: Trinidad and Tobago. In a global business environment, there are those who benefit from regional in-fighting. It undermines the individual and collective competitive strength. This is the Caribbean's Achilles heel.

Visitors to Barbados, from the region and from overseas (including the Diaspora), were all seen as viable market segments for community tourism enterprises. However, at that time, it was unknown if visitors coming for World Cup Cricket 2007 would want to do much more than watch Cricket. It was unknown to what extent Australia, South Africa, India and Pakistan would contribute visitors (England and North America were expected to be the primary source of visitors). A similar concern was expressed in Jamaica. It was also unknown if the number of visitors to Barbados would be as high as expected (estimates ranged from 12,000–30,000 or more) and how long they would remain in Barbados before and after the matches. The research on Hallmark events indicates that most visitors tend to spend cautiously at the beginning of their holiday but become adventurous financially at the end (Chalip, 2004). In this case, it was felt that Barbados and surrounding islands would gain from this as the Closing Ceremony was in Barbados. However, answers to these questions should have been addressed as part of the negotiating process so that existing and potential entrepreneurs could make reasoned decisions. Also, given the importance of preserving Caribbean unity it demands a regional strategy to encourage an even and consistent distribution of wealth, up and down the archipelago.

In the Barbadian context, it is important to note that improvements that were made in anticipation of World Cup Cricket 2007 were being presented as being for the people of Barbados, rather than just the visitors. It was felt by some interviewed that development of the community-based tourism sector needed to be in the long-term interest of the country. The visitors' interests also needed to be protected and to that extent there should be efforts made to quell the tendency to focus on short term gains by raising prices and decreasing quality in times of high demand. This type of action could have a negative effect on creating "push and pull" factors to the country. No recognition or acknowledgement of the regional image was raised in the Barbados interviews; notwithstanding the fact that the Caribbean was being marketed as one destination for World Cup Cricket 2007.

The impression gained from the interviews in Barbados was that World Cup Cricket 2007 was a good idea, but outside of the Local Organizing Committee which was formed for the purpose of staging the sporting event, the significance and the magnitude of the long term impact of the event had been missed or was minimized except for destination image. World Cup Cricket 2007 was viewed as a good marketing tool for the island's tourism but very little connection was made with "the islands'" longer-term developmental potential. Barbados was very concerned with its tourism image in World Cup Cricket.

Jamaica

In Jamaica, it was felt that countries hosting World Cup Cricket 2007 would be in the international spotlight. Most people interviewed felt that World Cup Cricket would offer good public relations for Jamaica. Yet, there was a fair amount of uncertainty about how many visitors would actually come to Jamaica and what they would do for entertainment aside from watching cricket. As was the case in Barbados, attendance estimates were required for planning purposes. Jamaicans felt, however, there was some business to be had because the World Cup Cricket event itself would bring a large security detail, press corps, players, and handlers. This alone was likely to significantly increase demand for services.

Some Jamaicans felt that the new stadium to be built in Trelawney would help jump-start tourism development in an area where little tourism presently exists. Others felt that Trelawney was too far away from Ocho Rios and Montego Bay (the location of most lodging/attractions) to be a viable location for the stadium. They felt that there would be a severe accommodation shortage in Trelawney and that the new stadium would be underutilized after World Cup Cricket 2007. That is, it would become a white elephant. They felt that World Cup Cricket would have been best played in Kingston at Sabina Park and that the money slated for the new stadium would be better spent to upgrade the press and parking areas at Sabina Park. This was an indication that the World Cup Cricket 2007 event was not seen as contributing to anything other than the sporting event itself. However, in reality the idea of erecting a stadium in the western end of the island would provide Jamaica with a future venue for music festivals and other large hallmark events. This is an example of futuristic planning but this idea was confined to one agency. Also, had there been sufficient thought given to poverty alleviation, the inner city areas surrounding Sabina Park could have been targeted for considerable development. This is particularly important given the high incidents of crime in these areas.

Most of those interviewed felt that the overall impact of World Cup Cricket on Jamaica's tourism would be dependent on who was in the semi-finals (i.e., if England were in the semi-finals then a large number of visitors could be expected, but if a smaller country (e.g., Sri Lanka) was in the semi-finals then the numbers could be much smaller). This uncertainly made planning difficult. Further anxiety stemming from uncertainty was caused because of the fear of an overwhelming number of bookings or cancellations which would then reflect negatively on the country's efficiency levels. Similar sentiments were expressed in both Barbados and Trinidad. This is yet another example of the failure to include these types of details in the initial negotiations. These are national and regional issues which require policy intervention.

In reality, the absence of this intention has a negative impact on the planning process and the "buy-in" from the various stakeholders. The launch of World Cup Cricket 2007 by the ICC may have been ideal for that organization but it created logistical problems for the countries. The launch came too late in the countries' planning process. The interviews for this research were held in Barbados and Jamaica prior to the July launch of World Cup Cricket 2007, so some of the issues that were expressed in Trinidad and Tobago were different because of the timing of the interviews in relation to the launch. The Jamaicans interviewed felt that they would be in a better position to understand fully the match schedule, mechanisms for purchasing tickets, and rules about licensing and merchandising agreements after the launch. They felt that subsequent to that announcement, Government agencies, tour operators, business owners and communities would be better equipped to plan for the event.

As was the case in Barbados, there was concern that the average Jamaican did not understand the rules of engagement. Information about time periods, geographic parameters, infringement penalties, and access rights needed to be carefully communicated to the public. Some people felt that the late release of the information could have possible social repercussions. Jamaicans, in particular, tend to react quickly to issues that limit their freedoms and so there was doubt that licensing and merchandising agreements could be strictly enforceable. A breach of the rules of engagement could ultimately lead to disastrous consequences for the countries. This concern was not confined to Jamaica. In these types of negotiations, knowledge of the host country/region's characteristics is an important factor in negotiating the time of the release of information. These peculiarities also shape trade negotiations. Managing the image of the destination is a critical aspect of a hallmark event. This is even more crucial in the light of the fact that large numbers of international press cover these events. A simple incident can be misinterpreted and have devastating long term consequences for a small nation. In the case of the Caribbean, if one nation fails, the Caribbean fails as it is being marketed as one destination. There was a clear and definite convergence with respect to the implications for social unrest in one or all of the countries resulting from insufficient and poorly disseminated information surrounding the event and/or real or perceived hijacking of traditional rights. Notwithstanding these high risks there was no one regional coordinating body for focal point to shepherd the project.

The Cricket authorities determined that the impact of World Cup Cricket on tourism in Jamaica was the responsibility of local tourism authorities and business owners. Windies Cricket and the LOC were primarily concerned with managing the World Cup Cricket 2007 event. However, Jamaica took a different approach from the other islands. Jamaica hired the company that managed World Cup

Cricket in South Africa to create a legacy strategy. This initiative was spearheaded by the Jamaica Promotions Corporation (JAMPRO), Jamaica's investment and promotion agency. The purpose of the Legacy strategy was to create a vision for Jamaica so that by 2012 Jamaica could be competitive. At the time of the interviews the Legacy strategy was in the making. It was therefore not clear what framework would be used to move from conceptualization to implementation.

The interviews revealed that there were a number of local initiatives and opportunities that would need further investigation if they were to be fruitful. It also revealed that many of the initiatives required policy decisions. These included:

- Reducing barriers facing those that wish to develop tourism enterprises during World Cup Cricket 2007 (e.g., lower taxes, ease in import restrictions/ duties, provide incentives for food production (especially to youth), set performance standards, provide low interest loans for new businesses, facilitate financing for renovating existing businesses).
- Allowing youth to produce crops on idle lands to meet the increased demand for agriculture produce during World Cup Cricket.
- Instituting a poverty alleviation plan in rural areas to help curb problems of tourist security and harassment. (People apparently move back and forth from the countryside in pursuit of handouts and easy money from tourists. Poverty and high unemployment in the rural areas were thought to be the cause).
- Organizing and coordinating the planning, development and marketing of tourism activities during World Cup Cricket across the various sectors (e.g., accommodations, attractions, transportation, food services).
- Coordinating information dissemination about events developed by communities by using the Jamaica Hotel and Tourist Association Chapters. In addition, the Association could provide training to those interested in developing B&Bs. A different approach from Barbados perhaps because of the size of the industry.
- Providing training in business plan development, finance, and business management through the Jamaica Business Development Centre to those interested in developing community tourism enterprises.
- Providing leadership in the effort to develop new attractions.
- Creating incentives for entrepreneurs to develop new businesses.
- Using the Jamaica Export Association's (private sector lobby group) Unique Jamaica campaign to play a role in promoting Jamaican attractions to World Cup Cricket visitors.
- Linking poor rural areas to resort areas through agriculture and micro-enterprise opportunities.
- Facilitating creativity; e.g., leasing land to youth with a view to producing agricultural crops for the event and based on their performance continuing the lease for export.

Jamaicans, like Barbadians, felt that it had a lot to showcase (e.g., Blue Mountain and its coffee plantations, Cockpit country, tropical flora and fauna (including a wide variety of flowers and tropical fruits), local sports matches, music, horse racing). However, it also felt that people needed to be educated about how they might engage in community-based tourism as the existing levels of production may be insufficient to meet demand. There was also a need to get information to those interested in farming so they can properly plan production. Again, the issue of creating a service culture and its link to security and poverty was noted. Jamaica seemed focused on both long and short term opportunities but again there did not seem to be a vehicle to link agencies, execute projects and parlay opportunities into concrete business ventures.

Trinidad and Tobago

In Trinidad too there was uncertainty about how many people would actually attend World Cup Cricket 2007 events, but it was thought that the Asian Diaspora linked to India, Pakistan, Sri Lanka, etc. living in both Europe and North America would be a good market for World Cup Cricket 2007 in Trinidad and Tobago. It is noted by many interviewed that research was needed that profiled the interests of the various visitor groups. It was felt that this information should form the basis for developing any tourism offerings in Trinidad. Planners would have needed to consider the unique interests of an Asian audience in terms of attractions (e.g., music, food services) that they may want to develop for World Cup Cricket 2007. The population in Trinidad is made up of a large percentage of people of East Indian descent. Trinidad, unlike its other regional counterparts, is an oil producing country and does not attach a high significance to tourism. Although its sister island, Tobago, depends solely on this industry.

Trinidad did not take the bidding process for World Cup Cricket 2007 as seriously as the other nations, for whatever reasons, which resulted in Trinidad and Tobago receiving what they called a "brown bag" package. Having received this package, their strategy then shifted focus from cricket *per se* to the Asian spectators, with a view to promoting long-term trade with this market segment. So by default, Trinidad saw the long-term potential and sought to convert this opportunity into reality ahead of the actual event.

Trinidad held trade missions to India and *vice versa.* They did not focus on either tourism or sports and seized the leveraging opportunity presented to them through their "brown bag package". Again, this was not strategic but in reaction to what was perceived as a poor cricketing opportunity. By the time this research had been conducted in Trinidad and Tobago, the July announcements about the match locations had been made but the uncertainty surrounding the rules of engagement remained. Trinidad was very nervous about making possible errors in attempting to interpret the 600-page document that constituted the contract for the rules of engagement. They hired attorneys to decipher the contract and were in a position to make strategic plans around this opportunity. Their LOC was also the executing agency unlike the LOCs in the other countries.

In Tobago, schedules of practice matches on the island were also unknown. In addition, there was perceived to be a history of Tobago being treated as a "lower economic development" priority by Trinidad and so there was no surprise to the Tobagoians that they did not know what was planned. Some individuals in Tobago were therefore skeptical about the degree to which World Cup Cricket 2007's impact would be shared with Tobago. In the past, they noted that some festival style events and large sports matches in Tobago had not worked well primarily because they had been imposed by Trinidad without local design/development considerations.

Tobago has a well-established image as a quality tourist destination and had more lodgings than Trinidad. It also had more direct fights from North America and Europe than Trinidad. Though the air-bridge between islands was problematic, the sea-bridge between the two islands was good. Tobago can therefore contribute significantly a lot towards the success of Trinidad and Tobago's hosting of the World Cup Cricket 2007. It can also provide needed air access to the region which supports the marketing image of One Caribbean. In addition, it was also felt that World Cup Cricket 2007 may present opportunities to advance aspects of the existing Tobago Development Plan. However, the rivalry between Trinidad and Tobago is so strong that it may require regional intervention to ensure that the regional image in not tarnished. For example, Tobago's established and on-going air access to Europe could well play a significant role in the future of Caribbean tourism. There is considerable "bad blood" between twin-island States of which there are three in the West Indies (Jordan, 2003). The question emanating from the interviews in Trinidad and Tobago is: given the rivalry between Trinidad and Tobago and the fact that policy for Tobago, though determined internally, requires genuine endorsement in Trinidad, can these regional opportunities really be realized? More particularly, the division is reflective of the jealousy that exists between islands throughout the archipelago. It is unlikely that the Caribbean can successfully complete and until these issues are addressed.

Trinidad and Tobago decided initially to focus their tourism efforts on the 15-day period during which preliminary matches were scheduled to be held in the country. Their main concerns were that if any of the countries scheduled to compete in Trinidad and Tobago progressed to the semi-finals, visitors might depart for other island venues where these matches were scheduled to be played, leaving decreased economic opportunity. Given the possibility that the greatest spend could come after the Closing Ceremony in Barbados, and given the proximity of Trinidad and Tobago to Barbados, it provided a chance for Trinidad and Tobago to try to entice tourists back after the final event. It is known that conversion of repeat visitors is dependent on their initial experience. A positive experience hinged on Tobago's willingness to guide Trinidad in the area of tourism strategies designed to yield repeat visitors. The challenge was also to generate good public relations for the country during the preliminary matches. This is difficult because Trinidad's mainstay of the economy is oil, not tourism. The placing and spacing of matches cannot be left solely to the discretion of the owners of the event as these decisions impact negatively on archipelagic regions. This is again a point for inclusion in negotiating the contract prior to agreeing to host the event.

The role that the LOC might play in promoting community tourism development in Trinidad and Tobago was also undefined. The LOC in Trinidad was an executing body unlike its counterparts in Barbados and Jamaica. The Tourism Development Corporation (TDC—an agency focusing on building/promoting tourism in Trinidad) at the time of the interviews had just been separated from the Tourism and Industrial Development Company (TIDCO). The new TDC had not commenced operations. Once active, TDC could play a key role in coordinating linkages supporting community tourism development. Yet, there was some doubt that TDC was the right organization to execute this mandate. In addition, it was felt that the Ministry of Tourism did not have the capacity to undertake this task. Community development requires a long-term commitment and its focus was different from tourism. Community groups need long-term supervision and assistance with training, finance, and management if the goal of micro-enterprise development was to be achieved. For strategic plans to be effective systems and structures need to be synchronized.

The LOC in Trinidad felt that the primary impact of World Cup Cricket would best be evaluated on either a country wide-scale or regional-scale but would be experienced after the event resulting from raised standards and new business linkages. This assumes a mechanism for measuring and evaluating the impacts. No, this mechanism was defined. World Cup Cricket 2007 could have provided the impetus to raise standards on issues related to immigration, health/sanitation, guest relations, and other quality control issues affecting the hospitality sector. There is also a recognized need to bring local standards up to international levels so that enterprises can be globally competitive. Yet, there was uncertainty regarding how global standards that would become used regionally for measuring lodging, attractions, food services, transportation, etc. This too was a point of controversy and debate in the region. The hotel industry has not endorsed traditional standards nor have they produced substitute standards. Therefore, the debate was which and what standards would be regionally enforced and would their absence lead to market confusion and product damage.

In Tobago, community tourism was seen as both an integrated approach and collaborative tool for the socio-economic empowerment of communities through the assessment, development, and marketing of natural and cultural community resources. These were seen to add value to the experiences of local and foreign visitors while simultaneously improving the quality of life of communities. It was felt by the interviewees that another opportunity to regional cooperation and competitiveness. The visitor finds appealing varied natural attractions, local resources and talents, and indigenous attributes of a community or area. Through visitor-community interaction, respective cultures are explored, ideas and information are exchanged, new friends are made and trade opportunities developed. Individually, Barbados and Jamaica were focused on tourism and image. Trinidad was focused on longer term international trade while, Tobago, inadvertently, provided the insights barriers into the underbelly of the regional cooperation. This lead to another question: Can disparate nations really be effectively marketed as one destination?

Lessons Learnt

In gathering data from within the region about possibilities for short and long term opportunities resulting from World Cup Cricket 2007, it became clear that there were cross cutting issues such as coordination, equity, ownership and planning that needed to be addressed. Some particularly interesting issues such as stakeholder conflict relating to the decision-making processes emerged, as in examples of site selection for new stadia by Trinidad, Tobago and Jamaica. Another area of stakeholder conflict was the likely shift in the balance of power in the hotel sector in Barbados. That became evident in the strong resistance to the introduction of bed and breakfast operations in Barbados. Such an action could threaten the base of the traditional hotel sector but could also widen the Barbadian stake in tourism. These examples represent but a few of the issues that have to be managed when the Caribbean as a region ventures into new areas of business opportunity. Industry disharmony impacts on destination prosperity.

Resistance to change as indicated by Holder (2001) is a characteristic of Caribbean people. It appears to be based on a lack of trust, leadership and strategic direction fostered over many years. All of these issues may well have their origins in slavery and the plantation system and are built on the concept of "divide and rule". A collective and informed policy intervention designed to foster and ultimately build Caribbean development seems necessary. Understanding many of these issues, putting them in their proper perspective and carefully crafting policies designed in a global context is an imperative for Caribbean economic survival: a must for leveraging hallmark events.

The goal is to create a win-win environment. For example, policies that are drafted to optimize the opportunities presented under the World Trade Organization's rules, hemispheric and bi-lateral agreements provide an opportunity for fostering competitiveness. The essence of negotiating a successful hallmark event begins with well-crafted regional and national strategic policies and plans, new business models based on Caribbean long-term goals, as well as a very sophisticated and experienced negotiating team. The negotiations should address issues relating to: information flow, intellectual property, creative industries, branding and all the elements of the tourism system that can yield data and subsequent analysis for creating new industries and prospects for linking sectors to tourism. Mason (2003) indicates that such policies must also address the following: political structure, value system, institutional framework, distribution of power and decision-making process. Hallmark events, like tourism, are a means to a carefully devised and managed strategic end. Data needed to begin the process is not easily identifiable but is embedded in the unique issues relating to the individual Caribbean countries. The interviews for this research helped to highlight some of them.

Bianchi (2002) points out that while tourism is very important to many countries it has not been included in discussions on international trade. He states that with globalization there will be greater decentralization and coordination of decision making. He uses the mergers and strategic alliances between and among global airlines in tour operations to show that more and more resources are being concentrated in fewer and fewer hands. However, unlike previous times the nationality of the owner is no longer an issue because the transnational corporations have access to all territories. Tour operators own and/or operate hotels and airlines that allow them easy access to the entire distribution chain (*ibid*). Bianchi notes that the fluidity of capital movement along with the emergence of transnational corporations has formed the globalised and transnational tourism political economy. Bianchi points out that as this phenomenon grows the owners of these transnational corporations will become more and more distant from the issue of culture and local needs. Their main focus will be economic growth for their corporations. Countries that manage scale and ownership issues by using incentives or disincentives to achieve developmental goals will emerge winners in this global competition. Also, the nature of the transnational tourism political economy can only best be managed through interventions designed around the management of the tourism system itself. From this comment it seems evident that Caribbean nations must have common goals if effective leveraging can result *en masse* to the region from Hallmark events.

Boxill (2003) suggests "emphasis should be placed on using and developing the intellectual and cultural capabilities of the people of the region, rather than simply exploiting the natural resources of the island (i.e., sea, sand and sun)". The Caribbean warmth and natural friendliness is an essential ingredient for creating competitive products based on individual country attributes and collective attractiveness. Weed and Bull (1999) state that leadership in the policy network is important and this usually falls to government. During the research, however, it became evident that while the Caribbean has had in excess of 30 years of working together as a trading bloc, this experience has not removed the distrust among and between islands. The research also confirmed and underscored that there are socio-cultural impediments to Caribbean economic independence. These have to be removed or at least minimized if economic success is to be achieved. The real opportunities lie in the effective management of the tourism system bolstered by policies designed to create a vehicle for moving a well conceived regional negotiated strategy from concept to reality. A suggested application of the system is set out below:

- Generating markets: all information related to the visitors, all elements of the tourism product must form part of the negotiating strategy. This is the essence of strategic analysis. These data must be retained by the host region for future trade purposes and new product development.

- Transit route: this, along with the information gained from the generating markets, is the essence of the global distribution system. Strategies for manipulating such data for the purpose of marketing and creating new products must be carefully crafted, monitored and evaluated on a continuous basis.
- Destination: This is the essential element of creating and maintaining the economic image of the country in the global market place. This is the engine that drives the previously discussed "pull" and "push" factors.
- Industry: At this level the market differentiation strategy must be designed around international standards for the purpose of using human and natural resources, the essence of the Caribbean, as a competitive tool.

The Local Organizing Committees (LOCs) in each country are only facilitators of communication not coordinators of development projects. Their primary function is to ensure that World Cup Cricket events meet ICC expectations. Though they are willing to help identify ideas for viable community tourism enterprises and bring the main players together, they do not have the capacity to help with project implementation. A missing ingredient is leadership. A regional entity with institutional links at the national level is necessary for creating a comprehensive and effective implementation strategy. World Cup Cricket 2007 is a one-off event. Hallmark events are continuous but can become a major industry for the Caribbean to either itself host periodically or provide services to other who wish to do so.

One of the essential results of Hallmark events is the development of a brand image. In this case, brand Caribbean. However, this result demands consistent and continuous cooperation not just for tourism and cricket but also for international trade. Old habits die hard. Resistance to change based on unscientific approaches to business and tourism, distrust and incoherent regional policies serve to undermine possible short and long term gains from World Cup Cricket 2007. The World Trade Organization rules of engagement require transparency, equity and cooperation. Head to head global competition means creating new business models based on competitive advantage, strategic and regional alliances. Only time will tell whether World Cup Cricket 2007 will cause the Caribbean to, in the long-term, indeed put meaning to its cricket anthem rally "round the West Indies".

Chapter 5

Intent versus Reality: Impacts of World Cup Cricket on Community Tourism in Barbados and Trinidad and Tobago

Ben Tyson, David Truly, Leslie-Ann Jordan and Carolyn Hayle

Introduction

Hallmark events have always been considered significant tools for cities and/or regions intent upon enhancing tourism development or revitalizing tourism efforts. Successful outcomes however are not guaranteed and there are numerous examples where original intentions were not fully realized (Hall, 1992). The announcement that the 2007 World Cup Cricket games would be held in the Caribbean signaled a significant opportunity for trade within communities in participating countries. While this region has a long history of tourism development, the region has also struggled with enhancing its image as more than just a sun, sand and sea destination, a product of mass tourism development (Hutchings, 1996). This has proven to be a challenge as the influence of large multinational tourism corporations throughout the region have to varying degrees stifled attempts to promote smaller-scale indigenous-types of community tourism development. This chapter examines the efforts of two countries to utilize a hallmark event to enhance community tourism development and discusses several themes that characterize the region's ongoing evolution as a tourism destination.

Prior to the staging of World Cup Cricket 2007 two research projects were conducted by the University of the West Indies (UWI) and Central Connecticut State University in March and August, 2005, in Barbados and Trinidad and Tobago. The research question addressed in each instance was: *how can communities and private sector entrepreneurs take advantage of World Cup Cricket 2007 to develop or enhance community tourism ventures that will attract visitors both during and after the event?* Trinidad and Tobago was scheduled to host warm-up and stage matches, where as Barbados was scheduled to host warm-up and play off matches as well as the World Cup Final match. Hence, Barbados had more at stake. Research methods consisted of focus groups with a total of 55 administrators of World Cup Cricket, tour/attraction operators, community development NGOs, community tourism specialists, small business associations, accommodations representatives, retail enterprises.

A report summarizing findings from the two research projects (plus findings from a third project in Jamaica) was issued in late 2005. This report was widely distributed throughout the region by the University of West Indies Institute of Hospitality and Tourism (Hayle, Jordan, Thame, Truly and Tyson, 2005). In addition a shorter version of the report was published in the *Journal of Sports Tourism* (Tyson, Hale, Truly, Jordan and Thame, 2005). The report included recommendations addressing:

a) Potential opportunities for community tourism/micro-enterprise development (including crafts, agro/culinary, tours/special destinations, festivals/special events, local sports, restaurants, transportation and lodging);
b) Equity issues;
c) Legacy issues;
d) Sector coordination;
e) Standards;
f) Service and safety;
g) Information needs; and
h) Environmental issues.

In early 2008, several months after the World Cup event, a follow-up survey was launched to assess what respondents to the 2005 studies perceived did and did not happen regarding recommendations presented in the 2005 report and what factors they thought helped or hindered these actions. A survey was conducted via mail, email, and/or phone with 20 of the same individuals that participated in the 2005 study. The ten page instrument used in the 2008 follow-up study addressed ten categories of issues: Research, Legacy Planning, Coordination, Community Tourism/Crafts, Community Tourism/Agro-culinary, Community Tourism/Special Events, Community Tourism/Lodging, Standards, Service and Safety, and Environmental Impacts. A three or four sentence summary statement based on recommendations from the 2005 report was presented for each category and after each summary statement, the following five questions were posed:

- When planning for the World Cup, what activities were conducted in your country to help with _____?
- What do you think were the key factors that helped make these activities happen?
- What activities were *not* conducted to help with _____ that you think should have been?
- What do you think were the key barriers that hindered these activities from taking place?
- Overall, on a scale of 1 to 5 very poor to very good, rate efforts in your country to use the World Cup as the impetus to help with _____.

The following section of this chapter discusses findings from the 2008 follow-up study for each of the ten categories of issues.

Findings

Audience Research

Conclusions drawn from the 2005 studies showed that there was general consensus among respondents that entrepreneurial opportunities stimulated by World Cup Cricket 2007 exist for lodging, attractions, crafts, foods, etc. Yet, there was a fair amount of uncertainty about how many visitors would actually visit, how long they would stay and what type of entertainment they would experience aside from watching cricket. Respondents agreed that audience research was needed to answer these questions so that existing and potential entrepreneurs could plan the community tourism enterprises they wish to pursue.

Results of the 2008 survey show that in Trinidad and Tobago, aside from the 2005 research associated with this project, most respondents were either unaware or felt no additional research had been completed. In Barbados, many respondents were also unaware that additional research had been conducted. Yet three individuals were aware that the Barbados Tourism Authority (BTA) and the Barbados Hotel and Tourism Association (BHTA) had sent research/promotion missions to India, Pakistan, and Sri Lanka. Respondents were aware that dozens of meetings had been held with food and craft vendors, small business associations and community groups to agree on structures and processes to accommodate the Cricket World Cup (CWC) authority. They were aware that research had been completed in key areas such as transportation and accommodations.

Respondents from the 2008 survey felt that market research was needed and that sub-committees should have been assigned to investigate their particular area of expertise. Areas of investigation should have included:

a) Better projections on expected attendance;
b) How previous CWC events had been conducted and effects on consumer spending;
c) Ways to attract Indian and Pakistan tourists; and
d) Ways to ensure that small vendors benefited from the event.

Some felt that criteria for the development of commercial enterprises that were set by the International Cricket Committee (ICC) were too restrictive and that additional research would not have been applicable.

Barriers to conducting research were said to have included the fact that multiple destinations hosted the event. This made it difficult to both coordinate regional research needs and forecast marketing variables at individual sites. No clear intra-regional transport plan had been developed to move large volumes of people and no clear regional product pricing strategy were ever devised. Most respondents felt that planners had a limited vision of potential impacts, both regionally and locally, and operated on the assumption that little research was actually needed.

On a one to five scale, very poor to very good, respondents in Trinidad and Tobago rated efforts to conduct audience research in anticipation of the World Cup Cricket 2007 an average of 1.71. In Barbados, ratings averaged 3.29.

Legacy Planning

Respondents to the 2005 studies felt that each country should have developed a legacy strategy that would have defined the overall goal to be achieved from World Cup Cricket 2007 including short-term impacts during the event and long-term impacts after the event. For example, one legacy might have been to help businesses within the region achieve better coordination with each other. Another legacy might been to advance community tourism (micro-enterprise development) and sports tourism initiatives.

Results of the 2008 survey show that in Trinidad and Tobago most respondents were unaware of any legacy planning activities associated with planning for the World Cup. Yet, several respondents did recognize that security for the event was well planned and that the country is now better equipped to host another large event like the World Cup Cricket 2007 in the future. Others feel that the event helped highlight the potential for sports tourism and that the refurbished facilities can now be used for other events. It is felt by some that the Trinidad and Tobago government relied too much on the local organizing committees (LOC) whose agenda did not focus on the legacy of the event. One respondent felt that "we sought to have it be too much of an international affair without putting a Caribbean flavor to it". Some feel that the stringent rules laid down by the ICC only helped large established businesses to benefit.

In Barbados, most respondents were aware that a detailed legacy plan was developed that addressed public safety, infrastructure development, traffic management, environmental and health planning, and standards/service in the hospitality sector. A major beautification campaign was also launched. Most feel that World Cup Cricket 2007 has left a blue print that can be used for future major events. A few respondents pointed out that this legacy is mostly on a large scale and has little impact on local communities and small businesses.

Barbados, however, was determined to reap long term benefits from its CWC investments. A focused legacy plan was coordinated by the government and folded into the national strategic plan. The government's main concern was to see a return on money spent refurbishing and expanding the Kensington Oval.

On a one to five scale, very poor to very good, respondents in Trinidad and Tobago rated efforts to use the World Cup as the impetus to plan a legacy strategy an average of 2.5. In Barbados, ratings averaged 3.29.

Coordination

Conclusions from the 2005 studies showed there was general consensus among respondents that World Cup Cricket 2007 could have been a catalyst for local people to improve coordination within and between their communities. Markets for community tourism enterprises are small. Hence, community enterprises need to cluster with each other to make packages for visitors that are worth pursuing. Respondents felt that agencies/organizations with small business and community development mandates should help coordinate this. They agreed that good coordination is also needed between those responsible for planning World Cup Cricket 2007 and the various development agencies/organizations in each country.

Results of the 2008 survey show that in Trinidad and Tobago about half of the respondents were unaware of any special coordination efforts associated with planning for the World Cup. The other half were aware that some level of coordination was achieved for national security, transportation and among the larger hotels. Respondents recognized that little coordination was achieved within and between communities to benefit local tourism enterprises. Though some felt that the LOC was partially successful in helping coordinate the activities of larger organizations, many respondents felt more work was needed in this area, including with those at a smaller scale. Respondents think that the ICC and LOC should have worked more closely with the Trinidad Development Corporation and the Ministry of Tourism to cluster and engage various stakeholders (e.g., craftsmen, tour operators, food vendors, youth groups) in the planning process. Many feel that ICC rules hindered involvement of many local groups and that this subdued visitors' experiences; i.e., the real vibrancy of Caribbean was missing.

In Barbados, many respondents were aware of the LOC's coordination efforts for security, transportation, accommodations, small businesses, etc. and that a legacy plan had been developed addressing public safety, infrastructure development, traffic management, and environmental impacts. Most feel that key areas (security, transportation, accommodations) were coordinated well. In addition, some communities recognized that opportunities existed and launched activities in their districts, churches, and community centers. Yet, several respondents feel that though a lot of initial brainstorming was done about community involvement in the early planning stages, very few concrete activities were actually organized in this "non-essential" area. Some feel that this was because coordination/communication was lacking and that people simply ran out of time to plan.

On a one to five scale, very poor to very good, respondents in Trinidad and Tobago rated efforts to use the World Cup as the impetus to improve coordination an average of 2.25. In Barbados, ratings averaged 3.13.

Community Tourism: Crafts

Respondents from the 2005 studies felt that increased tourism because of World Cup Cricket 2007 would likely increase demand for crafts and that this presented an opportunity for new artisans to get in the business. Respondents also felt that local crafts organizations needed to take charge of their own concerns and forecast demand and production needs. They felt that the industry lacked coordination, regulation and training and that World Cup Cricket 2007 represented an opportunity to rectify this weakness.

The results of the 2008 survey show that in Trinidad and Tobago nearly all respondents were unaware of efforts to help the craft industry. One respondent stated that opportunities were given to craftsmen to expose their crafts through merchandising agreements, but that because it was a branded event, "when potential clients came to us we could not properly assist them because of the branding process involved". In addition, some people felt that the price of a vendor's license was very high. Some respondents also felt that the government should have been more insistent with the ICC that local craftsmen should be given the opportunity to market their products and that the LOC should have coordinated this activity. In addition, some feel that the craftsmen should have been organized themselves better and tried to improve their entrepreneurial skills.

In Barbados, about half the respondents were unaware of efforts to help the craft industry, while others recognized that some efforts had been made. Some knew that the Barbados Industrial Development Corporation (BIDC) had conducted some work with small manufacturers and craftsmen to develop new products with mass visitor appeal but that little has been done to help with marketing. The main Pelican Craft Centre was not well promoted. Overall, respondents feel that it could have been a good opportunity to showcase crafts, but that craftsmen lost out because of "lack of creativity and poor marketing efforts". Most respondents believed that craftsmen were not considered a priority by the ICC and the LOC. Some respondents stated that they knew craftsmen that had made efforts to produce and market items and bought rights to use the WCC logo in the merchandise, but that they were not successful.

Using a one to five scale, very poor to very good, respondents in Trinidad and Tobago rated efforts to use the World Cup as the impetus to help the crafts industry an average of 2.00. In Barbados, ratings averaged 1.83.

Community Tourism: Agro-culinary

Conclusions drawn from the 2005 studies suggested that respondents felt that agro-tourism enterprises (e.g., farm stays and farm tours), culinary tourism enterprises (e.g., cooking competitions, food festivals, top-chefs tour), and cottage industries producing food items such as local candies, spirits, and spices were good ideas for possible micro-enterprise development. There was general consensus among those interviewed that plans are needed to better link rural areas and resort areas for production/supply of agriculture products and development of micro enterprise services/opportunities.

Results of the 2008 survey show that in both Trinidad and Tobago and Barbados nearly all respondents were unaware of efforts to help agro-tourism enterprises. One respondent in Trinidad and Tobago stated that the National Economic Development Corporation (NEDCO) did alert entrepreneurs in various communities about potential business opportunities in this regard and some meetings were held with some individuals, but little came of these efforts. One respondent in Barbados stated that efforts by the BIDC included individuals involved in agro-tourism enterprises. Respondents agree their country missed a perfect time to have a culinary festival to highlight the nation's foods and to showcase agricultural products. As with the crafts industry, licensing restrictions laid down by the ICC stifled smaller scale entrepreneurial activity.

On a one to five scale, very poor to very good, respondents in Trinidad and Tobago rated efforts to use the World Cup as the impetus to help agro-tourism enterprises an average of 1.83. In Barbados, ratings averaged 2.25.

Community Tourism: Special Events

Respondents to the 2005 studies felt that guided nature walks by local experts, garden tours, tours of the homes of Cricket legends, tours that showcase military history and night tours of music venues are ideas for possible micro-enterprise development would have been a good product. The development of "Caribbean Villages" showcasing local history, arts, sports, entertainment, crafts, and food/ drink were also felt to be a viable idea for new attractions.

Results of the 2008 survey show that in Trinidad and Tobago most respondents were unaware of efforts to help develop special events for tourists. Some were aware that the Tourism Development Company (TDC) did organize a few special projects (special dinners, demonstrations, displays) at the request of industry stakeholders. Respondents felt that because Trinidad and Tobago is so multi-cultural that special cultural events could have been created but no one took the initiative. Some respondents feel that the management of the TDC did not believe the CWC 2007 could generate significant new business and therefore did not focus on the development of sites and attractions. In addition, it is thought that tour operators did not identify the opportunity as profitable because visitors would not be repeat clientele and as such, they saw no sense in doing anything extra for the CWC 2007. Others feel that ICC rules and regulations were too restrictive and that this stifled development of local cultural special events.

In Barbados, most respondents were very aware of efforts to develop special events for tourists. For instance, legends activities, special events, and night-time activities were staged at St. Lawrence Gap, Oistins, Speightstown, and Bridgetown. These events were listed in the Barbados Civic Community Calendar. Private entrepreneurs saw the possible profits that could be made and invested their own money. Yet, several respondents agreed that "things were happening but there were not enough patrons to go around" and that "some special events were over-offered but many were under-subscribed". Many lost money. Several respondents stated this was because of poor marketing and transportation planning.

On a one to five scale, very poor to very good, respondents in Trinidad and Tobago rated efforts to use the World Cup to help develop special events for tourists an average of 2.13. In Barbados, ratings averaged 2.71.

Community Tourism: Lodging

There was general consensus among those that participated in the 2005 studies that the expected increased demand for accommodations during World Cup Cricket 2007 would exceed supply. Respondents felt that this issue would be exacerbated because the timing of World Cup Cricket 2007 coincided with high tourist season. Hence, they felt that there would be opportunities to develop more home-based bed and breakfast (B&B) lodgings.

However, the results of the 2008 survey showed that in Trinidad/Tobago most respondents were aware of efforts to help develop home-based B&B lodgings. The hotel association and the accommodations subcommittee of the LOC put a lot of effort into promoting the development of new B&Bs. In addition, the Tourism Development Company promoted the establishment and coordinated certification of new B&Bs and NEDCO provided a few loans for the refurbishment of these properties. As it turned out, the supply of rooms exceeded the demand. As several respondents agreed, "there was little need to develop B&B lodgings since the large hotels had sufficient capacity". Apparently, because large events are commonly held in the country (e.g., Carnival), there was already sufficient B&B capacity.

In Barbados, nearly all respondents were aware of efforts to help develop home-based B&Bs for tourists. The Government of Barbados through a mechanism called Fund Access set up a fund whereby property owners seeking to refurbish their properties could access financing. In addition, training was offered for B&B owners by the Ministry of Tourism. Persons interested in offering home accommodations were invited to register with the Barbados Tourism Authority (BTA). Their homes were inspected and if approved for such an operation, were marketed through a website. In addition, flyers were distributed in overseas markets as part of the regular marketing activities of the BTA.

On a one to five scale, very poor to very good, respondents in Trinidad and Tobago rated efforts to use the World Cup to help develop home-based B&B lodgings an average of 3.00. In Barbados, ratings averaged 3.88.

Standards

Respondents to the 2005 studies felt that World Cup Cricket 2007 could provide the impetus to raise standards on issues related to health/sanitation, guest relations, and other quality control issues affecting the hospitality sector. They agreed that there is a need to bring local standards up to an international level so that enterprises can be more globally competitive. Yet, respondents recognized that the industry needs to be careful about setting unrealistic standards—i.e., hygiene standards of food vendors and B&Bs cannot be raised too high/too quickly or people will be put out of business. There was general consensus among those interviewed that small scale, short-term, incentive programs designed to help businesses upgrade to meet international standards were needed.

Results of the 2008 survey show that in Trinidad and Tobago respondents were unaware of any efforts to help develop better standards for the hospitality sector. Several respondents recognized that the TDC already had a set of standards in place, implying that this was sufficient. They felt that local standards were already at an international level. Others felt that this issue needed a lot of attention and that the Trinidad and Tobago Hospitality and Tourism Institute should have been used for training.

In Barbados, this was a national priority and nearly all respondents were aware of efforts to help develop better standards for the hospitality sector. Standards set for B&Bs were at an international level. Guidelines for the licensing B&Bs were produced and disseminated. Inspections were carried out of hotels, apartments, guest houses and B&Bs. Increased awareness and customer service training initiatives were carried out through the National Initiative on Service Excellence. Roadside vendors also underwent training in food handling and food safety at Barbados Community College. As one respondent put it, "the whole country was aware through the media that we were putting on a show for the world and everyone, from the hotels to the farmers understood that quality control and standards were important for the World Cup be successful".

On a one to five scale, very poor to very good, respondents in Trinidad and Tobago rated efforts to use the World Cup to help develop better standards for the hospitality sector an average of 2.86. In Barbados, ratings averaged 4.00.

Service and Safety

Respondents to the 2005 studies agreed that untrained hotel and restaurant staff can negatively affect visitors' perceptions of the local tourism industry. They felt that some people who work in the hospitality sector do not know the difference between service and servitude. There was general consensus among those interviewed that there is a need to educate the community about the nature and impacts of tourism. Concern for visitors' security was also recognized as a major issue. In addition, one of the most critical problem facing retailers and restaurants is said to be the harassment of tourists (e.g., panhandling, aggressive selling tactics, taxi drivers cheating tourists). Poverty and high unemployment in the rural areas are thought to be contributing factors. Respondents felt that the World Cup Cricket 2007 could present an opportunity to deal with issues of visitor security and harassment.

Results of the 2008 survey show that in Trinidad and Tobago respondents were very aware of efforts to improve safety issues. Respondents recognized that there was great concern for the safety of cruise ship passengers because it is a very fragile industry that authorities did not want to jeopardize. In addition, they recognized that the government wanted to avoid anything that would have potentially embarrassed the country. Workshops were conducted by security agencies for port personnel.

More police patrols were instituted. Security was upgraded in hotels. Special buses were used for visitors so that they would not be subject to harassment. Training was done for volunteers recruited to assist visitors. Medical systems were tested and visa restrictions were tightened. In terms of service, most respondents felt that standards were already sufficient. Yet some felt that the media should have been used to educate the wider population about the importance of quality service. These respondents feel that there is a general lack of awareness and knowledge about what quality service means.

In Barbados, nearly all respondents were aware of efforts to help improve both service and safety issues. As one respondent put it, "The media did a lot to highlight security issues and to show the difference between service and servitude. Everyone recognized that Barbados was on show and people were on their best behavior. There were public awareness advertisements on television dealing with beautification of surroundings, friendliness, etc. so that the whole of Barbados was geared up to welcome many visitors". Respondents recognized that many hotels and restaurants made a special effort to cater to visitors' needs during CWC and there was a lot of sensitizing of staff on how to deal with persons of different cultures. In terms of safety issues, respondents agreed that the country paid a lot of attention to this to ensure that visitors remained safe. Hotel security personnel were retrained by the security forces and special constables were recruited specifically to police the World Cup Cricket 2007.

On a one to five scale, very poor to very good, respondents in Trinidad and Tobago rated efforts to use the World Cup to help improve service and safety issues an average of 3.09. In Barbados, ratings averaged 4.00.

Environmental Impacts

Conclusions drawn from the 2005 studies recognized that tourism in the region relied heavily on healthy natural resources. Respondents agreed that the ability to properly handle solid waste disposal, sewage treatment and provide a safe water supply is already stressed in many countries and that World Cup Cricket will add alarmingly to this stress. There was general consensus among those interviewed that standards are needed that specify the type of materials that can be used in the hospitality industry (e.g., biodegradable cups, plates, tableware). They believed that plans for how to better handle the waste stream need to be made prior to the World Cup and that new business permits that are issued need to specify how waste will be managed.

Results of the 2008 survey show that nearly all Trinidad and Tobago respondents were unaware of any effort to improve management of environmental impacts. Only one respondent was aware that additional rubbish bins and cleaning personnel had been added. Respondents felt that planners did not think the involvement of the Environmental Management Authority (EMA) was important. Several respondents made comments similar to the following, "we are extremely backward in our approach to this issue". Several respondents feel that the different stakeholders, including EMA, should have been brought together to plan proper environmental management and that a pubic awareness effort should have been launched.

In comparison, Barbados respondents were divided in their perceptions about efforts to improve management of environmental impacts. Some were aware that airport, seaport and marina waste management systems had been upgraded and that the Kensington Oval was linked to the sewage treatment plant which was upgraded and retrofitted. They felt that a good waste management plan had been devised and executed effectively throughout the World Cup. Others feel that the country does not have a proper solid/liquid waste management system and that they missed an opportunity to put something in place for the World Cup in the short-term and the country in the long-term. They feel that nothing was done to help reduce, reuse and recycle garbage during the World Cup 2007.

On a one to five scale, very poor to very good, respondents in Trinidad and Tobago rated efforts to use the World Cup to help improve management of environmental impacts an average of 2.33. In Barbados, ratings averaged 3.43.

Conclusion

This study offers important insights into the impacts that the 2007 World Cup Cricket event had on community-based tourism development in Barbados and Trinidad and Tobago. A survey in 2008 assessed the impact of recommendations from an earlier study in 2005. Results of the follow-up survey highlight differences between the two countries and the successes and difficulties encountered when trying to use a hallmark event to enhance community tourism development.

Both destinations were able to use the event as a reason to upgrade security measures in their countries. Security problems have been a deterrent to tourism in the region in the past. Security systems that were put in place for WCC 2007 should have a permanent dampening effect on crime in these countries and therefore a positive effect on tourism. In addition, both Barbados and Trinidad and Tobago were successful in using the WCC 2007 event to promote the expansion and improvement of their home-based lodging sector. These efforts should also have long lasting effects and help to develop a smaller-scale more community-based type of tourism. It appears from the findings that Barbados, probably because it hosted more WCC 2007 events of greater stature and therefore had more at stake, was more successful than Trinidad and Tobago in using WCC 2007 as the impetus for addressing issues associated with legacy planning, industry standards, sector coordination, and special events development. Both countries are certainly better equipped now to stage large scale events in the future because of the experience they had hosting such an attention-getting international event as WCC 2007.

Areas that both nations did not address adequately include crafts and agro-culinary development. The lack of success regarding crafts and agro-culinary development is distressing given the significance these factors could have had on community-based tourism development. The development of agro-culinary products and local crafts cannot only help offer economic relief to local communities but can also help promote cultural pride (Kessler, 2005).

The difficulties these countries experienced using the influence of the WCC 2007 event to promote community-based tourism development appear to be due in large part to: a) varying degrees of awareness among the various stakeholders about the potential for harnessing the power of such an event in each nation and across the region, b) obstacles that hindered the development of equitable policies, communication and coordination between international bodies administering the event, island governments, local organizations, community groups, and vendors and c) lack of formative research that could have provided the basis for sound strategic planning for each nation and across the region.

Lack of awareness seemed to plague community-based tourism development efforts as evidenced by the number of respondents who were "unaware" of attempts to address the ten categories of issues raised in this study. Community-based tourism development within the Caribbean region has not fully evolved because it has been overshadowed by a tradition of mass tourism (Weaver 2001). Diversifying the tourism sector by promoting awareness of community based tourism opportunities remains a challenge.

Organizational obstacles had a significant impact particularly regarding the interaction between the WCC 2007, ICC, the LOCs, and the other agencies involved. Respondents often commented on the "restrictive" nature of the ICC and some felt that the larger more established businesses benefited more than local businesses. While there were successful coordination efforts within the security and home-based lodging sector in both countries, the coordinating agencies often overlooked a potentially key stakeholder in these efforts—the local community. The inclusion of community based stakeholders is a fundamental premise of community-based tourism development particularly when it involves local products (Bossellman, Peterson and McCarthy, 1999).

A lack of research was identified as a general problem for both Trinidad and Tobago and Barbados. This lack of research affected several issues addressed by this study such as Special Events, Lodging, Crafts and Agro-Culinary development. In 2005, respondents agreed that there was a need for market research on visitor attendance and their needs/desires. While Barbados did make some effort to promote and assess markets overseas, the research that was conducted did not address many of the questions that needed to be answered.

Consumers are no longer content with the traditional sun, sand and sea image of the Caribbean (Vincent, Milne and Sarigollu, 1998) and tourism providers have struggled with a lack of research on Caribbean tourism to guide them in their efforts to develop alternatives, such as community tourism (Harrison, Jayawardena and Clayton, 2003). Although there have been some recent attempts to profile tourists to the Caribbean through benefit segmentation (Huang and Sarigollu, 2007), more extensive and targeted research is needed to adequately plan and promote community tourism development.

These three themes (awareness, coordination, and research) reflect the geographic reality of a region that is defined as much by its differences, as by its similarities. While the image of sun, sand and sea resorts still dominate the Caribbean landscape, the socio-cultural, economic, environmental and political variability of the islands within this region inhibit efforts to create a single model for community tourism development. Community-based tourism development cannot be homogeneous. In the case of WCC 2007, the multiple staging areas within the Caribbean complicated efforts to create a unified plan to promote community tourism.

The negative impacts of the well-financed mass tourism industry on Small Island Developing States like the Caribbean and have proven to be formidable obstacles in the development of smaller-scale indigenous-types of community-based tourism (De Kadt, 1979; Harrison, 1992). As someone once said, *money makes might and might makes right*. The power (might) of a hallmark event like the Cricket World Cup also appears to have overshadowed efforts to promote the development of lesser-financed community tourism. Even still, as discussed above, some progress was made in both Barbados and Trinidad and Tobago. Findings from the surveys discussed in this chapter identified both strengths and weaknesses of attempts to harness the influence of Hallmark events to stimulate community-based tourism development. Hopefully, lessons learned here will inform future efforts elsewhere.

Chapter 6

The Social and Cultural Consequences of Cricket World Cup 2007: Poor Spectatorship in Trinidad and Tobago

Anand Rampersad

Introduction

Cricket World Cup 2007 (CWC 2007) provided several Caribbean islands with the opportunity to host a major international mega-sporting event. A window of opportunity was provided to the region's social, cultural, economic, political and sporting appeal to the rest of the world through the arrival of thousands of cricket fans and television audiences across the global. The hosting of this mega-sporting event also posed several logistical challenges—legal, air travel, local transport and accommodation, security and sponsorship issues—to all of the organizing stakeholders given the size and geographical spread of the eight sovereign states. None of the previously staged World Cups were characterized with such logistical challenges of this magnitude. It is unknown that any major tournament was simultaneously held in so many countries in any other major sporting discipline. Hence, the Caribbean was truly undertaking a historical task.

The organization and rationalization of the tournament reflected the principles of Weber's rational-legal authority and Ritzer's McDonaldization thesis. It was multifaceted and comprehensive involving clearly defined rules and regulations to ensure that the tournament was successfully staged. The rules and regulations were implemented to protect the rights and interest of the several stakeholders—the International Cricket Committee (ICC), the ICC Cricket World Cup 2007 organizing committee, the West Indies Cricket Board (WICB), the various Local Organizing Committees (LOC's) sponsors, the media, regional governments and local and foreign spectators. The tournament offered a multitude of positive derivatives through job creation, visitor arrivals, media coverage and the development of the host territories and the region as an entire socio-politico economic sphere. The organization of the World Cup was premised squarely on the capitalist ethos of achieving profitability with economic profits being the main objective. This organization ethos was reinforced by the reality that regional governments had incurred large outlays facilitating modern cricket stadia as well as public knowledge of the enormous financial debts that the WICB.

Considering the socio-cultural impact of the mega-event, it can be argued that of all the stakeholders, the organizational ethos of the tournament impacted most negatively upon local (regional) live spectators. They appeared to have experienced the greatest level of disenchantment and dissatisfaction. A dialectical relationship between the organizers through their rules and regulations and local (regional) cricket fans through their social dispositions was created throughout the region. From the spectator perspective there seemed to have been an obvious lack of understanding of the dynamic social, economic and cultural aspect of live cricket spectatorship in the Caribbean by the organizers. Evidence throughout the Caribbean indicated that there was a woeful misapprehension of the habitus and social practices that define all that is cricket in the Caribbean. These social practices are deeply rooted in and shaped and reshaped by historical antecedents. On the other hand, it can be construed that normative principles governed the organization of the tournament, which assumed and expected the population especially avid traditional cricket fans to have been overwhelmed by the staging of the mega-sporting event in the Caribbean. In addition to being overawed, it was assumed that regional people would have responded uncritically to the rules and regulations of the tournament. In lieu, Caribbean cricket fans responded by staying away from the matches. Even those matches that involved the West Indies cricket team did not attract the overwhelming customary interest of fans. The reaction by perennial ardent cricket spectators seem to reflect a form of social, economic and cultural alienation that was created by the dialectical relationship between the organizers and people who view the sport as more than a game. In other words it was just not cricket!

It is the contention of this chapter that two major interwoven factors may have accounted for the poor local spectatorship (live/active) during Cricket World Cup 2007 in Trinidad and Tobago and by extension the wider Caribbean. Firstly, the rationalization or McDonalization of the tournament through the organization principles of efficiency, calculability, predictability and control through non-human technologies discouraged and prevented cricket fans from experiencing the World Cup with their unique Caribbean style. Secondly, the organizers, especially those from within the region (sadly so) failed to demonstrate a proper comprehension of the historical and contemporary sociology of Caribbean people—inclusive of cricket spectatorship—reflecting change and development and which is also fraught with complexities and contradictions.

Sport in Trinidad and Tobago

Sport is a secondary social institution in Trinidad and Tobago and can be characterized by amateurish principles and practices. Generally speaking, the institution is not a primary source of employment, social mobility and status. It is usually competed away by the quest for education and the search for permanent and guaranteed sources of income. As a result, most athletes pursue sport as a secondary social activity to school or work or a combination of both. However, sport provides great opportunities for recreational and leisure pursuits for the general population. The bedrock of most sporting disciplines manifest the social characteristics of kith and kinship ties, religion, social class, race and ethnicity all of which in some cases are tied to geographical factors.

Since sport is a secondary social institution, it is not startling that the industry is at the nascent stage of development. Most of the sporting disciplines save a few are not professionalized in structure and organization (although this may be vehemently dismissed by those who are involved), which, is reflected in the lack of proper facilities, professional coaches and trainers, lack of data, heavy reliance on the state and corporate entities for financial assistance and sponsorship, poor sport management skills and low membership. Even in the two most popular sporting disciplines—cricket and football—the level of professional development is mostly visible in the premier divisions of the respective sports.

The Study of Sport and Spectatorship

The sociological and scientific study of sport has mirrored the development of organized sport in the world (Coakley, 2004). In recent years, the growing number of sport sociologists in the developed world as well as in other areas of the world has countered the traditional view that sport had a life of its own which was dominant up until the 1970s, by arguing that sport reflects the social political and economic characteristics of society. Therefore, sport is seen as being worthy of detailed systematic analysis. However, the study of sport has received little or no critical analyses from Caribbean social scientists (McCree, 1995). Sport is seen as an uncritical, romanticized, utilitarian social activity. Whatever Caribbean literature on sport that is available have been written from journalistic, historical and or literary accounts (Beckles, 2006; Ferguson 2006; King and Laurie, 2004; Manley, 1995; James, 1963).

As a corollary, it is not unforeseen that there is no available empirical study of sport spectatorship (live or televised) in the region. The literature that exists relates to literary and historical narratives namely about cricket (Rohler, 1994; Beckles, 1999). Although outside of the Caribbean, spectators and spectatorship have received sociological attention, it has been limited primarily to football spectators (Giulianotti, 2005). Furthermore, the focus on spectators is relatively negligible when compared to the interest shown by social scientists in relation to sports participation (Crawford, 2001; Thrane, 2001; Ciupak, 1973). With reference to the benefits of studying spectators, Giulianotti (2005: 289) argues that:

> … sociologists have considered spectators with reference to subcultures of violence, and systems of social control; cultural politics, resistance and popular empowerment; demographic composition and the construction of taste communities; forms of gender or national identity; and media representation.

Available literature on sport spectatorship indicates that a variety of intertwined demographic and social characteristics may affect spectatorship at sports events. Some researchers have argued that there is a positive correlation between social and economic status and sport spectatorship (Crawford, 2001; Thrane, 2001; White and Wilson, 2001). Yet still some studies have indicated that other variables such as age and ethnicity may cut across class appeal. One such example is a comparative sociological study of football crowds in Western Europe that indicated that although the matches attracted predominantly young white males, there was a varied class appeal that may not have been perceived (Waddington, Malcom and Horak, 1998). Similarly, Famaey (1981: 94) in a study in Dutch-speaking Belgium states that age is an important determinant of sport spectators. Famaey, further states that "sport events are more regularly attended in the lower strata of society. Executive staff and university graduates stick to occasional unplanned pleasure trips".

Therefore, given the fact that there is a glaring absence of sociological studies on sport and spectatorship in the Caribbean, a number of salient questions arise. For instance, to what extent does the available empirical evidence derived from studies elsewhere, apply to the study of sport and spectatorship the Caribbean? Does sport provide a sense of class distinction in society as obtains in developed countries for sports such as tennis, ice hockey and American football? Are Caribbean people religious supporters of sport whether the performers are at the pinnacle of their game or at the pedestal or do they only ride the wave of victories and successes? Does age, gender and ethnicity factor into sport spectatorship? These are important questions that must be understood when studying sport spectators in the Caribbean. *Ipso facto*, the sociological understanding of sport and spectatorship is useful in the planning and managing of sporting events in the Caribbean. Therefore, the social and cultural impact of the absence of rigorous data and analysis in the planning and implementation of CWC 2007 has to be determined. Such social and cultural impact assessment is not only important for CWC 2007 but also for all future sporting events especially major international events.

Cricket and Cricket Fans in the Caribbean

Cricket in the Caribbean is more than a sport. Cricket has provided Caribbean people with an opportunity to transform a civilizing and social controlling sport of the masses into a social and cultural mechanism of resistance manifested in the style of play and festive dispositions of live spectators (Beckles, 1999; Burton, 1995; St. Pierre, 1995). Cricket allows for "proletarian camaraderie" where the masses overcome the trials and tribulations of the everyday life (Patterson, 1995). The cricket fields in the Caribbean unlike other venues in the cricketing world are likening to a carnival stage where various actors portray their different roles to make the overall performance a success. It is a social site where historical symbolic battles have been contested.

Caribbean cricket fans play an important role in the drama that unfolds at the cricket arena. Through their cultural traditions and practices they add fervour and energy to the happenings on the field of play especially when the actual cricket may be unexciting. The rich socio-cultural diversity of the region is manifested in the celebratory style each of the various islands, which makes Caribbean spectatorship experience even much more unique and dynamic.

According to Rohler (1994), West Indian cricket values are tied to its culture through its music and literature. For him, the survival of West Indies cricket is linked to the replacement of the white elites and their cultural dispositions with a black West Indian personality and sense of community (1994: 109). He further states that this personality reflects the creolization of West Indian cultural experiences, which translates into a "sense of 'West Indianess', which ensures continued support for the team" (1994: 109). Similarly, like Rohler (1994), Beckles (1999) sees cricket and its survival as an important social institution for the masses and the less fortunate to overcome the elites and their cultural practices in society. Cricket facilitates the expression of cultural freedom through music, dance and literature (Beckles, 1999). He forewarns quite clearly:

> It is this (culture and attributes) special contribution that requires careful attention lest its value be lost within a haze of elitist assumptions about the culture of the "lower orders" (Beckles, 1999: 115).

At the same time, the culture of Caribbean people reflects degrees of complexities and contradictions, which may be problematic for both rationalist and like-minded. For instance, Caribbean people may clamour for effective management and policy implementation on one hand and yet still be critical of both the policies and the administrators. The field of sport provides excellent examples of the cultural complexities and contradictions of Caribbean people. When the West Indies cricket team or individual players are riding high on the crescent of success, they are elevated to the statuses of prince's and even demigods but when performances fail to flatter, the same "subjects" become their major critics sometimes in the most verbally outlandish manner in the form of insular comments. Another example of the contradictions and complexities is in relation to the qualification drive of Trinidad and Tobago's national football team ("Soca Warriors") for World Cup 2006. At the initial stage, a high level of doubt and suspicion characterized the interest level and poor on the field performances compounded this. However, as the performance of the team improved and the light of qualification for the World Cup shone, the interest level magnified almost by the size of the population; 1.3 million. The interest level continued to soar not only in the realm of support for the team but also in the nationalistic spirit. However, the euphoric period subsided after the World Cup; the high level of suspicion and doubt about the team's ability that prevailed at the initial stage of the World Cup 2006 campaign dictates once again. Therefore, the sociology of Caribbean people makes it extremely challenging and problematic for unknowledgeable educators, uniformed planners and administrators.

Sociology of Pierre Bourdieu

The sociological concepts of habitus, capital and field as employed by Pierre Bourdieu (1978, 1988) may offer a theoretical insight into the poor spectatorship during the CWC 2007. Furthermore, it may also provide important lessons to be considered when similar events in the future are to be organized. Bourdieu employs the concept of habitus to serve as mediator between structure and agency. Habitus regulates the social practices between institutions and actors. He notes that habitus is not only a "structuring structure but also a structured structure" (Tomlinson, 2004). Therefore, there is social dynamism within the interactive process. The concept of capital refers to a form of power social groups possess to enact change and control (Tomlinson, 2004). Social practices are mediated by the degree and type of capital that an individual or group may possess. These include economic capital (income, wealth, spare time) (Wilson and White, 1999), cultural capital (expression of taste), educational (qualifications) and symbolic (image and reputation). The interplay between these types of capital will inform the practices of social groups and classes. The term field refers to social settings where there are objectively defined positions, which may be in opposition to each other. Therefore, fields are social sites of struggle between those who want to preserve the status quo and those who want to engender change through transformation.

According to Bourdieu, lifestyle choices are influenced by the access to various forms of capital. The various types of capital help to reinforce the class relations of domination and subordination (Wilson and White, 2001). Cultural, educational and symbolic capital enhances individuals or groups ability to engage various forms of social consumption and taste. Therefore, sport participation and sport spectatorship can be affected by access to the various forms of capital. The "rules" of the game may serve as a deterrent for interest or participation for some groups such as the lower class.

In this study, the field is the sport of cricket with specific reference to spectatorship. Within the field there are written and unwritten "rules", which define what is valued and legitimate and what is not. Historically, as indicated by Beckles (1999), the elites in society thrust their acquired colonial values and practices over and above the values and social practices of the lower classes. These superior values and practices are manifested in every facet of life from speech, attire and mannerism. Hence, there is a structure of power relation between the dialectical positions of what is valued as acceptable and non-acceptable behaviour, which is aligned to the dynamics of class, race, ethnicity and gender.

The cricketing crowds in Trinidad and Tobago and the wider Caribbean have their own habitus, which has been shaped by their daily-lived experiences. Their daily experiences would have been shaped by the extent of the degree of economic, cultural, educational and symbolic capital they possess. Cricket has predominantly been a sport of the masses and for the masses, which has shaped both the type and kind of attending crowds. Therefore, cricket emits high symbolic capital to the lower classes in society not only in terms of participation but also attendance. At the same time, cricketers and spectators in the Caribbean may not necessarily display the high levels of educational capital as their counterparts in England and Australia. Therefore, although cricket may offer symbolic capital it is not enough to serve a means of economic distinction in society.

ICC Rules and Regulations—Rationale

The ICC rules and regulations were enacted to ensure that the tournament was executed with a high degree of integrity and safety to all stakeholders involved. As a result, legislation through the passage of the Sunset Legislation attempted to protect the rights of legitimate sponsors of the competition against any exploitation from unofficial sponsors through "ambush marketing". Additionally, safety measures had to be put in place at each venue to protect the players, officials and the public from potential harm especially after the horrific events of 9/11. As such, a list of clearly defined "do's" and "don'ts" were identified for the public to take into consideration when attending the matches. How did these rules and regulations impact upon the social behaviour of the local public?

The Social and Cultural Consequences

Purchasing Mechanism for Tickets

Traditional live spectators of cricket have always used the queuing mechanism for purchasing tickets. For CWC 2007, the traditional and optional means of purchasing tickets via the queuing system was fully replaced by the on-line system via the Internet. For the traditional average cricket fan this method was totally lost upon them as it was not customary. Traditional cricket fans emanate from the masses who may lack not only the economic capital to afford the credit rating to obtain credit cards but also may not have the cultural capital taste—as a result of low educational capital—for the consumption of computers and internet access. Furthermore, the general distrust of authority—which is related to, the historical impact of colonialism—may have further served as major disincentive for live crowd participation by the lower classes.

Prices of Tickets

Cricket in the Caribbean is a kith and kinship activity. It is an opportunity for family members to spend a day together enjoying a favorite pastime. The average price of tickets for One Day Internationals (ODI's) involving the West Indies in Trinidad and Tobago is about US$32 (TT$200). However, the CWC 2007 prices ranged from US$25 to US$90 even though the West Indies was not playing. Therefore, it meant that in addition to having to purchase tickets online and in US currency, the traditional cricket fan was discouraged by the high prices of tickets. When questioned about the high prices of tickets, Malcom Speed the Chief Executive Officer of the ICC, indicated that the offer was made to the respective LOC's to set their prices. In an interview with the *Sunday Express* columnist BC Pires, Speed indicated "... the West Indies Cricket Board came back to us (ICC) with the ticket pricing". Therefore, it seemed that the major concern was meeting the budgeted revenue from ticket sales as well as assisting the WICB meet its large financial debt.

A comparison to the FIFA Under-17 World Cup that was staged in Trinidad and Tobago in 2001 indicates that tickets were priced TT$10–20 (US$1.66–3.33) (preliminary stages) and TT$40–60 (US$6.66–10.00) (final stages). Most if not all the games were sold out, even the ones that did not include Trinidad and Tobago, as it was affordable to everyone. Similarly, Cricket South Africa responded to the questions about the high-ticket prices for CWC 2007 by ensuring that the 20/20 World Cup that was staged in September 2007 did not suffer the same fate of high prices and restrictions.

Concession Prices

One of the major aspects of cricket in the Caribbean especially in Trinidad and Tobago is its celebratory culture both on and off the field. Off the field, the jovial culture of music and dance is reinforced and fueled by excesses of food and beverages, which may range from being non-alcoholic to alcoholic. Furthermore, it is a tradition for spectators to take prepared food and drinks to the cricket grounds. However, some of the restrictions impacted on this established practice. The option of purchasing the items that otherwise would have been brought from their homes was not alluring given their price structure. The prices of the items that were on sale were unaccustomed to the traditional cricket fan. At the practice matches, prices for the concessions were as follows:

Doubles	TT$6.00 (US$1.00)
Guinness	TT$36.00 (US$6.00)
Carib Beer	TT$18.00 (US$3.00)
Coconut Water	TT$24.00 (US$4.00)
Sandwich	TT$30.00 (US$5.00)
Nuts	TT$6.00 (US$1.00)
Water	TT$12.00 (US$2.00)

These prices were met with resistance in the form of protest. Not accustomed to paying so much for water, spectators opted to fill zip lock bags with water to enter the sporting arena. After much protest there was a reconsideration of some of the prices, which after the re-pricing would still have been steep for the traditional cricket fan. For the first official match, the prices range was:

Carib Beer	TT$18.00 (US$3.00) to TT$12.00 (US$2.00)
Water and soft drinks	TT$12.00 (US$2.00) to TT$8.00 (US$1.30)
Cashew nuts	TT$12.00 (US$2.00) to TT$9.00 (US$1.50)
Rum	TT$30.00 (US$5.00) for a drink
Roti	TT$42.00 (US$7.00)

Cricket is a family event and given the various unaccustomed prices, there would have been a high disincentive to attend the matches.

Rules and Regulations

The checklist that was provided by the ICC for spectators infringed upon the traditional Caribbean way of celebrating cricket. The restrictions involved a ban on entering the stadia with alcohol, which is an integral part of celebrations that takes place in the region. Restrictions were also placed on bands and musical instruments (such as the trombone, bottle and spoon), except where approval was given by the LOC after receiving a request from the potential bearers of the instruments. Furthermore, patrons were asked to remove caps on their bottled water before entering the ground. These rules and regulations are unheard of in the Caribbean and the sudden imposition was interpreted as yet another attempt to control and manipulate who they are and how they celebrate a sport that means more than a sport.

The rules and regulations stifled the cultural atmosphere. In Trinidad and Tobago, at major sporting events spectators are treated to the antics of nuts vendors by way of how they get the nuts to the buyers. At a practice game nuts men were informed that they, "… can be ejected for throwing packs to … customers, since they can be considered missile" (*Express*, March 7: 7). The rationale for such an action was printed on the tickets with reference to Terms and Conditions, which stated, "… that the throwing of objects might cause damage to people or property is reason for ejection". Furthermore, questions of uniformity and consistency in the application of the rules and regulations were evident as some patrons entered the facility with caps on their bottled water and other bottles containing various liquids while others were prevented as the rules stated. Hence, the questions of discrimination of treatment based class, status, race and ethnicity surfaced in the application of the rules.

The rules and restrictions were evidently admitted by the organizers to be problematic and discouraging to those locals who were prepared to pay the prices to attend the matches. As a result, there was a relaxation in some of the rules and restrictions as were manifested from the second round of the tournament.

Absence of the Future (Children)

One of the major disappointments of CWC 2007 was the absence of children, especially school children, at the matches even though throughout the region, especially during the first round, there was an expanse of empty seats at the cricket grounds. This was troubling, as West Indies cricket has been on the decline for a number of years without many answers being offered to arrest this development. The history of the development of West Indies cricket is rich with schoolboys' teams throughout the region. However, this was not evident in the planning of CWC 2007. Furthermore, the other disincentives of high prices both for tickets and concessions would have further worked against the presence of children at the matches.

Ethnic Factor

Trinidad and Tobago were awarded the Brown Package, which included first round matches in Group B. This group included three of the four Asian teams: India, Sri Lanka and Bangladesh. One of the potential rationale of hosting these teams here in Trinidad and Tobago was the large Indo-Caribbean population. Therefore, it seemed that ethnic appeal would have drawn large crowds to the matches. This thinking may have hinged on historical evidence such as when India won the test match at the Queen's Park Oval in 1976 and received rapturous support from the local Indo population. However, socio-economic and political changes have taken place amongst the Indo population, which is reflected, in a greater contemporary nationalistic interest than in past. As a result, there is a greater appeal to see the West Indian players' especially local batting maestro Brain Lara rather than Sachin Tendulkar, Rahul Dravid, Sanath Jayasuriya or Mohammed Ashraful. The societal changes are reflected in the behaviour of spectators, which reinforces CLR James claim that cricket goes beyond a boundary in the Caribbean (James, 1963).

Public Relations

A proper sociological understanding of the behaviour of Caribbean people would have facilitated greater effort being taken in communicating the rules and regulations and their reasoning. An understanding of sport spectators would have assisted the LOC in marketing the tournament in a manner that would have reached the public in a more effective manner. Informed knowledge of the social and cultural habitus especially of traditional cricket fans may have allowed the LOC to enhance its marketing drive in such a manner that they may have been able to attract greater local attendance. As much that some would argue that the extensive marketing was unnecessary; given the uniqueness of the event, greater effort should have been made to ensure that the general community appreciated fully the significance of cricket as a major social institution in the region. There was a need to bridge the gap between the organizers and the general population especially given the history of public distrust for authority.

Discussion

The social and cultural uniqueness of the West Indian crowds were stifled for an extended period during the World Cup much to the chagrin of Caribbean people, visitors, cricket commentators and even some of the players of the participating teams such as Australia. The Caribbean socio-cultural flavour was glaringly absent as a result of the over-rationalization of the tournament (which was recognized by the start of the "Super Eight") and a failure to understand the habitus of the people who attend cricket in the region.

It seemed that Allen Standford (an American) had a proper understanding of Caribbean peoples' socio-economic cultural dynamics. The Standford 20/20 competition manifested the cultural diversity of the people throughout the region without all the rules and regulations of the World Cup. The Standford 20/20 tournament allowed spectators to express their cultural narcissism of the respected islands through the use of colour, music, flags and other paraphernalia. In addition there was the obvious sight of women and children of all ages throughout the duration of the tournament. There was no gainsaying that the tournament marketed in an unfettered manner the cultural diversity of the region, which was so gloweringly missing for the CWC 2007.

The interplay between habitus, capital and field is quite useful in understanding the social and cultural effects of the rationalization of CWC 2007 in Trinidad and Tobago with reference to spectatorship. The rationalization of the tournament affected many of the social and cultural aspects of the average cricket fan in Trinidad and Tobago. Most of the rules and regulations served to highlight the historical struggle between the elites and the lower classes; the dominant and the subordinate and "high" culture and "low" culture. Although the tournament was brought to the Caribbean to be experienced by the people of the region, in the end, cries of social and cultural alienation were quite evident.

Unlike sports in developed countries, members of the lower classes dominate in participation and spectatorship. Therefore, the high prices and the means of purchasing tickets would have been contrary to their habitus and social practices and therefore they responded by staying away from the matches. A similar understanding could also be drawn for the rules and restrictions on the historical, social and cultural behaviour—music, dance—at the matches, which was in opposition to the normal habitus of the fans.

The rationalization of the tournament would have been interpreted as yet another attempt by an external/foreign agency (ICC), facilitated by local agents (regional governments, the WICB and the regional organizing committee) of neo-colonialist practices. It seemed that the population construed the rules and regulations as another attempt by those in authority to control and exploit: the unequal relationship between the core and periphery was highlighted. Such interpretation triggered cricket fans with a response of empowerment by staying away from the games or following them via the television or radio.

In Trinidad and Tobago, people may have been additionally encouraged to stay away from the matches because the restrictive features of the CWC 2007 would have been in blatant contradictions of the free and expressive cultural behaviour associated with the Carnival Season. Additionally, the economic and social development of the society has facilitated greater social and cultural options and choices of expression. Therefore, although CWC 2007 was a mega-sporting event, its organizational restrictions may have serve as an incentive to the population to find established means of unfettered expression of self.

The staging of World Cup matches in Trinidad and Tobago did not automatically mean that people would have gravitate to the games as there is no established or predictable culture of sport spectatorship. Success and affordable entrance fees does not guarantee spectatorship. For instance, even though the national cricket team has been very dominant in the region over the last five years; they have not been able to draw consistently large crowds when they play at home other than if they are playing in a final. Therefore, it would become even more problematic to predict crowd response where prices of tickets go contrary to their usual expenditure. However, it would have been predictable that people would not have been attracted to pay the entrance fees to see Bermuda play especially since they are not a top ranked cricket team. It is in this light that one has to appreciate that sport is amateur in Trinidad and Tobago. There is no professional fan that would fork out monies weekly to see any team play.

Conclusion and Recommendations

The major legacy of the CWC2007 is that it made a profit of US$53.9 million more than any of all the previous tournaments. Additionally, US$31.4 million was derived from ticket sales, which is also the highest, compared to all previous tournaments. At the same time, it is ironic that the World Cup with highest ticket revenue also reflected poor local spectatorship throughout the region.

The rules and regulations of the World Cup interwoven with the complexities and contradictions of Caribbean people contributed to poor spectatorship in Trinidad and Tobago and the wider Caribbean. The sociological understanding of Caribbean people reflects complexities and contradictions, which may present a formidable task for the rational organization of any event. The task becomes even more problematic if there is an underestimation of the socio-cultural strength of the people as was experienced by the organizers of the CWC 2007.

There is no guarantee that had the rules and regulations not been restrictive that attendance would have been high but given the historical importance of cricket, every attempt should have been made to encourage wider participation of the general public in the World Cup. The receipts from ticket sales may have been greater and more importantly, the social and cultural value of the region would have been displayed. The legacy of the tournament would not have been measured mainly in economic profits but also in social and cultural gains.

Based on the above it is recommended that:

1. There is need for a sociological understanding of sport in the region. An understanding of the social and cultural factors that influence involvement in sport is required.

2. The sociological understanding of spectatorship if undertaken would provide insight into the issues and concerns of spectators who participate in live sporting events.
3. The sociological understanding of sport and spectatorship would provide invaluable information to sports administrators and management personnel. This is critical to the region as the sports management and sports tourism are fledgling fields.

Acknowledgements

The author would like to thank Jay Coakley for his constructive comments on drafts of this chapter.

Chapter 7

Cricket, Lovely Cricket? The Views of Urban Locals and their Participation in Sports Tourism: The Case of the 2007 Cricket World Cup in Kingston, Jamaica

Shenika McFarlane

Introduction

Tourism is the largest industry in the world. In Caribbean countries, in common with many other Small Island Developing States (SIDs), tourism has been the chief foreign-exchange earner. It is therefore hardly surprising that McElroy (2005) views the Caribbean as the most tourist-dependent Region in the world with numbers increasing from 10 million stop-over visitors in 1990 to 21.8 million in 2004 (Caribbean Tourism Organization [CTO], 2006). In Jamaica, tourism has proven to be the most indispensable industry especially since the agricultural and bauxite sectors have been faced with adversities in recent times. Despite the vulnerability of the island's tourist industry to global variables such as terrorist attacks and natural hazards such as hurricanes, Jamaica has managed to sustain growth in visitor arrivals increasing by 15.3 percent in 2006 to reach the 3 million mark (Planning Institute of Jamaica [PIOJ], 2007).

The hosting of mega-sporting events is seen as the ultimate opportunity to achieve "the promise of an economic windfall" (Matheson and Baade, 2003: 2) within cities. It is therefore no wonder that cities such as London, Moscow, Havana and Madrid were racing each other to host the 2012 Olympics. With thousands of tourists scheduled to touch Jamaican grounds, the economic prospects of hosting the Cricket World Cup was certainly appealing to all. Additionally, the seasonal nature of the Jamaican tourist industry, has lead the island's tourism developers and planners to warmly embrace sports tourism as this serves to diversify such seasonality. In common with many other mega-sporting events, the Cricket World Cup was seen as a means to leave lasting positive legacies in the Kingston urban space. But as demonstrated in the last Cricket World Cup hosted in Southern Africa in 2004, the prospective legacies are not always achieved. It was during this time that cricket tourists and citizens who have been oppressed, hoped that the World Cup would serve as an instrument to loosen up the region's tight political regime. This chapter, illustrates that the potential benefits of hosting the Cricket

World Cup in Kingston were achieved only to a limited extent. The main aim is to test these potential and achieved legacies as expressed by the urban poor, a group which is often overlooked as significant stakeholders in tourism development.

Sports Tourism: There is no single definition for sports tourism. It can, however, be conceptualized as "arising from the interaction of activity, people and place" (Weed, 2006: 305). As earlier mentioned, sports tourism in Jamaica is seen as an important means of combating the seasonality of the island's tourist product and the capital city has been the island's biggest mecca of such events. Past hallmark events include the Commonwealth Games of 1966 and the World Championships in Athletics in 2002. The Cricket World Cup, however, has been the largest and probably the most culturally significant spectacle to be hosted in the city of Kingston. Traditionally, studies on mega-sporting events—otherwise called "Megas" (Roberts, 2004: 108)—tend to focus solely on the economic legacies which are garnered from such spectacles. But these events have the ability to renew the social fabric of any city, leaving long-lasting impacts or legacies (Kearney 2005). However, Bull and Lovell (2007), drawing on their hindsight, note that while event organizers and sponsors may accrue substantial benefits, it is usually not clear how residents are involved such events.

The Study Area in Context

The Sabina Park, which was the match venue for all Group D matches, is located in the capital city of Jamaica—Kingston. In terms of geography, Kingston is a coastal town which has the Blue Mountains Range as its backdrop to the north and the Kingston Harbour to the south, the seventh largest in the world. Kingston, the second largest city of the English-speaking Caribbean has a total population of almost 600,000 (579, 137) according to the Statistical Institute of Jamaica (STATIN, 2003). However, the effective urban area extends throughout the Kingston Metropolitan Region (KMR), with a total population of close to one million. Much of the population increase in Kingston is attributable to increased birth rates, as well as the continuous rural-urban drift which largely occur for economic reasons. In an effort to more effectively manage this rapid expansion in the urban centre's population, Kingston was, in 1923, amalgamated with urban St. Andrew to form the Kingston Metropolitan Area.

There is a central point of agreement in literature on Kingston that this city has a characteristic Uptown-Downtown dichotomy (see Dodman, 2006; Clarke and Howard, 2006; Gray, 2004) in which the dominant socio-economics of these areas is in turn reflected in the dominant spatial structure. The more affluent members of the city tend to live Uptown whereas the less affluent—many of which are poverty-stricken—occupy Downtown. With this feature in mind, Kingston cannot only be viewed as a "postmodern transgression" (Austin-Boos, 1995) but also a "postmodern perfection".

Research Methods

Several methods of collecting data were employed. Qualitative data were collected from March 2006 to March 2007 and took the form of focus groups, interviews and textual analyses. The focus groups and interviews were carried out with local stakeholders such as the vendors of the Kingston Craft Market and residents of the Social Development Commission's selected Theme Communities. Semi-structured interviews, lasting over two hours each, were conducted with locals as well as planners from governmental organizations. These individuals included the Regional Director for Kingston and St. Andrew at the Social Development Commission (SDC); a Senior Planner at the Urban Development Corporation (KSAC); the Urban Development Corporation (UDC); the Chief Executive Officer at the Kingston City Centre Improvement Committee (KCCIC) as well as representatives of the Tourism Enhancement Fund (TEF) and the Tourism Product Development Company (TPDCo). Textual analyses were an important part of the desk research and mostly entailed the evaluation of the stories in the local newspapers such as *The Gleaner* and *The Observer* which pertained to the participation of Kingston's poor in the staging of the Cricket World Cup. Some vendors were initially reluctant to participate in the study as they were either tired of being interviewed or were afraid that I may have been from "government".

The focus groups, consisting of eight individuals each, proved to be an effective means of "facilitating others' analysis ... [and] handing over the stick of authority" (Chambers, 2002: 132). Residents were empowered by virtue of allowing them to analyse specific issues, complemented by my role as a moderator. Important views were garnered from these discussions concerning their level of participation in the Cricket World Cup. In agreement with Babbie (2004), the focus group can indeed be understood as a method of bringing individuals into a laboratory for observation. Both the focus groups and the interviews proved to be pertinent means of collecting *qual*ity data. However, a major limitation of these methods of investigation, as seen through the eyes of Positivists is that they are non-scientific and may therefore create problems of representability.

Discussion

Whose Reality Counts? An Overview of Participation in Tourism

The 1970s saw a shift in the approach to the conceptualization of "development" in general. This philosophical turn was facilitated by an increasing critique of the top-down and "centre-out" planning (Potter et al., 2004; Potter, 2003). The current definition of the concept of participation is:

> An essential means to empower communities to identify their priorities and to
> ensure their control over the actions and resources needed to achieve their goals

... participation offers a new approach to the governance of societies (United
Nations Economic and Social Council-UNESCO, 1998: 3).

The work of Robert Chambers was most influential in the bid to facilitate bottom-
up development in his 1983 and 1997 books. In the latter entitled *Whose Reality
Counts?* He asserts that the preferences, values and social realities of the poor
contrast to those of the more wealthy.

Deflecting attention from Chamber's rural appraisal tourism, it is clear that
participation has been a part of the most recent debates in tourism sustainability.
This is reflected in the coining of terms such as Community Based Tourism (see
Murphy, 1985) and Community Participation in the Tourism Development Process
(see Tosun, 2000 and 2004). Participation in tourism as used in this chapter, takes
off the definition given by Dallen Timothy (1999) who, after conducting studies in
Indonesia concludes that this is a two-fold process. He believes that if locals are
not included in the decision-making process and the benefits generated from the
tourism activities—especially in economic terms—then participation in tourism
is handicapped. Thus, it was significant to incorporate the views of the residents
of Kingston in the quest to assess the extent to which an event of this magnitude
could facilitate participation as a panacea.

As reflected in the Ten Year Master Plan for Sustainable Tourism Development,
locals are theoretically incorporated in the tourism development process. The
Plan, which was prepared for the Government of Jamaica by the Commonwealth
Secretariat, has five main tenets, two of which directly speak to the inclusion of all
in the benefits to be had from the tourist industry:

- The third goal of the Plan is:

    For sustainable development, local communities must play a major role
    in defining, developing and managing the tourism experience so that
    they take ownership of the industry ... planning should be bottom-up,
    not top-down.

- The fourth goal of the Plan is:

    An inclusive industry. From its current perception as an exclusive
    industry that benefits the few, the Jamaican people should come to
    view the industry as inclusive ... this calls for measures that ensure that
    the benefits of tourism are spread widely (Commonwealth Secretariat,
    2002: vi).

The staging of the Cricket World Cup in Kingston was marketed and presented
as a passport to prosperity or at the very least, a nudge to the development of
community tourism in a city which is desperate for any form of development. So,
to what extent were these tenets realized during the staging of the biggest event

to have ever been hosted in the island? The answer to this question lies in the perceptions of local individuals and local communities which are reflected in the following sections.

Views of the Residents of the Theme Communities

Since one of the pillars of sustainable tourism development is community-based planning (Timothy, 1998), it does not come as shocking that Tosun (2004) sees members of host communities as "the main actors of development" (Tosun, 2004: 336). In order for this bottom-up or participatory planning to be achieved, then the way for participation to occur in its fullest sense, there first has to be a fair balance of power in the decision-making process among the actors of tourism development. It is against this backdrop that select governmental agencies of Jamaica claim to have attempted to empower poor communities of Kingston before and during the Cricket World Cup of 2007—both in an economic and social sense. This claim is underpinned by the selection of Theme Communities as well as having on paper, plans to refurbish the Kingston Crafts Market.

The Theme Communities were thus called "because they offer something that has been going on traditionally, not just for World Cup but for the longest while", explained Mr Wilfred Talbert, field officer at the Social Development Commission (SDC) in an interview with a media personnel (JIS, 2006: 1). These communities were Allman Town, Trench Town, Port Royal, Rae Town and Tivoli Gardens. Each of these places is characterized by at least one aspect of the urban heritage tourism product that was poised to enrich the experience of the hundreds of domestic and international cricket tourists who were scheduled to flood the city. Allman Town, the host community, has Black revolutionary Marcus Garvey as its first parish councillor; Trench Town has a rich music heritage and is known for its association with Bob Marley; Port Royal for its history of piracy (especially in the aftermath of *Pirates of the Caribbean*); Rae Town for its old hits and Tivoli Gardens for Passa Passa, a dancehall affair. The chief facilitator for the involvement of communities in the Cricket World Cup was the SDC, which has as its Mission Statement:

> To facilitate the empowerment of citizens in communities, enabling their participation in an integrated, equitable and sustainable National Development Process (The Social Development Commission).

From as early as 2006, these Theme Communities were being sensitised and informed about the Cricket World Cup. The prospect of hundreds of tourists visiting a city that is not normally first on the travel itineraries of tourists, certainly instilled a certain level of exuberance in these locals. However, as time for the start of the tournament drew closer, the sentiments of most of these residents also evolved. These views were essentially mirrored in the local newspaper. For instance, towards the end of 2006 the headline of *The Gleaner* for October 26 read: "Communities Prepare to Reap Rewards from Cricket World Cup" and

"Culture Plaza to Benefit Communities around Sabina Park" in the December 24, 2006 issue of the same newspaper. A sharp contrast in the sentiments of the urban locals was reflected just before and even during the World Cup including threats to disrupt the tournament.

Allman Town   Of all the Theme Communities, Allman Town was probably the community that was most distinctly poised for incorporation in the participatory process. Allman Town, like some of the other Theme Communities, has been marred by spates of violent crimes, poverty, among other social ills over the past few decades. Any chance of participation in tourism development would have therefore prospectively served as a means of empowerment. In accordance with the precepts of the participatory approach, the residents of this community were allowed to produce locally-defined goals for the SDC, but the extent to which these were achieved is where the real concern lies. Through focus group discussions, it was concluded that the community members were fully incorporated in the planning process. For this community, consultation with the residents started from as early as 2005 with a series of meetings with the other stakeholders, including the West Indies Cricket Board, the police, the Local Organizing Committee (LOC), the Jamaica Public Service (JPS) and the National Water Commission (NWC) and the Urban Development Corporation (UDC).

The residents indicated that before March 2007, which was when the tournament started, they were made to feel a part of the planning for the city's staging of the tournament. Their comments and concerns were recorded at these consultation sessions but were not, at least for the most part, reflected in reality. But could the fact that Allman Town was the host community means that what initially seemed like participation was indeed what Few (2003: 32) terms "containment" (2003)? Although not specific to tourism, Few (2003) in his studies on the protected areas in Belize concluded that the authorities only "incorporated" the residents of this territory in the project in order to prevent any disruption to the project by them. With the match venue, Sabina Park, being in such proximity to the area, it would not come as shocking if authorities were trying to prevent any possible disturbance from these neighbours.

In addition to the series of consultative meetings, the residents expressed that they were appreciative of the social and spatial renewal which took place in sections of the Allman Town area as they prepared for the event. Direct participation in the spatial revitalization of their community made them feel as though they were indeed participants in the preparations. Under the Lift Up Jamaica Programme, residents collaborated with members of the Jamaica Defence Force (JDF) to rid the community of derelict walls, old zinc fences and overgrown trees along what was scheduled to be the "Park and Ride Route" in January 2007. According to one resident of the community, "the zinc fence no really look good … wouldn't mind if two more World Cup come" (*The Gleaner*—January 27, 2007). A community representative explained that some residents eventually rejoiced as the HEART Trust/NTA provided the Allman Town Benevolent Society members with training in capacities such as health and safety, budget management and conflict resolution. To this end, residents explained that a general increase in the literacy of its residents was the area in which the community benefited most distinctly; many even learned how to fill out simple forms such as bank slips.

In an interview, a community leader and executive member of the Allman Town Benevolent Society, Miss Tamara Reynolds, explains that the greatest disappointment came close to the tournament when the community's proposal for a Culture Plaza was dissolved by the SDC. The Culture Plaza, scheduled to be set up in close proximity to Sabina Park, was meant to be the community's project involving the display of wares made by residents to the cricket tourists. Mr Courtney Brown, Regional Director at the SDC, explained in an interview that the budget for the project which was initially approximately J$40 million was cut down to between J$7 million and J$9 million. Furthermore, the community was not able to secure sponsorship. According to Miss Reynolds:

> We were told our plans are going to be scrapped by the SDC and that the One Love Village was now the main focus, not our plans again.

That the cancellation of the Culture Plaza project a few days before the start of the event came as a big blow to the residents, was reflected in their threats to disrupt the matches by means of protest if they were not made to feel a part of the process as much as a year or so before. It is against this background that the General Secretary for the Greater Allman Town Benevolent Society, Mr. Lawman Lynch, echoed sentiments similar to those of many other locals that the World Cup failed in empowering the poor. In an interview he confirms, after finding out about the dissolution of the project that, "this thing about community tourism is a façade" (*The Gleaner*—March 5, 2007*)*. Some of the residents who were scheduled to vend in the Culture Plaza were instead instructed to pay a sum of J$20,000 to J$30,000 for one booth and venture to the Uptown district of New Kingston which was the location of the One Love Village. This venue, being located in very close proximity to the three top hotels—which all recorded a 70 percent occupancy level—in the city meant that the prospect of earning profits from vending was good. However, like the dilemma of the Kingston Craft Market vendors, very few tourists visited the village.

Residents of Allman Town such as Sheryl Smith, was angry at the fact they had to borrow huge sums of money in order to purchase stocks, which only lead to a loss rather than a profit as few tourists visited the Village. It was in this regard that these locals saw their relocation to the new venue as one of the most inappropriate decisions that any top-down stakeholder could have made for them. This sentiment was captured in the issue of *The Gleaner* two days after the start of the World Cup, "Not Feeling the Love" (March 15, 2007). Vendors waited for the influx of tourists which was promised, but none came. As such, they had to discard perishable items such as cooked food on a daily basis, with no profits being accrued.

Trench Town   Trench Town, one of the most socio-economically depressed Communities of West Kingston, is known locally and internationally for its association with the Jamaican music heritage. It is in this regard that it is described by David Howard as:

> The stamping ground of a young Bob Marley [which], more than any other downtown district has clearly marked its place on the world cultural map (Howard, 2005: 125).

This space, which played its part in producing the greatest reggae superstar on earth (in addition to other performers as Dean Frazer, Peter Tosh, Alton Ellis and Wailing Souls), was positioned to benefit from the city's staging of the 2007 World Cup. However, as in the case of the other Theme Communities, plans fell through the cracks of the floor. Trench Town has been the nesting ground for not only the "King of Reggae" but also for a myriad of reggae artistes who have made their mark on the musical culture of Jamaica.

Even though there were no mass clean up projects, the residents of Trench Town echoed similar sentiments to those of Allman Town; they were disgruntled about a number of things. Firstly, the J$4.8 million which was approved by the Ministry of Tourism, headed by the then Minister of Tourism, Aloun Assamba was not granted. The money was supposed to come from the Tourism Enhancement Fund (TEF) for the upgrading of the Trench Town Culture Yard and Museum, Bob's former home which has been transformed into a tourist attraction. The residents of this community had hoped that the money would have been granted so that at least Bob Marley's first vehicle, now a wreck, could have been repaired. While the Projects Manager at the Tourism Enhancement Fund, Mr Christopher Miller is of the view that the Culture Yard had a huge potential to benefit from the tournament, "the project did not get started in time for the Cricket World Cup". Culture Yard, as opposed to the Uptown Bob Marley Museum which receives thousands of tourists per year, it receives only 30–40 visitors per month. This level of under-use of any attraction undoubtedly has serious implications for its sustainability. As underpinned by McKercher and Ho (2006: 473), "both over- and under-use pose threats to the sustainability of cultural tourism products".

Secondly, they believed their community was not being given a fair chance to benefit from the tournament. In this regard, the residents here lamented that the Social Development Commission in particular, had failed them before they were given a chance "to pass the test". Put in the words of Sonia White of the Trench Town Development Committee (TTDC) who explained her point of view:

> No, dem gi' we failing grade before we even start di test. So why dem nuh gi' we di exam and mek we pass it?! That's all we ask fo', gi' we di pencil, di pen and mek we pass before yuh fail we!

Thirdly, the residents of Trench Town not only thought that the authorities were deliberately discouraging tourists from visiting the community, but also that the significance of the community's attraction was being downplayed. According to them, cricket tourists were scheduled to visit Trench Town on March 17, 2007 according to the Local Organizing Committee's official calendar of events. As one worker of the Trench Town Culture Yard reflected, "all was in place for the Roots Rock Reggae Kingston 12 Tours". The residents lamented that the staging of such a large event brought no benefits to such a culturally rich community. In the words of one member of the focus group:

> World Cup was the most devastating t'ing wha' could happen to any community in my point of view.

It is not clear as why no funds were provided for the materialization of Trench Town's project. However, the sentiments of the citizens have led one to question whether the facilitation of partial participation was mere tokenism or was it just done because incorporating grassroots in decision-making was just the right thing to do? It seems as though the required human and social capital were already in place for the reaping of the economic and social empowerment that the hosting of the World Cup had to offer.

Tivoli Gardens   Jamaica has been dominated by dancehall and ragga. In the words of Sonjah Niaah, "The 'dance' provided physical, ideological and spiritual shelter for a generation of lower-class Jamaicans" (Niaah, 2006: 14). Just as the more affluent of Jamaica identify with prestigious clubs, the masses find their identity in the lyrics of dancehall alongside the physical space of the "dance". Tivoli Gardens is probably most associated with violent, gang-related crimes. But this small West Kingston community has, since the 1990s, developed a brand for themselves- Passa Passa, a type of street dance held in the community every Wednesday. Even though the majority of attendees are the masses, it should be noted that tourists —especially the Japanese—and Jamaicans from all strata of society can be found there. It was this brand that the community members were hoping to market to the expected influx of visitors to the city during the World Cup.

Like those of the other Theme Communities, however, the residents of Tivoli Gardens were sensitised and were made to feel that they were a part of the planning for the tournament as their community representatives were invited to several planning meetings leading up to the event. The community members felt secure and increased their hopes when they were told to create and submit a budget for their Passa Passa project which had as its pivotal role to attract as many cricket tourists as possible. But even though the community members, in preparation to reap economic rewards, purchased and made souvenirs (such as hats, T-shirts and buttons with Passa Passa, Tivoli Gardens written on them), the proposal failed to receive the funding which was required. This is the reason why the residents of this community have been resentful about the city's hosting of the World Cup. As pointed out by Wayne Bartley, a member of the Tivoli Gardens Development Committee, "nobody no benefit from World Cup, Tivoli Gardens did not benefit!".

The community members were not only disgruntled at the fact that they got no sales for their goods but also that promises of participation in the Bed and Breakfast Programme remained unfulfilled. Consequently, they had to seek local buyers for their wares as soon as the World Cup ended. When asked about their perceptions of the major way in which Tivoli Gardens have benefited from the tournament, it was explained that the answer to this lies in the temporary employment which was provided via the beautification exercise which occurred along Marcus Garvey Drive. It was also observed by these locals that the social capital of the community was put under some amount of strain as some blamefully got into confrontations with community leaders and representatives over the notion that Tivoli Gardens was excluded from the promised benefits of the tournament.

Port Royal   Port Royal is probably the most internationally acclaimed town in Jamaica (especially in the aftermath of *Pirates of the Caribbean*). Port Royal has been called the "City that Sank" since up to two-thirds of it sank beneath the Caribbean Sea during the earthquake which occurred in 1692. Also known to tourists as "The Wickedest City on Earth", the town is considered the most significant underwater archaeological site in the Caribbean. It is presently described as "a singularly unspectacular little town" (Pawson and Buisseret, 2000: xiii). According to these authors, it is disappointing that a place with such an extraordinary past has such scanty evidence of it on display today. Heritage tourism plans have been developed for the town from as early as 1965. However, as argued by Waters (2003, 2006), the residents here are not equipped with the necessary resources to counter the level of exogenous decision-making experienced over the years.

Like those of the other Theme Communities, the residents of Port Royal indicated that they were fully involved in the series of consultations and planning meetings up to one or two years before the World Cup. However, Mr Brown of the SDC, explained that the locals of this town were not as enthusiastic as members of the other communities and this alleged level of lethargy had a direct bearing on the level of participation which was achieved. Interestingly, discussions with the residents here have revealed that many of them did not attend these meetings which were being facilitated by the stakeholders in their community and were therefore not well informed. Additionally, many a times there were more disagreements than consensus at these community gatherings, which only served to defeat the purpose of meeting in the first place.

Politics, as conveyed by the members of the focus group, seem to have had its place in the decision making both as a means and as an end. The year of the World Cup (2007), also being the year of the Jamaica's General Elections, meant that the political atmosphere was profound. It was against this background that the variable of Party affiliation was being played out at some of these meetings where individuals of one political Party tended not to listen or co-operate with persons of the other. Even though Port Royal is deemed as one of the most peaceful and united communities (see Waters 2003 and 2006), it must be understood that a portion of it is usually unenthusiastic about tourism development and the consequent influx of visitors in their small community in general terms.

The Port Royalists indicated that they did not benefit economically from the tournament, even though they were made to believe they would. In this regard, the few fish vendors who purchased extra fish for preparation were greatly disappointed that no tourist came. The residents further lamented that Port Royal, like Trench Town, was scheduled to host activities during the time of the tournament in addition to promises by the Tourism Product Development Company Limited (TPDCo) to participate in the Bed and Breakfast Programme. As one resident stated "everybody went to New Kingston for entertainment instead". Another expressed that "nothing happened, nothing happened at Port Royal or Kingston. I don't know if it's the crime or what that kept the tourists in".

Like the residents of Allman Town and Tivoli Gardens, the Port Royalists believed that the only way in which the community benefited from the World Cup was via the clean up project which went on for about two months before the start of the tournament. They explained that many residents earned stipends from working on this venture. The residents were, however disappointed that no beautification in the community was initiated—especially at the entrance to the town. The fact that plans to mount a monument at the site where the first coconut tree in Jamaica was planted did not come through also wreaked resentment, but to a much lesser extent.

Views of the Kingston Craft Market Vendors

The Kingston Craft Market, located on Pechon Street, Downtown Kingston, is known to be the nation's first craft market. This is due to the fact that Kingston was, in the 1960s and 1970s, Jamaica's chief port-of call for cruise ships. The craft market vendors of Kingston, represent one group of local stakeholders who were expected to participate directly in the prospective profits of the Cricket World Cup. One main reason for this level of expectation is that the market is in close proximity to the drop off and let off points for the cricket tourists. By March 5, a few days before the start of the tournament, these vendors, however, were lamenting that sales were worse during the tournament than before. All the support they had was from their usual—customers buying presents for relatives and friends. As one vendor stated, "World Cup was for the rich and famous, it wasn't fo' people like me ..." This statement hints that the inverse of goal four of the Ten Year Master Plan for Sustainable Tourism Development, which seeks to increase the inclusiveness of the industry, came into play. Another vendor explained that the tourists:

> Jus' came, took their cars and buses and jus' left ... we didn't even see what they look like ... we draw out everything out of we bank book and stock up fi

nothing. We were preparing to get a piece of the pie, but if a pie we de wait pon we woulda starve!

It would appear that the significance of proximity to the points of arrival of tourists in the vendors' economic survival has decreased over the last three to four decades. Kingston's hosting of the Cricket World Cup has done little to change this situation. The vendors were of the view that in addition to the apparent failure of the Jamaica Tourist Board (JTB) to market the Craft Market to the visitors, the Cricket World Cup's authorities on a whole discouraged the tourists from walking in and around Downtown. This is, at least in part, the reason why the upgraded Kingston Waterfront remained unused by visitors during the tournament.

Not gaining the expected income from the Cricket World Cup was one aspect of failure in local participation. Not being incorporated in the pre-World Cup decision-making phase was another disappointment. The vendors indicated that while they were consulted on issues that were affecting them and their recommendations, they asserted that these views were not reflected in the final decision-making and tourism policies. So, was the planners' facilitation of participation in the first place mere tokenism? Or was this recognition even participation any at all, since according to Cleaver (2001) true participation ought to make locals the focus of development? It can, in this regard, be argued that their power to participate in decision-making is weakened by their comparatively weak social capital. Some amount of disunity exists among these vendors, which is reflected in the breakdown of their local crafts association. Scholars such as Tyson, Hayle, Truly, Jordan and Thame (2005) had hoped that the staging of the Cricket World Cup would have strengthened the vendor's social relations. However, this was truly not a benefit.

The vendors indicated that what served to discourage them was the fact that none of the plans for the massive face-lift of the market was carried out in time for the tournament, with the exception of the painting of the outside of the walls. This exercise proved to be more useful in providing a suitable backdrop for the cricket-goers' park-and-ride waiting than to bring clientele walking past their stalls. They complained that the inside of the walls were left unpainted and that the roofs leaked badly. Mr Christopher Miller of the Tourism Enhancement Fund explained that while his organization had pledged the revenues for the re-roofing exercise, there was still the question of when it would commence. He further pointed out that it should be understood that the Urban Development Corporation failed to deploy the necessary manpower to fix the roof.

Just as the vendors thought that they were going to permanently benefit from the World Cup, their hopes were bowled out. They pointed out that new light poles with electricity were installed just before the tournament along Pechon Street. But as soon as the tournament was over, the lights were out. This occurrence has convinced them that the World Cup was only for tourists, and perhaps Kingston's wealthy but not the city's locals. A senior planner at the UDC, Mr Paul Griffith, when asked about the issue, indicated that the real reason for this power disconnection stemmed from faulty electricity poles. He was also quick to clarify that since the World Cup ended, it has been the responsibility of the Kingston and St. Andrew Corporation (KSAC) to see to the reconnection. Whatever the explanation given, the market vendors still see tall new light poles, but receive no light. If the locals are not made to feel a part of the tourism development then any potential for sustainability is greatly affected. As pointed out by Kearney (2005), mega-sporting events should last a lifetime by virtue of the city not only hosting an event but also building a legacy.

When asked who they thought was responsible for their seeming exclusion, a number of answers were given. Firstly, they believed that the relevant marketing authorities failed to market the Kingston Craft Market to the cricket visitors. Also, they insisted that the tourists were not made aware that a craft market was located in such close proximity to where they are let off and picked up on match days. Secondly, they believed that it was the larger establishments of Uptown that acquired most of the profits from tourists who spent money on crafts. One vendor explained that the souvenir shops at the hotels as well as those shops in urban St. Andrew got the sales that should have been shared with them.

Conclusion

Kingston's hosting of the largest sporting event to be held in the city seemed to have acted a sound tool of spatial regeneration, especially at the Sabina Park itself and parts of its immediate surroundings. However, from all indications, there were many glitches in the attempt to use the city's staging of a mega-event as a tool of social renewal. These obstacles to participation include undelivered promises and miscommunication at all levels. Additionally, it was uncertain as to whether the act of incorporating the grassroots in the planning process in the first place was just another means of improving the imaging of governmental agencies (Few, 2003; Mosse, 2001).

Clearly, millions of dollars were spent on, before and during the start of the matches, but not on the projects of the city's poorest community members. The views of the main local stakeholders (the vendors of the Kingston Craft Market and the Theme Communities) were presented in this chapter as case studies. One of the main arguments of the latter part of this chapter coincides with that of Pal (2006), of who advocates that real devolution of planning power to locals will only occur if the political and administrative bodies allow them to do so by giving their ideas and needs precedence. Findings of this research have suggested that there is no doubt that the residents of Kingston, like those of Sheffield (England) expressing sentiments in the aftermath of the 1991 World Students' Games, believed that the massive spending on the tournament and little or none on the Theme Communities' projects, was, in the words of Bill Bramwell, "municipal stupidity" (Bramwell, 1997: 175).

124   *Sports Event Management*

Acknowledgements

The author is grateful to the University of the West Indies (Mona Campus) for supporting this research, Dr James Robertson and Dr David Dodman for their supervision as well as to the postgraduates of the Department of Geography and Geology for their comments on my 2008 Brown Bag Seminar presentation. The assistance from Dr Ashok Sookdeo and Mr Robert Kinlocke during the early stages of this study as well as the support of Dr Damion Morris, Ms Saundra Wilson and Mr Donald McFarlane during the final stages of the study is well appreciated. The input of all interviewees and focus group participants is also recognized.

PART III
Event Logistics and Marketing

Chapter 8

Work of the Sports Agronomy Team (SAT) for Cricket World Cup 2007

Francis Lopez and Louis Chinnery

Introduction

The Sports Agronomy Team (SAT) was set up to provide consultancy services to the CWC 2007 West Indies Inc. on matters related to pitch and field. Initially, SAT consisted of staff members of the University of the West Indies Sports Agronomy Research Unit (SARU), Department of Biological and Chemical Sciences, Cave Hill Campus, Barbados. A program was set up to help ensure that cricket grounds selected for play and practice during Cricket World Cup 2007 were of the required standards expected for competition and preparation at the highest level of the game. The involvement of a local team involving scientists and cricket experts interacting with overseas consultants was especially important in providing a legacy of technical skills and research and development infrastructure for sports grounds in the Caribbean. Assessments and advice given on site were supported by appropriate scientific data, and SARU continues to be involved in the development and verification of various grounds testing techniques at the University of the West Indies. Members of the team interviewed venue representatives at summit meetings and made periodic inspection and advisory visits to all countries in which games were scheduled. During the period of venue development, information was provided to grounds staff/management for improvements, and to the organizers for evaluation of the progress to event readiness and follow-up action where needed. Inadequate priority to pitch and field matters was identified as the main reason for late or non-completion of scheduled work on some practice areas. There appeared to be communication gaps and unclear management control lines between the many stakeholders leading to late-stage pitch and field concerns at some venues. This chapter outlines the main components of the work of the SAT, shares some of the experiences, including successes and shortcomings, and makes suggestions on possible improvements to be considered in future strategic planning.

Sports Agronomy and Cricket World Cup 2007

The Sports Agronomy Research Unit

Sports facilities of the highest standards are necessary to both attract international sporting events and related tourism to the Caribbean, and encourage the development of local world-class athletes who can further promote the region as a tourist destination. In order to support this, there is an urgent need for a scientific approach to the development and maintenance of these facilities that meet the expectations of athletes, sports governing bodies and sports tourists in a resource-efficient manner and with adequate consideration for environmental protection. To address these issues, the Sports Agronomy Research Unit (SARU) was established during the academic year 2002–2003 (UWI, 2003) in the Department of Biological and Chemical Sciences, Faculty of Pure and Applied Sciences, the University of the West Indies, Cave Hill, Barbados.

Agronomy is defined as the theory and practice of crop production and soil management (Beard, 2005). Following from this definition, we can further define sports agronomy as the body of knowledge and skills that underpin the development and maintenance of living playing surfaces and amenity areas. It is an applied science that involves the use of biological, chemical and physical principles to arrive at the best package of practices to achieve the desired appearance and performance characteristics of these facilities.

SARU is intended to be a hub for sports agronomy and to provide much required research and support services for the expanding sports facilities in collaboration with other agencies within and outside the region. The Unit currently has a Research Fellow in Sports Agronomy who works with academics in ecology, plant sciences and horticulture and has access to others in a wide range of disciplines within the Faculty.

Since Cave Hill has been designated by the University of the West Indies as the lead campus for cricket (UWI, 2006), this was the first sport to be addressed. SARU was first involved in the 2002–03 upgrade of the cricket field (3Ws Oval) at UWI, Cave Hill. This was first laid out by Sir Frank Worrell (Professor Hilary Beckles, *Pers. Comm.*) who along with another of the three Ws, Sir Clyde Walcott, is buried overlooking the field. Further improvements were made to the ground before the warm-up games for Cricket World Cup 2007. The field provides a convenient site for the development and evaluation of technological innovations. SARU has also developed strong linkages with the local organization overseeing sports in Barbados (National Sports Council), which has administrative control over most of the sports fields on the island. Therefore, SARU is well-positioned in terms of expertise and access to local fields and other resources to provide leadership in research, training and support services for the improvement of sports fields in the region. SARU is seen to complement other academic cricket activity at Cave Hill, including the teaching of cricket history since 1992 (Beckles, 1998) and the introduction of the M.Sc. in Cricket Studies in 2006.

Table 8.1   Individual Members of SAT

Team member	Specialization	Country
Professor J. Atherton	Horticulturist, UWI	Barbados
Dr L. Chinnery	Ecologist, UWI	Barbados
Dr F. Lopez	Agronomist, UWI	Barbados
Mr A. Roberts	Former Cricketer Cricket Pitch Consultant	Antigua

The Sports Agronomy Team

After several months of discussions between SARU and the organizers of Cricket World Cup 2007 (CWC 2007 West Indies Inc.), the contract formalizing the Sports Agronomy Team (SAT) was agreed in April 2006. Under this contract, SAT would continue to provide consultancy services on matters related to pitch and field for the event. Initially, SAT consisted of members of SARU, however, a cricket pitch consultant was subsequently included (Table 8.1) to strengthen the team's experience and ability to deal with pitch preparation issues. At the time SAT was established, cricket grounds to be used during the competition had already been selected by the International Cricket Council (ICC). Nevertheless, considerable work was still required on these fields and SAT was asked to help ensure that these grounds reached and maintained the required standards during the event.

The involvement of local scientists and cricket experts in SAT was critical to provide a legacy of technical, research and development infrastructure for sports agronomy in the Caribbean region. This was considered to be very desirable to reduce the dependence on foreign experts for maintenance of the facilities beyond the development period and in the preparation for future world-class events. SAT was expected to gain valuable experience working side-by-side with the overseas consultants to tackle the numerous sports agronomy issues associated with an event of such magnitude. Coping with the largest Cricket World Cup to date was uncharted territory for the West Indian nations, eight different jurisdictions with little previous experience handling global sporting events (Cozier, 2007). The main components of the work of the SAT are outlined in this Chapter along with the experiences on and off the field during preparations for Cricket World Cup 2007, and suggestions are made for improvements in the planning for future events.

Work Components of SAT

Advice to Local Organizing Committees

Cricket World Cup 2007 activities in each of the eight host countries were coordinated by a Local Organizing Committee, which was headed by a Chief Executive Officer and included a Venue Development Officer and a Cricket Operations Officer. SAT obtained information and provided advice on preparation activities, specific problems and future plans at each venue by the following means:

Interviews with Venue Representatives at Summit Meetings   Summit meetings were held at regular intervals in one of the eight host countries. Venue representatives from each host country were brought to a central location for interviews with various consultants and dissemination of information on the progress of preparations and the state of readiness of persons, methods and facilities. SAT carried out the interviews with regard to pitch and field matters with a team that included the coordinator of Cricket Operations from the central office of Cricket World Cup West Indies 2007 Inc.

Phone and Electronic Communications   A frequently updated list of phone numbers and electronic mail addresses was made available by Cricket World Cup West Indies 2007 Inc., this included their staff, consultants and members of the Local Organizing Committees. Persons on this list were also given electronic mail addresses specifically established for communications with regard to the event. The designated contact person for SAT in each host country was generally the Cricket Operations Officer of the Local Organizing Committee.

Site Visits to Individual Countries   By December 2005, initial site visits had been made by SARU to all host countries to review the state of the grounds at the main competition venues and also at the designated practice grounds. Follow-up visits were made on request to address specific problems. A grand tour of all the venues took place in November 2006 to assess their readiness for the event, and this included quantitative evaluation of pitch and field at the main competition grounds. It is only during these country visits that SAT had direct contact with the grounds staff at each venue. Countries were visited at other times to deal with particular concerns, e.g., possible negative effects of saline irrigation water. Some of these were at the request of Cricket World Cup 2007 others by the Local Organizing Committee.

In order for SAT to provide meaningful advice when requested, or to predict problems that may crop up at a later time, it was necessary to have accurate knowledge about the construction and maintenance activities occurring on each field. Information requested by SAT from the LOC and grounds staff included details on:

•   Soil type and drainage on the outfield.
•   Grass species and cultivar(s) on pitch and outfield.
•   Provision of a technical package by the field developers.
•   The presence and nature of a grass supply nursery to facilitate rapid field repair.

- Irrigation type and water source, supply and quality.
- Facilities for safe storage of agrochemicals.
- Number and general construction of pitches.
- Source, analysis and storage of clay used on pitches.
- Local availability of technical support and advice.
- Records kept with regard to pitch and field management and cultivation.
- Available field equipment, covers and facilities.
- Health and safety concerns of the grounds staff.

SAT also had the opportunity to gauge the quality of the grounds staff in terms of skill and initiative level, willingness to use new techniques and strategy for pitch and outfield operations. The initiation of a system for keeping records at each ground was a priority for SAT, as such a system can allow a better diagnosis to be made when any problems arise and provide valuable information even when no changes or small improvements are observed. Important information to be captured by a records keeping system include weather data, agronomic inputs, field operations, sports use and field performance.

The advice provided by SAT was based on on-site field assessments, information provided by the LOC and grounds staff and the desirability of having equivalent performance characteristics across all grounds in a particular host country, i.e., the pitches at the practice grounds should be as similar as possible to those at the competition venue. Such advice included details on the agronomic operations required, current field status and standards to be achieved. Following the completion of development works and ICC approval of the grounds, SAT was expected to continue working with the LOC and grounds staff to help ensure that the field quality was, at minimum, maintained for the event.

Interactions with Organizers and Other Consultants

Written reports of field visits and consultations with venue representatives were submitted to Cricket World Cup West Indies Inc. and copied to the relevant LOC personnel and to the ICC pitch and field consultant. These reports advised on the progress made so far, work still required to be completed, specific problems and the recommended way forward. The status of preparations at each site was rated using a colour coded scheme with green (all systems go) indicating excellent performance, blue indicating satisfactory performance, yellow (caution) indicating unsatisfactory performance and red (danger zone) indicating unacceptable performance (Charles, 2007). Some of the field visits were made jointly with the ICC pitch and field consultant and SAT also had access to pitch and field reports submitted by this consultant. It was envisaged that SAT reports and consultations with ICC personnel with regard to field quantitative assessments would support the ICC's final approval process for the various grounds.

The administrative structure for the cricket grounds varied throughout the host countries especially with regard to the designated practice grounds, and there were cases in which additional pitch and field consultants were retained for individual grounds. SAT needed to liaise with these and other consultants involved in Cricket World Cup 2007, cricket club officials, field developers and maintenance contractors. In particular, consultants involved in the positioning of video cameras, boundary perimeter signage, on-field logos and the sight screens needed information on the order of use of pitches during the competition. Pitch numbering needed to be standardized across all host countries and agronomic considerations needed to be taken into account in deciding on the order of use for the pitches. There was some discussion with consultants with regard to agronomic factors that can improve the stability of the outfield sand for holding on-field logos in place using nails. The adverse effect of reduced light due to stadium shadows on the growth of the turf grass was a problem at a few of the main venues, and SAT liaised with private consultants and maintenance contractors to address this issue. SAT was also expected to liaise with other experts for international accreditation of field testing protocols.

Development of Assessment Tests and Guides

SAT was asked to develop tests and "expert guides" to help ground staff improve and maintain pitch and outfield performance. Equipment for these tests and assessments were funded by UWI and Cricket World Cup 2007 Inc., however, most of the ordered equipment did not start arriving until September 2006. This was too late to adequately address all the issues involved, therefore, SAT concentrated on the development and testing of only selected pitch and outfield assessment tests. Such quantitative assessments are critical to provide objective support for the assigned field ratings and advice on methods needed for improvements. The work of SAT in the development and verification of various grounds testing techniques at the University of the West Indies has continued since Cricket World Cup 2007. This will provide a sound basis for judgments with regard to field ratings and thereby stimulate competition among the various venues leading to overall improvement in standards. Scientific field assessments also provide a means of evaluating the impact of various agronomic innovations, which can promote a culture of continuous improvement.

Pitch Tests Performance characteristics of cricket pitches and the possible effects of soil type, moisture content and grass cover have been described previously (McIntyre and McIntyre, 2001), though, methods for quantifying such characteristics still require considerable research attention. Cricket pitch characteristics are commonly described using terms such as pace, bounce, turn, cut, consistency and durability. There are some variations in the definitions given for these terms (McIntyre and McIntyre, 2001; James, 2004), and modifications have been suggested (James, 2004) to avoid ambiguity. Definitions used by SAT of pitch characteristics and possible quantification techniques are as follows:

Pace of a cricket pitch is the degree to which ball speed is maintained following impact. This is likely to be related to surface hardness measurements made with the Clegg Impact Hammer (Lush, 1985), a portable instrument developed in Australia. Pace can also be indicated by the rebound speed (or height) of a cricket ball dropped from a standard height, usually 4.9m (Stewart and Adams, 1968), and these measurements can be facilitated by use of a high-speed video camera.

Bounce (or lift) of a pitch is given by the ratio of the angle of rebound to the angle of impact of the ball with the pitch. This is also likely to be related to surface hardness measurements made with the Clegg Impact Hammer, and can also be measured with the aid of a high-speed video camera.

Turn is indicated by the degree to which a pitch responds to spin bowling. Turn characteristics of a pitch can also be measured directly with the aid of a high-speed video camera and a bowling machine that imparts a standard level of spin to the ball.

Cut can be defined as the degree to which a ball is deflected from its trajectory due to the effect of the raised seam on impact with the pitch. This can occur consistently when the bowler is able to keep the seam of the ball oriented in the same direction through out its trajectory (often called "seam bowling").

Consistency can be defined as the degree to which pace, bounce, turn and cut characteristics are maintained over the surface of the pitch. This can be determined by statistical techniques, e.g., coefficient of variation.

Durability is the degree to which acceptable pitch performance characteristics are maintained over time on a pitch. This can be determined by similar statistical techniques over the period of a match.

Outfield Tests   Especially for television, a uniformly green surface with healthy growth of a single grass type is highly desirable and is visually attractive for spectators and players alike. In addition, the speed and evenness of ball movement are important features that influence the quality rating of the cricket outfield (Adams and Gibbs, 1994). Some terms that can be used to describe cricket outfield characteristics include appearance, ball speed, traction, consistency and durability. Some explanations of cricket outfield characteristics and possible quantification techniques are as follows:

Appearance. In order to exhibit a consistent colour, outfield turf must be free from pests, diseases and nutrient disorders and there should be uniformity of surface cover and plant density across the field. This can be quantified by visual observations, use of a chlorophyll meter or analysis of images taken with a digital camera at different points across the field.

Ball speed. This is the speed at which the ball will move across the field to the boundary when dispatched in a standard manner and should be consistent in all directions from the Square. It is likely that this will be affected by height and textural characteristics of the turf species, and the evenness, slope and hardness of the outfield surface. Standard ball speed tests are available in other sporting areas such as golf (Nikolai, 2005) and soccer (FIFA, 2006), and a similar ball roll distance test should be used to obtain a measure of the ball speed on a cricket outfield.

Traction. Turf shear strength and surface slipperiness determinations will provide a measure of the traction of the outfield. An acceptable level of traction is required for the safety of players and will encourage more entertaining play since it is likely to boost the confidence of the fielders.

Consistency. Consistency is given by the degree to which turf characteristics are maintained spatially across the outfield, and the level of variability (lack of consistency) can be estimated statistically.

Durability. Durability is the degree to which acceptable levels of field appearance and performance are maintained over time on the outfield. This can be determined by measurements on the outfield over the period of a match or following a simulated wear treatment, and statistical techniques can again be applied.

Impact of SAT

SAT was able to bring several issues to the forefront during field visits and some recommendations that feature prominently in the submitted reports include:

Increased Attention to Pest and Weed Problems

Pests and weeds lead to patchiness in grass colour and density across the outfield which adversely affects the appearance and performance characteristics of the field. Most of these problems were already noted by the grounds staff and SAT assisted by identifying the problem species, suggesting control measures and referral to other experts for advice where necessary. Emphasis was placed on proper maintenance of the surrounding vegetation (immediately outside the cricket field) which can serve as a reservoir for weed seeds, pests and diseases. It was suggested that, whenever possible, these areas should be planted with the same grass type as on the outfield.

Improved Grass Culture Practices

The new sand-based outfields developed for Cricket World Cup 2007 minimize the incidence of play interruptions and cancellations due to rainfall but require a higher level of management than the traditional soil-based fields. Increased frequency of irrigation and fertilizer application is necessary in these sand-based fields, and SAT highlighted any instance where adequate fertilizer storage or water supply arrangements were not in place. Recommendations were made on fertilizer type and application rates to be used after consultations with field developers and/ or maintenance contractors.

Attention to Surface Levels and On-field Safety Issues

There were instances where surface levels on the field needed adjusting such as depressions in the outfield, a too steep bowler's run-up, pitches below the level of the outfield or sharp drops along an edge of the square. These problems were generally more prevalent on the practice grounds, which were soil based, and SAT drew attention to the presence of any on-field feature which was considered to be unsafe or not in line with ICC guidelines. In many cases there were long delays in addressing these problems on the practice grounds, which were probably due to insufficient resources or administrative commitment to these grounds.

Practice Pitches Development and Proper Pitch Preparation Methods

In addition to on-field facilities, practice pitches with nets were required at the main venues for Cricket World Cup 2007. There were long delays in the establishment of these practice pitches in most cases, which were largely due to stadium construction activities in progress. SAT drew attention to the potential problems very early and provided advice on cricket pitch preparation options as the delays became more extensive. A cricket pitch preparation expert was on hand to advise grounds staff on pitch preparation techniques during most SAT visits to the various host countries. Delays in the construction of these practice facilities meant that the goal of matching the characteristics of these pitches to those on the Square was not achieved in time for the competition.

SAT highlighted the above issues to the appropriate staff of the relevant LOC and Cricket World Cup 2007 Inc., and thereby helped to ensure that adequate resources were provided to address the problems. The request by SAT for very specific information from the LOCs about on-site facilities for maintenance of the turf grass helped to ensure that adequate plans and provisions were made. SAT reports would have also served to prepare personnel at other grounds to deal with particular problems that were likely to be encountered across the region. The grounds staff and other personnel at the various venues would have benefited greatly as a result of these interactions, and the experience and new linkages developed should lead to greater expertise and training capacity for sports agronomy in the region.

Demonstration of Quantitative Assessments

SAT carried out detailed observations on selected pitches and outfields in the months prior to Cricket World Cup 2007. Based on ongoing studies at UWI Cave Hill, a system of sampling on the outfield was developed to allow a thorough sampling of field characteristics and compare different sections of the field (see Figure 8.1, end of this chapter). Measurements were made at 24 locations on the outfield and parameters measured included moisture content, grass height, soil penetration resistance and chlorophyll index (a measure of field greenness). Ball roll distance was also determined on some fields using a modified stimpmeter currently under development at UWI Cave Hill.

Quantitative assessments done on the outfield were used to draw attention to any management problems on the field and data were provided in simplified map diagrams generated using the common spreadsheet software, 'Microsoft Excel'. Although fields are depicted as square due to the limitations of the software, such diagrams can provide useful information on the level of variation that occurs across the field, the approximate location of particular problems and possible causes. Coefficients of variation (COV) were used to determine the level of field consistency with regard to greenness, and actual values of field moisture content, soil compaction, grass height, etc. were useful for diagnosis of possible problems.

An example of an on-field drainage problem that was detected for the main venue in Trinidad included high moisture content to the south of the field due to blockage of the drainage system as a result of stadium construction activities in the vicinity. Another example of a problem, this time for the field at Trelawny, Jamaica, was detected where the chlorophyll index (greenness) was high in the southern section of the field, decreased towards the north and was especially low towards the north east. Such a pattern can possibly be due to non-uniform fertilizer application, variation in grass height due to mowing having been interrupted by the weather on one day and being completed the next day or high on-field traffic due to construction activities that were then in progress north of the field. These problems were diagnosed during the preparation phase and there was sufficient time for remedial action prior to the start of the competition.

Pitch characteristics were determined based on observations at 20 sampling locations (McAuliffe and Gibbs, 1993) with measurements of slope and surface hardness at each location and soil moisture content at selected locations on the pitch. Observations commenced on each pitch with the placing of a measurement tape down the centre of the pitch from middle stump to middle stump. Ten observations were made at 2m intervals along the western side starting 1m from the stumps at the northern end and 0.5m from the center line, followed by ten corresponding observations along the eastern side of the pitch. Pitch slope at each location was determined in the east-west and north-south directions using a digital leveling tool, and the true slope and direction of slope were calculated from these measurements. Pitch surface hardness was determined using a 2.25kg Clegg Hammer (Model 95049, Lafayette Instrument Company, USA), and data for pitch parameters were presented in simplified map diagrams generated in a similar manner as for the outfield.

Pitches were considered to be unacceptable if the slope at any location exceeded 1.5 percent. Pitches that are highly variable in terms of slope and slope direction can indicate problems with regard to the techniques and/or equipment of the grounds staff. Such pitches are also likely to show high variability with regard to surface hardness due to differential compaction by the rollers, non-uniform wetting of the surface and the resultant patchiness of grass growth. This will affect the way the ball comes off the surface during a game, often manifested as inconsistent bounce.

Mean surface hardness (Clegg) readings were deemed to indicate pitches that were too soft (below 150g), slow (150–250g), medium fast (250–350g) or fast (over 350g). These values were determined empirically for West Indian pitches based on SAT's measurements with the 2.25kg instrument. Such quantitative assessments provided benchmarks and a means to determine progress towards ideal tournament conditions and allowed the grounds staff to gauge the effectiveness of their pitch preparation efforts.

Suggestions for Future Strategic Planning

It was very advantageous that the SAT included a person with both grounds staff experience in the region and experience of playing cricket professionally at the highest level along with scientists with expertise in agronomy and plant sciences. If the process were to be repeated, the services of a soil scientist as a member of the team could also be very beneficial especially with regard to cricket pitch related matters. Sports agronomists who were former players, umpires or who have strong interest in the game could also strengthen the power of such a team. But, the dangers of increasing the size to the point where efficiency is reduced and the probability of contrasting advice would need to be taken into account.

The involvement of overseas experts working alongside local sports agronomists with a deep commitment to the region will definitely help to build a legacy of skills and knowledge in the field. There are also advantages for the participation of a regional tertiary education institution such as UWI, particularly with regard to the potential for rapid expansion in sports agronomy training and the adaptation of programs to suit local requirements.

An earlier involvement of sports agronomists in the planning process for Cricket World Cup 2007 would have been very beneficial. By the time SARU became involved, the grounds to be used during the competition had already been selected and construction of field infrastructure and buildings had already commenced. Long delays for the removal of construction items from the playing field created problems at the main venue in Grenada, while shadows from stands and media centres too close to the boundary at the southern end adversely affected grass growth at three venues. This was an important oversight since the sun was to the south of all the venues in the months leading up to the Cricket World Cup. The SAT was informed by one LOC that the structure had been moved closer to the playing area to save money!

Maintenance of the irrigation water supply, drainage system integrity and access for grounds preparation equipment are also critical when field development is occurring alongside hectic building construction activities. Agronomists need to be involved at an earlier stage in planning the layout and construction to avoid or plan for likely associated problems. Additionally, the procurement of equipment, fine-tuning of methods and general planning of field procedures could be better facilitated by early involvement of sports agronomists.

The structure that was put in place for SAT's interactions with the various venues appears to have worked well. The Cricket Operations Officer from each Local Organizing Committee was the designated contact person for SAT in each host country, and these officers and SAT interacted closely with the Cricket Operations Manager from the central office of Cricket World Cup 2007 Inc. There were several instances where other officers of the LOC's, such as the Chief Executive Officer and the Venue Development Officer, were also directly involved to ensure that the work of SAT proceeded smoothly.

Particular challenges were experienced with regard to the transport of field testing equipment across the region and the cooperation of other agencies including airlines and airport Customs officials is vital. That procedures varied from country to country did not help.

Information from SAT was distributed very efficiently through the networks created and there was opportunity for feedback from the LOC's directly to SAT or through the offices of Cricket World Cup 2007 Inc. SAT only had limited direct contact with grounds staff at the various venues and training sessions at central locations were envisaged at the start of the programme. One training session for grounds staff was held in St. Kitts with the ICC pitch and field consultant and SAT used documents made available from this event to assist grounds staff to improve and maintain pitch and outfield performance and conform to ICC requirements. Up-to-date books dealing with pitch and outfield construction and maintenance (e.g., McIntyre and McIntyre, 2001; Tainton and Klug, 2002) should be readily available in each country. A greater number of training sessions and the development of "expert guides" tailored to individual grounds would have been, and still could be, very helpful to grounds staff. The provision of a technical maintenance package by the field developers and the training of grounds staff alongside maintenance contractors should be insisted upon for future events. Too little of this happened during CWC 2007. There was insufficient time for SAT to develop all the required field assessment tests and this work should continue so that appropriate protocols will already be in place when planning for the next major event. Collaborations with other experts are critical for international accreditation of field testing protocols.

Efforts toward initiating a system for keeping records at each ground should be continued. Such records could ideally be entered directly into a computer spreadsheet to facilitate calculations and distribution by electronic mail as required, however, a simple handwritten diary at each ground can provide a good start. The additional skills and work involved should be taken into account in the recruitment of grounds staff and appropriate compensatory packages should also be considered. To facilitate the keeping of records, there is a need for a system of assigning numbers/names to pitches and other field sections, and it will be advantageous to standardize this system across the region. Efforts to select practice grounds with equivalent performance characteristics in a particular host country will be enhanced by the availability of records at each ground. Further harmonization of field practices can be brought about by bringing the grounds staff together regularly for training sessions or meetings that promote general information exchange.

A greater level of priority needs to be given to pitch and field matters in the strategic planning for future events. Detractions such as late-stage pitch and field concerns and inadequate preparation or non-completion of practice facilities could possibly have been avoided. One can understand the urgency to get the buildings, and seats for the paying spectators, completed on schedule but the actual playing areas are central to the whole event and should be given adequate priority. Some of the construction related problems included storage of construction materials and the presence of surveying pickets on the field, interruptions in field water supply, blockages of the drainage system and delays in the removal of construction debris from sites earmarked for the establishment of practice pitches. The perception that engineers in charge of venue development are likely to be more concerned with building construction and less with pitch and field matters is not necessarily correct but needs to be addressed in future strategic planning.

Some problems arose because of the wide variation in administrative structures for, and ownership of, cricket grounds within and between the different host countries, with control in the hands of private cricket clubs, governmental ministries or local cricket boards. A further complication was brought about by the hiring of private field maintenance companies at some grounds in addition to the regular grounds staff. Communication gaps and unclear management control lines sometimes delayed the carrying out of work recommended by SAT, with disastrous consequences which almost caused one venue to be eliminated from the competition. It will be helpful for future events of this magnitude to use a participatory approach with the various stakeholders in the planning process so as to ensure acceptance of the overall plan for management of the facility and funding for improvement works. Greater involvement of the local and regional boards for the sport and players' representatives in the planning process could help to ensure that pitch and field matters and related players' issues are given sufficient consideration.

Acknowledgements

We wish to acknowledge the contributions of Professor Jeff Atherton (formerly of UWI, Cave Hill, Barbados) and Mr Andy Roberts to the work of SAT. Helpful discussions and guidance were provided by Mr Andy Atkinson and other ICC consultants. Our work was facilitated by the support of Mr Don Lockerbie and staff of Cricket World Cup 2007 Inc., and the cooperation of the various Local Organizing Committees and grounds staff across the region. Field and laboratory equipment was obtained with funding from UWI Cave Hill and Cricket World Cup 2007 Inc.

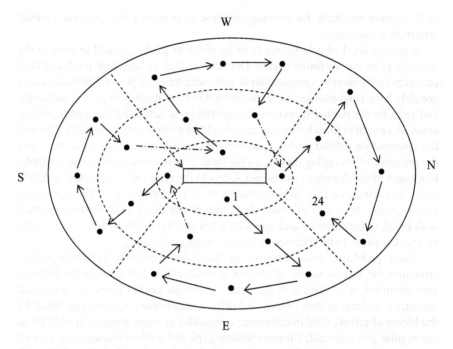

**Figure 8.1   Diagram Showing the Locations of Cricket Outfield Tests and
the Pathway Followed During Sampling**

Chapter 9

Accommodating Spectators: Community Attitude and Response to the Barbados Home Accommodation Programme

Cristina Jönsson

Introduction

Accommodation shortages can sometimes be an obstacle to hosting mega-events. With the planning for the ICC Cricket World Cup (CWC) 2007 hosted by the West Indies, the island of Barbados faced a major challenge with regard to accommodation. In preparation for the CWC, the number of available rooms in Barbados' accommodation sector was assessed, and it was recognised that available room capacity to accommodate the extra tourist flows generated by the mega-event would be diminished by rooms contracted out by tour operators and rooms sold to non-cricket visitors. The accommodation shortage was seen by the Government of Barbados as an obstacle in hosting the event and the government of Barbados found it necessary to developed additional accommodation in order to accommodate the influx of visitors and cricket participants to the island during the event.

A Bed and Breakfast/Home Accommodation Loan Fund of US$2.5 million was created by the government for the purpose to encouraging the development of community-based accommodation, alternatively described as Home Accommodation. This Loan Fund was available to property owners in Barbados who wanted to develop their homes or part thereof into Home Accommodation/Bed and Breakfast type accommodation. With this, the Government was hoping that a considerable portion of the room stock deficit could be provided and at the same time give residents the opportunity to play an active role in the development of CWC. The Home Accommodation Programme (HAP) had to be carefully planned before implementation since it could lead to an oversupply of accommodation after the event, especially if there was a lack of special demand (Cho, 2004). While the government wanted to include the community in the preparation of accommodation for the event, it was found important to understand residents' attitudes toward the government's Home Accommodation Programme.

To date, no (or little) published research has explored residents' attitudes towards major tourism events or initiatives in Barbados. Particularly, no research (academic or applied) has been generated with respect to residents' attitudes and views of the Home Accommodation Programme in Barbados. This chapter investigates this unexplored area of study, in an exploratory and descriptive fashion. It is expected that the findings not only follow academic lines but also assume practical and "applied" significance for policy makers in Barbados, particularly in the areas of tourism development and the importance to include the community, and major event planning. The purpose is to measure community response to the Home Accommodation Programme developed by the government of Barbados. The study seeks to explore whether differences in attitudes towards the programme exist with respect to various demographic factors such as age, gender, educational level and income. Furthermore, it also seeks to investigate whether frequency of contact with tourists, awareness of the programme, area of employment and perceived obstacles facing the Home Accommodation Programme are related to attitudes towards this initiative. Finally, the chapter identifies factors that are associated with these attitudes, and assesses these outcomes in the context of social exchange and contact theory.

Tourism and Mega-sports Events

Mega-events are a unique form of tourist attraction such as large internationally known events like the Olympic Games and World Fairs (Bowdin et al., 2006). Whenever sport is the primary purpose of a trip it is referred to as sports tourism (Mallen and Adams, 2008). The term has become increasingly common in the tourism industry over the past ten years and it is a lucrative segment of the tourism business. There is evidence that tourism is a major beneficiary of sports by enhancing local communities' image and providing activities and spending outlets for both locals and visitors and as such mega sport events play a considerable role in communities' lives (Getz, 1993). These events are usually viewed as a major economic tourist asset for the host area that also brings new facilities and infrastructure, renovation of facilities, creation of employment and cultural exchanges.

Events can be subdivided in four different categories (local, major, Hallmark and Mega-events) by using the size of the event and its impact (Berridge, 2007). Mega-events are one component of the tourism industry and it has been defined by Ritchie (1984: 2) as "major one-time or recurring events of limited duration, developed primarily to enhance the awareness, appeal and profitability of a tourism destination in the short and/or long term". Although there are one-time and short-term events, they have long-term positive consequences for the cities and communities that stage them (Roche, 1994). These consequences include growth of tourism and increased attention to the host city. The intentions of hosting an event are to renew investment in host cities, usually in the tourism sector, by projecting a positive image of the city (Berridge, 2007). Therefore, mega-events often inspire municipal or national governments to improve the appearance of the host city, usually on a very condensed timeframe.

With mega-events serving as mechanisms for physical redevelopment, considerable input of public support acting as a major means for physical redevelopment is needed. In the years prior to a mega-event, when the host city is preparing for international attention and a massive influx of visitors, it will often witness a lot of construction activity. However, during preparations for a large event, the distinction between short-term and ongoing development is unclear. Infrastructure such as hotels, stadiums and entertainment complexes are constructed for the purpose of the event, but these constructions are often related to a broader renewal or development plan.

In order for physical redevelopment to be successful, residents' support and involvement is imperative. Gursoy, Jurowski and Uysal (2001) argue that, since tourism depends heavily on the support of local residents, it is essential to understand residents' reaction and factors influencing these in order to achieve the goal of favourable support for tourism development.

In the context of this chapter, sports tourism will be viewed as "travel to participate in a passive (e.g., sports events and sports museums) sport holiday or an active sport holiday (e.g., scuba diving, cycling, golf)" (Ritchie and Adair, 2004: 8).

Community Attitudes Toward Mega-events

An increasing number of literature on event and impacts of events exists in the scientific literature (e.g. Mallen and Adams, 2008; Bowdin et al., 2006; Berridge, 2007). However, limited research has been undertaken to investigate community perceptions, attitudes and support towards the impacts of mega-events. The research focus has been mainly on impacts and outcomes of events, such as improvement of a destination's image, enhanced tourism development and community pride, increased employment, economic injection and increased visitation to regions (Jago and Shaw, 1998). Costs and benefits for communities and host destinations have been increasingly examined (Burgan and Mules, 2000; Carlsen, 2004; Crompton, Lee and Shuster, 2001; Mules and Faulkner, 1996).

Resident perceptions of pre- and post-impacts of the 2002 World Cup Games have been examined by Kim, Gursoy and Lee (2006). Their study was based on an exploratory factor analysis in order to identify perceived impact dimensions while the differences in perception before and after the games were analysed by performing repeated tests. The results show significant differences in benefits of cultural exchange, economic benefits, social problems, natural resources, pollution, price increase, construction costs, cultural exchange and social problems. However, there is a lack of literature on accommodating sports participants and its affect on the tourism development in a hosting destination.

Resident Attitudes towards Tourism Development and Their Participation in Planning

There has been substantial research on residents' attitudes and its influencing factors, towards tourism development (e.g., Williams and Lawson, 2001; Scholl,

2002). With regards to social psychologists and consumer behaviourists the term "attitude" has a technical meaning, while in the tourism literature this "attitude" is often used in its colloquial sense (Williams and Lawson, 2001). In other words, what is often described as an attitude in tourism would be termed as an opinion by a social psychologist. However, these terms are used interchangeably in the tourism literature.

Resident attitudes to tourist flows and tourism development has been studied and analysed by using various approaches. Davis, Allen and Consenza (1988) clustered residents into five groups: haters, cautious romantics, in-betweeners, love 'em for a reason and lovers. Residents were similarly clustered into three categories in Ryan and Montgomery's study (1994). They labelled the residents as middle of the roaders, somewhat irritated and enthusiasts. A well-established theoretical framework for investigating local communities response to the increase in tourist flows is that of Doxey (1975). This theory consists of a four stage model including Euphoria, Apathy, Annoyance and Antagonism. The model is an *ad hoc* index of irritation, "Irridex", to measure the changing attitude of communities to tourism development.

Furthermore, Harill and Potts (2003: 3) suggest that "attitudes towards tourism development range along a continuum from negative to positive". Various researchers have chosen to approach this continuum in a number of ways. Attitudes can be discussed within the context of the tourism development cycle, the segmentation approach and social exchange theory (Hernandez, Cohen and Garcia, 1996). While these are distinct and separate viewpoints it is also noted that these frameworks are complementary, rather than conflicting approaches. The authors argue that none of the approaches are complete by themselves and that each offers insight toward tourism.

Additionally, a modelling of resident attitudes toward tourism was performed by Lindberg and Johnson (1997). They introduced a broad, synthetic conceptual model of attitudes by which they evaluated survey data using structural equation modelling. The hypothesis that demographic variables affect attitudes indirectly through values was supported by the data. The study indicated that the strength of resident values regarding economic gain better predicted attitudes than values regarding disruption within the community. Perceived economic and congestion impacts had greater effect on attitudes than perceived crime and aesthetic impacts. The study provided strong indication that residents who find a growing economy important are likely to have positive attitudes toward tourism. Finally, the study also strongly indicated that resident attitudes are associated with the level of perceived economic and congestions impacts.

Gursoy and Jurowski (2004) classify the factors that influence residents' opinion about tourism as economic, social/cultural and environmental impacts. They argue that favourable impacts have been described as "benefits" while unfavourable impacts are considered "costs" (Gursoy and Jurowski, 2004: 296). The perception of costs and benefits can be a significant influencing factor when determining residents' attitudes to tourism in their community (Gursoy et al., 2001). Theoretically, Gursoy and Jurowski (2004) believe that if individuals perceive that benefits outweigh costs, they would make a logical and rational decision to support tourism development.

Gursoy et al. (2001) modelled host community support for tourism development based on the factors found to influence reactions towards it. They found that the host community support was affected by the perceived costs and benefits of the tourism development, utilization of resource base, and level of concern and ecocentric values. The findings show that community support for tourism development is affected by six factors: perceived benefits of tourism development, state of the local economy, perceived cost, use of the tourism resource base by local residents, level of ecocentric values of local residents, and level of community concern of local residents.

Factors which may alter residents' perception include the concern residents have for their community, their emotional attachment to it, the degree to which they are environmentally sensitive and the extent to which residents use the same resource base that tourist use (Gursoy et al., 2001). One can suggest that this argument gives a theoretical basis for the social exchange theory and builds on the works of earlier research. In this case, social exchange theory assumes that individuals select exchanges after an evaluation of rewards and costs. In light of this notion, attitudes are altered by the perceptions of the exchanges people believe they are making. Consequently, individuals who evaluate the exchange as beneficial perceive a positive impact, whereas someone who calculates the exchange as harmful will perceive a negative impact.

Social Exchange Theory

It is believed that social exchange theory offers an underlying framework for all of the approaches because it addresses how residents assess the expected costs and benefits of tourism. The issue of how this assessment changes through time is considered in tourism development cycle theories. For instance, in their study Hernandez et al. (1996) postulates that there may be a wide range of reasons for the changes in residents' attitudes including the level of tourism development, or a threshold occurrence of the social carrying capacity. Cooper, Fletcher, Gilbert and Wanhill (1998) identify social carrying capacity as the level at which tourism creates impacts that are unacceptable to residents. With the segmentation approach, cost and benefits variations for different segments of the population are considered. A study using this approach is that of Madrigal (1993) where the results show that those who work in the tourism industry and have more frequent contact with visitors and other social groups would have more positive attitudes towards tourism.

Contact Theory

Contact theory is based on the view that increased contact between social groups can result in favourable attitudes (Baron and Byrne, 2003). Applications of contact theory range from research investigating ethnic/racial conflict, where it is found that favourable intergroup contact leads to improved intergroup relations (Amir, 1998), to studies focusing on attitudes toward homosexuals (Herek and Capitanio, 1995). However, Amir (1998) highlighted that for this contact to lead to favourable attitudes, certain conditions must be present including the positive character of the situation, the positive character of the contact participants and common interests between participants, among other factors. Few studies on tourism issues have focused on the implications of contact theory (e.g., Weaver and Lawton, 2001).

In their study Weaver and Lawton (2001) investigated, among other things, the impact of residents' level of contact on their attitudes towards tourism; as expected, they found that residents' perceptions of tourism were related to the level of contact they had with tourists in their community. The authors stated that, "Members ... are more likely to work within tourism and have more frequent contact with tourists, and express a desire to share the community with non-locals ... the findings support the contention that those involved with tourism and tourists will be more positively inclined toward that [tourism] sector" (454). This and other studies (Etter, 2007) have shown that, under contact theory, persons with higher levels of contact (particularly those employed in the tourism sector) have a more positive disposition towards tourism and related initiatives, and other cultures.

Resident Involvement in Accommodation Development

Little research has been carried out on issues relating to the provision of accommodation for events, and residents' involvement in the development of accommodation for tourism and the hosting of mega-events. Cho (2004) assessed the role of Korean-style small Inns and the use of these as an alternative accommodation to tourist hotels for the 1986 Asian Games and the 1988 Olympic Games. The study showed that the small Inns played an important role in the preparations for the 2002 FIFA World Cup. The analysis focused on elements that made the preparation of the small Inns successful such as owner concerns, information exchange and resource availability. Results of this study indicated that Korean-Style small Inns can be used as an alternative type of accommodation in future Korean special events.

An investigation of the development and constraints upon South Africa's emergent small black-owned accommodation sector in the form of B&B establishments was undertaken by Rogerson (2004). The study concluded that for the successful growth of tourism small-enterprise's policy makers need to address issues relating to the marketing of tourism products and the spaces where black entrepreneurs are running businesses; training of entrepreneurs; improving access to finance and to available support networks of business information and advice.

In sum, these studies examined residents' perceptions, attitudes or opinions towards tourism development including mega-events and to a lesser extent alternative accommodation for a mega-event. Although the studies examining residents' perceptions or attitudes on the impacts of mega-events have been limited, there have been other efforts (Deccio and Baloglu, 2002; Mihalik and Simonetta, 1998; Ritchie and Aitken, 1985; Ritchie and Lyons, 1987; Soutar and McLeod, 1993; Waitt, 2003). However, there still exists a scant body of research exploring resident's attitudes towards participating in the preparation and development of alternative accommodation for a mega-event. With respect to the literature reviewed here, this chapter goes a step further by employing two theoretical frameworks, the social exchange and contact theories. This approach will provide a theoretically sound assessment of the results, in hope of contributing to a stronger conceptual model capable of explaining residents' attitudes and opinions towards tourism related development initiatives in the Caribbean.

Barbados Tourism

The island of Barbados is one of the southernmost and most easterly islands in the Caribbean with a small, open economy driven by external forces. The country has a long-established tourism industry dating as far back as the 1940s when the West Indian Royal Commission recommended tourism as a way to "create employment, diversify the economy, promote infrastructural development and help maintain the balance of payments of the colonies" (Dann, 1996: 118). In the 1960s international hotel chains and tour operators began to show interest in Barbados as a tourism destination and the government embraced tourism as the engine for economic growth. Since the 1960s the number of tourist arrivals has increased dramatically and tourism in Barbados has evolved into the largest industry in the country's economy and contributed with 12.4 percent to the country's GDP in 2004 (Central Bank of Barbados, 2005).

Since Barbados has very few natural resources, tourism continues to receive increased attention as an important sector of the Barbados economy and has provided a much-needed boost to the country's economy. The Barbadian government has come to recognise tourism's actual and potential contribution to their economy and are giving the sector a higher political priority than before. As a result, economic policy objectives increasingly centre on tourism's ability to generate employment, earn foreign exchange and contribute significantly to government revenue. The GDP composition by sector in 2004 according to the Central Bank of Barbados (2005) is 30.5 percent.

Barbados reaps a distinct competitive advantage of its airport being the main air-transportation hub for the Eastern Caribbean region. Although Barbados has a fortunate record of tourism growth, the country is vulnerable to external shocks and loss of competitiveness in the tourism industry due to the high volatility demand in the industry. Today, the status of Barbados' tourism development is suggestive of Butler's (1980) saturation stage. Development is currently taking place to rejuvenate and differentiate the existing tourism product and its infrastructure. The country's tourism industry is mainly made up of all-inclusive resorts/hotels and 3S tourism (sun, sea and sand). In 2005 the accommodation sector comprised approximately 180 establishments, out of which six were Bed and Breakfasts with a total of 10,770 beds (Caribbean Tourism Organization, 2006).

With the hosting of the CWC 2007, Barbados invested US$150 million in the construction of infrastructure alone (Scotia Economics, 2007). It was predicted that the country would receive more than 20,000 visitors during the event and accommodation would be one of the major challenges in hosting the event. Since the event was being held during the tourism high season there was a need for additional accommodation. Barbados' room stock was estimated at 8,000 rooms and according to Ernst & Young (2004) the anticipated total room requirement for the World Cup was approximately 12,000 rooms. Even with the Home Accommodation Project there was an estimated deficit of 2,200 rooms. Consequently, the government of Barbados borrowed US$15 million to charter the cruise ship Carnival Destiny as a floating hotel for a 19-day period.

During CWC 2007, the government struggled to fill the chartered cruise ship while land based accommodation providers endured one of the worse winter seasons on record. The accommodation sector had expanded with the Home Accommodation Programme and the newly constructed properties. Visitor numbers to Barbados during the first quarter of 2007 decreased by 39,315 arrivals compared to the previous year 2006 (CTO, 2008). Although the final game of the CWC was played during the first quarter the visitor numbers were not significantly affected.

The Home Accommodation Programme (HAP) was developed in order to accommodate the predicted increase in visitor numbers to Barbados during the CWC. The programme is also referred to as the accommodation home-stay programme, Bed and Breakfast accommodation programme, and home accommodation project. This category of visitor accommodation is offered by individuals and families outside of the realm of the traditional commercial tourism setting. It is part of an overall thrust in which the government aimed at developing and encouraging what they call community tourism. The homes which form part of the new HAP are registered by the Barbados Tourism Authority (BTA) and monitored by its Quality Assurance Department. There are three classification categories; Room(s) to let, Bed and Breakfast, and Family apartments, all accommodation developed in Barbadian homes.

The main objective of the programme was to increase the numbers of rooms available to visitors to Barbados during CWC 2007. With an average occupancy rate of 51 percent during high season (Loveridge, 2008), Barbados was not in need of additional rooms, therefore the need for an increase in room numbers was solely for the CWC. Other objectives of the programme were to allow visitors to experience what it is like to live in a Barbadian home and to provide visitors with an alternative choice of accommodation. The government also wanted to encourage Barbadians to become involved in the tourism industry by providing rooms within their homes as a small business.

Barbadians were informed about the HAP through national media and a town hall meeting held by the Ministry of Tourism. The meeting was lead by the Minister of tourism and had a wide cross section of participants. There was also information about the programme on the Barbados Tourism Authority (BTA) website. Since the programme is ongoing, information is still available on the BTA website. The main encouragement to participate was an initial attractive interest rate on the home improvement loans available to HAP participants. Another way Barbadians were encouraged to participate in the HAP was through the BTA stressing that, by participating in the programme Barbadians would own a piece of the tourism industry. Although the HAP is ongoing and a training session was held as late as August 2008, there was no outline of a long-term plan for the programme. This was one of the shortcomings of the HAP.

The government provided training to participants by offering a training series comprising five moduels: marketing, introduction to tourism, food and fire safety, record keeping, and basic housekeeping. Loan takers benefitted from additional training in business management. The modules were delivered by the Ministry of Tourism, the BTA, Poomarin Hotel in Barbados and MCM Caribbean Tours.

Properties that sign up for the HAP are certified and approved by the BTA. In order to gain such approval the properties are required to satisfy governmental stipulations relating to things such as service and hospitality, safety and security, health and sanitation, room sizes and facilities, the buildings and the environment, signage and parking.

Participants benefit from having their property promoted mainly by MCM Caribbean Tours, who was appointed to sell the home accommodation packages for the CWC. Visitors were primarily informed about the Home Accommodation through MCM and the BTA. There was no website developed specially for potential visitors. The MCM Caribbean Tours website is the principal place to book a home accommodation on the internet. The Ministry of Tourism developed a website specifically for the programme which contains information about the HAP and caters mainly to Barbadians interested in participating in the programme. Additionally, information about the registered properties were published by the BTA in a special annual booklet, and distributed to travel agents worldwide.

The programme has approximately 150 registered rooms today, and is ongoing. Seventy-one properties are listed on the official Barbados Tourism Authority website however, according to the BTA there has been no fallout from the programme since CWC 2007 (Cosier, 2008). There were no initial plans put in place to measure the success of the programme, however the success and the occupancy for the properties in the HAP is according to Cosier (2008) currently under investigation by MCM Caribbean, hence no data is currently available.

Research Methods

A structured questionnaire was developed for this study containing 27 questions, where 13 of these were designed to measure participants' attitudes toward the HAP (see Table 8.2), and the initial seven questions were demographical. A five point Likert scale was used for these 13 items (Strongly disagree to Strongly agree). Sample items include: "The Home Accommodation Programme would enhance my community" and "I would enjoy having a tourist stay in my home". The items were combined as an index, where higher scores reflected more positive attitudes toward the programme. Negatively worded items were reverse coded. Relevant demographic information was also elicited such as participants' age, gender, income and educational level. Items relating to frequency of contact (1 = Very Infrequent to 5 = Very Frequent) with tourists in the community, awareness of the HAP, area of employment and perceptions of obstacles facing the initiative were also included in the questionnaire. These variables were examined to determine their effects on participants' attitudes toward the initiative.

Sample and Procedures

Six hundred Barbadian residents were targeted via telephone interviews, a response rate of 54 percent was secured (n = 322). All members of the sample were homeowners. Of the 322 completed surveys, 207 were women and 115 were men. Persons who were employed in the tourism sector accounted for only 8 percent of the entire sample, while the remaining 92 percent came from other sectors including agriculture (n = 11) manufacturing (n = 20), financial (n = 68), education (n = 20), and health care sectors (n = 22), among others. Table 9.1 shows the demographic profile for the sample.

The sample population was determined by the utilization of a stratified random sampling technique. Population information for each parish of Barbados was accessed from the Barbados Statistical Service (BSS) and a proportionate sample was selected from the sampling frame. Using a systematic sampling procedure (a random start was chosen due to the alphabetical listing of sampling frame), a telephone directory was used where every tenth person was selected from each parish. Persons were then interviewed over the telephone; the telephone survey method was adopted because of its efficiency and ability to access participants who were geographically scattered over the island. However, the interpretation of these findings should be cautioned due to the relatively small sample size (under 400 persons) and that the telephone survey method usually "reduces anonymity and introduces potential interviewer bias" (Neuman, 2003: 290).

Table 9.1   Demographic Data for Sample

DEMOGRAPHICS	N	%
Home owner		
Yes	322	100
No	-	-
Gender		
Male	115	36
Female	207	64
Age		
18–25	16	5
26–40	119	37
41–60	173	54
>60	14	4
Education Level		
Primary	4	1
Secondary	85	27
Tertiary	233	72
Income		
<$1000	23	7
$1000–$2000	35	11
$2001–$3000	48	15
$3001–$4000	70	22
$4001–$5000	60	18
>$5001	86	27
Area of Employment		
Tourism	27	8
Other	295	92
TOTAL	**322**	**100**

Research Results

The 13 items, which measured attitudes towards the HAP, were examined by a principal component analysis (PCA), with a varimax rotation. Table 9.2 shows the results of the PCA. One factor was extracted and explained more than 40 percent of the variance. Factor loadings for 12 items were above the criterion of 0.4. The item eliciting whether participants agree with the significant and dominant role that tourism plays in the economy was dropped from the scale (<0.4); this item appears to measure participants' attitudes toward tourism in general, rather than on the HAP. The final scale (12 items) yielded a Cronbach's reliability coefficient of 0.88, indicating high internal consistency (Morgan, Leech, Gloeckner and Barret, 2004).

Table 9.2   Principal Component Analysis of HAP Attitude Scale

Items	Component
Tourism plays a significant and dominant role in the economy of Barbados	
I would enjoy having tourists stay in my home	.80
I would enjoy interacting with tourists staying in my home	.77
The HAP will enhance my community	.69
My community is a good place for the HAP	.67
The positive impacts of the HAP outweigh the negative impacts	.74
All my community will benefit significantly if the HAP is developed	.59
My social standard will be enhanced by developing my home into a Home Accommodation	.79
Home Accommodation will diminish the space in my home and this is of great concern to me*	.45
The HAP can erode social values in my community*	.43
The HAP can bring unwanted activity to my community*	.55
I think the future of my community will be bright if the HAP is developed	.69
My overall quality of life will be enhanced by developing Home Accommodation in my home	.79

Note: Varimax rotation method. Factor loadings shown. † The first item was dropped from the scale due to the low factor loading (< 0.4). * Negative attitude items.

Table 9.3   Demographic Factors and Attitudes towards the Home Accommodation Programme

Gender	Mean	SD	T
Male	3.35	.51	1.60
Female	3.25	.50	

Age	Mean	SD	F
18–25years	3.13	.61	0.66
26–40 years	3.27	.53	
41–60 years	3.31	.48	
> 60 years	3.30	.43	

Educational level			
Primary	3.21	.40	1.68
Secondary	3.20	.52	
Tertiary	3.32	.49	

Income			
< $1000	3.34	.45	1.37
$1001–$2000	3.30	.51	
$2001–3000	3.12	.51	
$3001–4000	3.32	.48	
$4001–5000	3.26	.42	
> $5000	3.34	.55	

Note: Higher mean scores reflect more positive attitudes towards the Programme.

Table 9.4   Attitudes towards the Home Accommodation Programme with Respect to Awareness, Perceived Obstacles and Area of Employment

Awareness of the HAP	Mean	SD	T
Aware of the HAP	3.34	.48	3.23*
Not aware of the HAP	3.10	.53	
Obstacles Affecting the HAP			
Obstacles perceived	3.23	.49	2.17*
No obstacles perceived	3.36	.52	
Area of Employment			
Tourism Sector	3.49	.54	2.21*
Other Sectors	3.27	.49	

Note: *p<0.05.

Overall, the mean attitude score for the sample was 3.30 (SD = 0.50), which reflected that the participants generally expressed a moderately positive attitude towards the HAP. Table 9.3 reports mean attitude scores and inferential statistics for gender, age, income and education level while Table 9.4 reports mean attitude scores and inferential statistics for variables such as frequency of contact, awareness of the HAP and area of employment.

Demographic Variables and Attitudes towards the Home Accommodation Programme

Independent ANOVAs were used to examine the effects of age, income and educational level, whereas an independent t-test was used to examine gender differences in attitudes towards the HAP. No significant differences in attitudes were found for age, gender, income and educational level. Means for the various sub-categories highlight moderately favourable attitudes towards the initiative.

Frequency of Contact and Attitudes towards the Home Accommodation Programme

Since frequency of contact was measured on an ordinal scale (a violation of the assumption of normality), a Spearman (non-parametric) correlation analysis was employed to ascertain the relationship between this variable and attitudes towards the HAP. Frequency of contact was significantly and positively related to attitudes toward the initiative (*rho* = .22, p<0.001). This result suggests that higher levels of contact with tourists in the community were associated with more positive attitudes toward the HAP.

Awareness and Attitudes towards the Home Accommodation Programme

An independent sample t-test was conducted to determine whether there was a significant difference in attitudes between persons who were aware of the HAP and those who were not. A significant difference emerged between these two categories of persons (t = 3.23, p<0.001, r = .17), indicating that persons who are aware of the initiative possessed more favourable attitudes. ["*r*" represents an effect size (point-biseral coefficient) for t-test analyses, where r =√t²/t²+df; r =.10 is a small effect size, r =.30 is medium effect size and r = .50 is a large effect size (Cohen, 1988)].

Perceived Obstacles and Attitudes towards the Home Accommodation Programme

In order to determine whether perceived obstacles affected attitudes towards the HAP, a t-test was computed between persons who perceived obstacles and those who did not. A significant difference was found. The results revealed that persons who perceived obstacles facing the initiative expressed less favourable attitudes towards the HAP (t = 2.17, p<0.05, r = .12). This result is supported by Doxey's "Irridex" (1975) in that resident attitudes towards the HAP would be similar to those of annoyance and antagonism. Similarly, Davis, Allen and Consenza's (1988) residents described as haters, cautious romantics and in-betweeners supports this result.

Area of Employment and Attitudes towards the Home Accommodation Programme

An independent t-test was conducted, investigating whether persons who work in the tourism sector differ significantly in their attitudes towards the HAP from those who work in other sectors. The results highlighted a significant difference between the two categories of workers; those employed in the tourism sector (*M*= 3.49), compared to those employed in other sectors (*M* =3.26), expressed more positive attitudes towards the initiative (t = 2.21, p<0.05, r = .12).

Discussion

The results of this study suggest that community response to the HAP across different demographics was moderately positive. The study does however highlight that residents' attitudes towards the programme was not influenced by demographic differences. The study also raised the question about significant relationships between frequency of contact with tourists and attitudes toward the HAP. Residents with high levels of tourist contact were more likely to express positive attitudes toward the programme; this finding is corroborated by past studies (Fredline and Faulkner, 2002; Weaver and Lawton, 2001). According to the principles of contact theory, increased contact between members of different social groups can ultimately lead to positive attitudes (Baron and Byrne, 2003). Residents' desire to open up their homes to tourists by developing part of their homes into Home Accommodation might be motivated by a strong link to, and previous exposure and contact with tourists. However, this contact must be under favourable conditions. Conversely, Doxey (1975) argues in his "Irridex" that residents with more tourist contact expressed negative feelings towards tourism. The first reaction of residents to any area of tourism development is euphoria, which involves a welcoming attitude towards any initiative promoting an influx of tourists. The "Irridex" represent the rising irritation of residents as the impact of visitor numbers increases. Since the HAP facilitates for residents to be part of a new tourism development project, the findings in this study are consistent with the euphoric stage of the "Irridex" (Doxey, 1975). One of the factors influencing the ability of host communities to accommodate or tolerate tourism, and the attitudes consequently formed is determined by a number of factors, one of them being the cultural distance between hosts and guests (Doxey, 1975). This is an area that has not previously been scientifically studied in the Caribbean context and it would add greatly to the existing gap in the research on Caribbean host communities and their tolerance towards tourism. Furthermore, the respondents readiness to participate in the HAP if benefits are gained without any major cost is supported by the social exchange theory which suggests that residents will be willing to enter into an exchange with the tourist if they can benefit from it without unacceptable costs. Consequently, residents who perceive the exchange as beneficial will support tourism development initiative while residents who perceive the exchange as damaging will be in opposition to the development (Ap, 1992).

Along with frequency of contact, awareness was also seen as an important factor that could enhance attitudes toward the HAP. It is important to understand that people who are not made aware of planned developments or initiatives are more likely to react negatively toward these when they are implemented. This is consistent with the findings of Keogh's study (1990) which found that there was a relationship between residents' familiarity [awareness] with proposed tourism development initiatives and positive perceptions of the initiatives. A major implication highlighted in this study was that governments or those directly responsible for implementing a major tourism initiative must ensure that residents (those directly affected by the initiative) are fully informed about the initiative and the associated benefits. Consistent with social exchange theory, the awareness of attached benefits is likely to lead to favourable perceptions toward the particular initiative (Gursoy and Jurowski, 2004; Madrigal, 1993). Furthermore, communication between parties is essential (in this case, government and residents) because those readily informed about proposed developments and initiatives are likely to show commitment towards the same and would be motivated to ensure that they are successful. A post-CWC 2007 study needs to be undertaken in order to examine participants' commitment to the programme and to study the motivational level and its effect on the successfulness of the HAP.

The Home Accommodation Programme can be seen as a win-win scenario where both the community and the tourism industry benefit. The possibility of participating in the development of alternative accommodation for the country's tourism industry might be a reason why the community supported the programme (Boyd and Singh, 2003). However, the extent of residents' reactions and attitudes toward tourism development is often influenced by economic dependency on tourism. Studies show that residents who benefit from tourism have a higher level of support for it (Lankford, 1994). With tourism playing a vital role in the Barbadian economy, it is a major contributor to foreign exchange earnings. Approximately 35 percent of the workforce is employed in tourism in one way or another (Barbados Ministry of Tourism, 2003), and directly benefitting from tourism. This study shows that this dependency might contribute to the high support level of the HAP. It would be interesting to examine if this dependency affects the community's irritation index.

Those residents employed in the tourism sector were only 8 percent of the respondents. It is important to clarify here that the Barbados Statistical Services sees tourism a separate industry from hospitality, transportation and restaurant industries. Consequently, it is impossible to know if the 8 percent is a representative figure. Those residents employed in the tourism sector were more likely to exhibit favourable attitudes toward the HAP, compared to those in other sectors. This finding is supported by the arguments of Madrigal (1993) who asserted that under the theory of social exchange, those employed in tourism industry would be more likely to perceive tourism development initiatives in a more positive light, due to their heavy dependence on tourism. The main explanation offered was that this category of persons who are economically dependent on the tourism industry are more likely to recognise the benefits of tourism development initiatives, compared to those in other sectors. Another plausible explanation for this finding is that those employed in the tourism sector have more extensive contact with tourists, compared to others, and under contact theory, would be more comfortable with the concept of accommodating tourists in their residence. This interpretation would be consistent with Weaver and Lawton's (2001) study, which shows that residents who were involved in the tourism industry were more likely to express favourable views toward the initiative, due to the high levels of contact with tourists. Finally, the knowledge about the tourism industry and its benefits is more existent among those employed in the tourism sector as a result they would be more likely to display favourable attitudes toward the Home Accommodation Programme.

Moreover, the study showed that residents who perceived obstacles in the HAP expressed less positive attitudes towards the programme. The obstacles were mainly concerns about the continuity of the HAP and future occupancy. Additionally, respondents expressed concern for the government's positive prediction of visitor numbers. The main fear in this regard was to invest in the HAP and not being able to maintain occupancy after the CWC. Most respondents felt that the HAP was a good initiative, yet they were reluctant to take loans and end up in debt with difficulties to repay.

According to social exchange theory, perceived costs associated with a tourism initiative are a major predictor of negative attitudes towards the initiative. If benefits are perceived to be greater than the costs in relation to a particular initiative or event, persons are more inclined to support the initiative (Gursoy and Rutherford, 2004; Madrigal, 1993). These benefits may include economic (e.g., employment opportunities), social (e.g., incentives to preserve national culture) and cultural (e.g., development of cultural activities by locals) dimensions (Gursoy and Rutherford, 2004). Participants in the HAP were given loans as part of the programme, however no organised marketing of the properties was developed in order to maximise occupancy of the properties. The possibility of the HAP properties becoming superfluous after the CWC 2007 was one of the reasons for negative attitudes toward the programme. With a proper marketing programme this risk could be reduced. In order to discuss this issue further an empirical investigation into residents attitudes post-CWC 2007 needs to be undertaken. A focus group discussion with HAP participants would be an interesting method to use in such a study.

Another interpretation of this finding is that persons who expect obstacles are less likely to embrace the programme based on the view that although perceived costs (in this case, negative impacts) may not be a factor, there remains a perception that the benefits attached to the initiative would be financially undermined or limited to the period of CWC 2007.

Cricket is the national sport of Barbados and also part of the country's culture. The HAP developed as a result of the hosting of CWC 2007, consequently the majority of the visitors during the period of the games were expected to be Cricket fans from all over the world. This cultural familiarity might have influenced residents' positive attitude toward the programme and the event.

Studies show that positive benefits are significantly related to personal benefits from tourism (e.g., Pearce, Moscardo and Ross, 1996). The non-significant gender effect findings in the present study are conflicting with studies by Pizam and Pokela (1985) and Ritchie (1988) who found that gender has an influence on the support for tourism. Other factors would, as previously discussed, influence the support for tourism, hence these factors would have to be examined in relation to gender in order to see if the factors differ between the genders.

Conclusion

This study highlights that the Home Accommodation Programme may have initially been welcomed by residents of Barbados. In order to gain positive response and have the local community supporting an initiative like the HAP it is necessary to have some form of public awareness program in place. Tourism initiatives or programmes should ideally not occur prior to some form of co-operation between government and the local community. This is of great significance from the perspectives of contact and social exchange.

Programmes and initiatives should be integrated into the government's public policy, especially relating to major tourism initiatives and events. The Barbados Ministry of Tourism should ensure that residents understand and appreciate the benefits of the Home Accommodation Programme and that before any initiative is communicated to the public, all obstacles (and perceived costs) be reduced significantly, if not eliminated. The local community is what makes a destination and if residents are not part of or feel part of the country's tourism development and initiatives it will negatively affect the overall destination as a tourism product.

One limitation of this study was that although the sample was randomly selected, the generalisability of the findings is still questionable due to the relatively small sample size, compared to the general population of Barbados (over 266,000 residents). Another limitation was the absence of in-depth qualitative interviews and focus groups with residents, along with the structured survey approach adopted here, to further corroborate the results and understand fully the fundamental reasons behind these attitudes with respect to the Home Accommodation Programme. A post-CWC 2007 study needs to be undertaken in order to examine participants' commitment to the programme and to study the motivational level and its effect on the successfulness of the HAP. Finally, an interesting area to be further explored is Caribbean host communities and their tolerance towards tourism. This is an area that has not previously been scientifically studied in the Caribbean context and it would add greatly to the existing gap in the research area.

Chapter 10

Image, Logo, Brand and Nation: Destination Marketing, Nationalism and the 2007 Cricket World Cup

Leanne White

Introduction

The 2007 CWC represents "the largest single sporting event ever held in the Caribbean" (Gemmell, 2008: xvi). It was estimated that an audience of more than two billion people in more than 200 countries watched the event (Hawkes, 2007: 8). The 2007 mega-event marked the ninth Cricket World Cup. Previous tournaments were staged in England (1975, 1979 and 1983), India and Pakistan (1987), Australia and New Zealand (1992), India, Pakistan and Sri Lanka (1996), England, Ireland and the Netherlands (2000) and South Africa, Zimbabwe and Kenya (2003).

The logistics of the event were relatively complex with teams playing at: Queen's Park Oval in Trinidad (the largest and most picturesque ground), Warner Park Stadium in St Kitts, the Sir Vivian Richards Stadium in Antigua, Providence Stadium in Guyana, the National Cricket Stadium in Grenada, the Beausejour Cricket Ground in St. Lucia, Sabina Park in Jamaica, and Kensington Oval in Barbados (the most historic cricket ground in the Caribbean). Each of these countries has their own governments, flags, anthems and currencies and "to complicate matters even further, they are separated by water" (Cozier, 2006: 194).

There was no secret made of the fact that the West Indies hoped to stage nothing less than "the greatest Cricket World Cup the world has ever seen" (Jordan, 2006: 37). As cricket is regarded as "the king among all sports in the Caribbean" staging an impressive and memorable World Cup was considered imperative (Sandiford, 2004: 82). There was also considerable hope that the West Indies might win the World Cup, as at no time in the history of the game had a host nation managed to win (Lloyd, 2006: 6). Following the literature review and methodology, an analysis of the images surrounding this significant event will be undertaken.

This chapter examines mediated images surrounding the mega-event that was the 2007 Cricket World Cup (CWC)—the biggest sporting event ever to take place in the Caribbean. The chapter closely examines the many signs and symbols surrounding the 2007 CWC held across eight countries in the Caribbean from February to April. While more than 425,000 cricketing fans passed through the turnstiles, millions more watched or listened to the mediated event via television, radio and the internet.

Key organizations involved in staging the mega-event included the International Cricket Council (ICC), the West Indies Cricket Board (WICB), the Caribbean Community (CARICOM), national governments and their tourist boards, Local Organizing Committees, and the ICC CWC WI 2007 Inc. (Jordan, 2006: 19-20). These groups effectively organized the event and importantly, arranged the associated rights to sponsorship, licensing, display of corporate logos, mascots, trademarks and other event branding issues. The national symbolism associated with the 16 teams participating in this key event will be examined. The 2007 CWC has played a central role in the way the world's cricket fans, and the global community more generally, perceive the countries involved in the event and more generally, the Caribbean as a tourist destination.

Close textual analysis, in particular semiotics (examining how signs generate meaning) and content analysis (studying what is actually evident on the page or screen), are useful methodologies for deconstructing mediated representations of national imagery and branding. A combination of primary and secondary research, semiotic analysis and content analysis will be undertaken to analyse the way in which a range of images generated by this cricketing event were imagined, created, replicated and relayed (often for commercial purposes) across the world. The images examined in this chapter will be explored through the dual theoretical frameworks of nationalism and destination marketing.

Nation, Nationalism and Imagined Communities

The term "nation" encompasses more extensive thinking than simply the borders of a particular country. Theorists on the topic of nationalism have acknowledged that the term can incorporate political, social, cultural, historical, economic, linguistic and religious factors. "Nation" originated from the Latin term *natio*—meaning community of birth. While the focus of this study is on representations of nationalism at the 2007 CWC, sometimes overlapping areas include: nation-state, nationality, national identity, national consciousness, national sentiment, nation-building, patriotism and citizenship.

While numerous theorists have analysed the term "nationalism", Benedict Anderson's ground-breaking 1983 work (revised in 1991) *Imagined Communities: Reflections on the Origin and Spread of Nationalism* has reconceptualised the way scholars have come to think about nationalism and related terms such as those outlined above. Anderson popularly conceptualised the nation as an "imagined political community". He argued, "It is *imagined* because members of even the smallest nation will never know most of their fellow-members, meet them, or even hear of them, yet in the minds of each lives the image of their communion" (Anderson, 1991: 6).

There is common agreement amongst academics that the phenomenon of nationalism emerged in late eighteenth century Europe, and strengthened with the events of the French Revolution in 1789. In terms of pin-pointing any possible demise of nationalism, Anderson asserts that "nation-ness is the most universally legitimate value in the political life of our time" and that the end of nationalism "is not remotely in sight" (Anderson, 1991: 3).

Nationalism can be considered as either a positive or negative force. On the positive side, it is regarded as a source of distinction, while those in the negative camp claim it to be a source of aggression. Hobsbawm (1990: 169) raises the negative aspect of nationalism when he states, "nationalism by definition excludes ... all who do not belong to its own nation, that is, the vast majority of the human race". However, Seton-Watson (1982: 13) explains that nationalism is intrinsically neither good nor bad. He claims national identity is at least "passively treasured by nearly all citizens of modern societies, even if they don't know it". After the September 11 attacks in the United States in 2001, the citizens of the nation showed their patriotism and stance against "the enemy" by proudly flying the flag. Some might perceive this as a proud gesture while others might argue that it may either deliberately or inadvertently promote aggression. Across the United States, around New York City and what became known as "Ground Zero" in particular, the stars and stripes were prominently displayed in an almost defiant stance.

The intensity of an individual's feelings about their national identity seems to be directly related to their level of national sentiment. Sentiment for the nation involves a sense of personal identification and empathy with something larger than oneself. As a particular level of emotion is involved, national sentiment is a highly subjective feeling and can vary enormously in different circumstances. To illustrate the point, while it is possible that possessing citizenship might not register any emotional involvement, it is often the case that being a member of the nation-state does carry some meaning, even if it is regarded as one of the more abstract identities which the individual possesses. Additionally, national sentiment might be more concentrated when the citizen is younger and possibly more impressionable, than when they become older and increasingly aware of various manipulative forces such as multinational corporations using nationalism to sell a corporate message, product or service. That the young may be more easily influenced by national sentiment might best be demonstrated by the propensity of some sporting fans to wear their country's flag as a proud (sometimes jingoistic) cloak.

Nationalism and Sport

The complex relationship between sport and the media remains relatively under researched. Boyle and Haynes (2000: 7) note in *Power Play: Sport, the Media and Popular Culture*, that "it has only been relatively recently that a sustained engagement with the sport/media/society nexus has taken place". The authors point out that academic research into relationships between television and sport is relatively new. They also note that it is surprising that it took until the 1990s for academic research to recognise "one of the most pervasive aspects of our popular culture" (2000: 11).

Televised sport has been a powerful magnet for viewers for many years. Media magnate Rupert Murdoch states that sport overpowers film and everything else in the entertainment industry. This observation was entirely correct in the case of the 2007 CWC. At a global event such as this, the industries of tourism, sport and the media are intimately connected and all contribute to the overall experience that is consumed by the visitor to the venues and (in a different way) the television viewer. As Hall (1997: 14) argues, the study of hallmark events is a relatively new area of research and is "marked by significant differences between researchers in definition, method and theory". Hall calls upon researchers to closely examine hallmark events "before, during and after the event", given the central place of the event in the context of wider marketing strategies (1997: 15).

By closely examining national images, logos and brands at the Caribbean's most significant event in its history, this chapter will add to the overall literature on events with particular reference to mega-events as explored through the dual theoretical frameworks of nationalism and destination marketing. As Gemmell (2008: x) argues, as cricket evolves on a global scale "it has become increasingly associated with national identity". At this event the people of the West Indies were able to successfully unite around the common theme of unity, sport, and 'their' cricket team in particular. Indeed the West Indies team is often cited as a successful model of regional integration for the many Caribbean nations. The 2007 CWC is an incredibly rich text to examine. It is also a text which says much about the national identity of the 16 teams. This iconic text helped to create key archival images that will continue to shape individual nations and their sense of identity into the future.

Destination Marketing

In recent years, the number and range of events occurring around the world has increased substantially. This has lead researchers to investigate various aspects of events. Jago and Shaw (1998) note that most of this research has focused primarily on the impacts and outcomes of special events. Other benefits of events have been identified as an extension of the tourist season and enhancement of community pride (Getz, 1997).

Recent studies in tourism have considered the role of particular attractions in assisting with the creation of a national identity. Pretes (2003) notes that tourists receive messages sent to them by the creators of the sites they visit, and these sites of significance, presented as aspects of a national heritage, help to shape a common national identity, or 'imagined community' among a diverse population. Pretes also argues that a shared identity is often an official goal of countries comprised of many different cultures where there exists a common urge to create a national identity to overcome diversity and difference within the nation-state. If sites can help create a common identity or imagined community among a diverse population, can a series of sporting events held across a series of countries in the Caribbean represent aspects of an overall culture and help to develop a common identity in the region?

The Australian Tourist Commission (ATC), now known as Tourism Australia, made it clear that it saw the Sydney 2000 Olympic Games as an opportunity to shift attitudes towards Australia. The ATC wanted to use the Games to remove the "Crocodile Dundee" image of Australia (Rivenburgh, Louw, Loo and Mersham, 2004). In 1995, the ATC embarked on a new way to promote Australia—known as "Brand Australia". In this campaign, a unified and cohesive image of Australia was developed for the major markets—Asia, Europe and the United States. Australia's personality was presented as youthful, energetic, optimistic, unpretentious and genuine. In their cross-cultural study of foreign attitudes towards Australia before, during and after the Sydney Games, Rivenburgh and her co-writers (2004: 13) argued that "the ATC saw the Opening Ceremony as an opportunity to sell Sydney and Australia to the world" and to get Australia recognized as an exciting and desirable travel destination. Mega-events such as the 2007 CWC are extremely sought after by cities and nations because they are "a powerful travel lure" (Hall, 1997: 32).

Research Methodology

This chapter is concerned with examining national images circulated in the public arena during the 2007 CWC. How these images intersect and change depending on the use to which they are put is explored. The chapter will undertake a close analysis of the images by applying aspects of semiotics and content analysis—key qualitative and quantitative research methodologies. Combining different research methodologies is particularly relevant to this chapter as content analysis can be used to substantiate semiotics. In this case, the quantitative analysis can work to further validate the qualitative analysis. Both qualitative and quantitative research methodologies have particular strengths and using both methods reinforces the final research outcome. The strengths and weaknesses of these two approaches will now be explained further.

Semiotics is the study of signs, codes and culture, and a methodology for reading 'soft' data such as representations of nation. Semiotics will be integrated into this chapter as it is a useful tool for examining the sometimes multi-layered images of a nation. Semiotics is the study of how signs operate in society or "the study of the social production of meaning" generated from sign systems (O'Sullivan, Hartley, Saunders, Montgomery and Fiske, 1994: 281). Meaning in this context is the dynamic interaction between the 'reader' and the message. Meaning is influenced by the reader's socio-cultural experiences, and the reader plays a central role in any semiotic analysis. Semiotics is a particularly useful methodology for deconstructing our daily experiences and attempts to capture those experiences more permanently. The search for various representations of nation as presented in the Caribbean in 2007 can be discovered through a close examination of the symbols and images televised during the momentous global event.

Content analysis is a research methodology that is concerned with the frequency of content contained in a particular data set. Berelson (1952: 15) defined content analysis as "a research technique for the objective, systematic and quantitative description" of communications. Content analysis will be integrated into this chapter as it is a useful tool for examining the larger picture. Content analysis is effectively a counting strategy and is put forward as an objective method for counting content. It is a useful research tool for identifying, categorizing and describing trends. Content analysis is primarily concerned with studying what is actually evident on the screen. Quantitative content analysis of this kind does not concern itself with questions of quality or interpretation but can easily detect systematic patterns.

Semiotics is a valuable methodology for undertaking a close analysis of a particular text—whether that be a particular shot in a television program, a specific scene, or an advertisement. On the other hand, content analysis is able to perform analysis over a larger sample and thus detect similarities, differences and possible trends. When semiotics meets content analysis, we can interpret key features of the text and also measure the frequency of the specific phenomenon under investigation. These combined research tools (qualitative and quantitative) will be applied to the data examined in this chapter as they provide a rich base from which to undertake a close and thorough analysis of various images presented at the 2007 CWC.

ICC Logo, Mascot, Song and the Sponsors

The official logo for the 2007 CWC in the Caribbean was designed by Minale Bryce Design Strategy (MBDS). The company has produced other well-known logos including the Sydney 2000 Olympic bid logo which consisted of an impressionistic treatment of the sails of the Sydney Opera House in the five colours of the Olympic rings (blue, black, red, yellow and green). The transition from one colour to another was made using an Aboriginal dot painting technique. The logo also represented the "dawn of a new century" and the Olympic flame. Its design was said to evoke "the informal vitality of Sydney" with its blending of colours suggesting "unity among nations" (Yew, 1996: 390).

For the CWC, the design company was given the task of creating a logo that would immediately "reflect the aspects of Caribbean life, resonate with an international audience and encapsulate the spirit of cricket" (ICC, 2007). The logo that MBDS developed is said to "express the joy and exuberance of cricketers and cricket fans worldwide, in a Caribbean setting" (ICC, 2007). The logo was featured prominently at all venues, promoting a level of consistency and easily identifiable branding of the mega-event, both for those attending the venue and for viewers watching the event across the globe.

The design team also created the ICC CWC 2007 mascot named "Mello". While the mascot was neither an object, an animal nor a person, that didn't stop people from attempting to classify the character. Mello might best be described as a human-like teenage orange mongoose with a big smile and bright eyes. The character is dressed in a white T-shirt, colourful shirt sporting the red HIV/AIDS ribbon, shorts and runners while he holds a cricket bat with one hand and ball in the other. Some thought that Mello looked more like a raccoon or a meerkat, than the much-maligned Caribbean mongoose. Mello was presented as a socially aware cheeky and curious personality with a zest for life. The mascot's main objective was to educate children in the fight against AIDS, and CWC 2007 organizers were aware that the game of cricket operates as a successful vehicle for communicating this important message to the world. Mello received a mixed reaction from the cricketing public. The deliberate ambiguity of the character was a source of annoyance for some, while others perceived the mascot as being too laid back and perhaps inadvertently promoting the Caribbean in an overly casual manner.

To further reinforce and brand the event, an official theme song for the CWC 2007, *Game of Love and Unity*, was commissioned by the ICC. The overall message of the song is of "love" and "unity" in this beautiful "game". During the course of the song, the word unity is heard 11 times, the word love is heard 12 times, while the word game is heard no less than 25 times! *Game of Love an Unity* was performed by Shaggy (from Jamaica), Rupee (from Barbados) and Faye-Ann Lyons (from Trinidad). The content of the song, along with the nationality of the singers, works to emphasize a theme of harmony and unification for the Caribbean nations and the world game of cricket.

Other logos which featured prominently at all venues, in a highly consistent manner in terms of placement around the venues, were those of the four main sponsors: LG (Lucky Goldstar), Pepsi, Hutch and Hero Honda. On the sides of the grounds was signage for other key sponsors including Gatorade, Scotiabank, Visa, Servo, and Cable and Wireless.

The National Teams, Colours, Images and Logos

As 16 countries were to contest for the first time, the teams that qualified to play in the 2007 CWC were divided into four groups—A, B, C and D. Group A comprised Australia, South Africa, Scotland, and the Netherlands; in Group B was Sri Lanka, India, Bangladesh and Bermuda; Group C consisted of New Zealand, England, Kenya and Canada; while finally, in Group D were Pakistan, West Indies, Zimbabwe and Ireland. The teams that made it to the final 'super eights' were Australia, Sri Lanka, New Zealand, South Africa, England, West Indies, Bangladesh and Ireland. In the semi-finals, Sri Lanka defeated New Zealand, while Australia defeated South Africa. For the 2007 CWC final (and after 50 matches) Australia played Sri Lanka and the Aussies emerged victorious for their record fourth win of the nine World Cups contested to date—winning in 1987, 1999, 2003 and 2007.

The imagery surrounding the 16 cricketing nations in Groups A, B, C and D will now be examined.

Group A—Australia, South Africa, Scotland and the Netherlands

Being the most successful team in the history of the World Cup, Australia went into the 2007 CWC as favourites. Australia also has the honour of being the "most successful Test-playing nation of the past 130 years" (Derriman, 2006: 117). The attitude of the seemingly invincible Australians might have been best reflected by the tattoo on Michael Clarke's left arm—"Carpe Diem" or seize the day. However, with the absence of Shane Warne, and with a much-publicised aging team, some cricket aficionados were sceptical that Australia would be able to repeat its previous performances. With the advertising of the principal sponsor Emirates clearly displayed, the Australians sported their yellow and green uniforms.

The green and gold (with red gloves) boxing kangaroo flag became popular with Australia's success at the 1983 America's Cup yacht race. Hutchinson (2002: 72) explains that since 1983, the flag has become "a kind of unofficial Australian sporting flag—but was officially endorsed for waving at the Sydney Olympics". As explained by Cashman, spectators supporting Australia at major sporting matches wave almost as many boxing kangaroo flags as the national flag, and the 2007 CWC was no exception. Cashman (2001: 9) also argues that it is likely that "sport is contributing to the current debate on flag reform".

The current Australian flag became the nation's official flag in 1954. Almost in defiance, many Australian sporting teams choose to wear green and gold rather than the red, white and blue of the nation's flag. Horne (1981: 67) has claimed that it was in the 1960s that a discourse emerged in Australia about severing constitutional links with Britain, changing anthems and flags, examining the symbolism of stamps and currency, and generally re-assessing the images projected by Australia in many forms of national symbolism. Horne asserted that Australia experienced a genuine "cultural awakening" which essentially consisted of Australian participation in the arts and entertainment, and in works produced by intellectuals. It was an acceptance that there was nothing embarrassing in being an Australian and that our country's themes and legends were as valid as any others. Unfortunately Australia has yet to officially endorse a flag with its own unique identity (as opposed to projecting the image of an English colony). The union flag of Great Britain has been associated with Australia since Captain James Cook first flew it in 1770. However, on the sporting field, the fresher images of green and gold are as close as the country currently gets to projecting a distinctive Australian identity.

Also in Group A was South Africa (also known as the Proteas), who entered the World Cup tournament in 1992. The uniform of the South African cricket team is predominantly green with some yellow. Green is the central colour of the South African flag which was adopted in 1994 and with the colours—red, blue, white, black and yellow—is said to represent all South Africans. The logo of primary sponsor Standard Bank was also displayed. As expected, South Africa performed well at the 2007 CWC making it to the semi-finals.

Scotland made their World Cup debut in 1999. Unfortunately, Scotland did not progress very far in the 2007 CWC as they played Australia, then South Africa, and lost both matches. Consistent with the national flag, the uniform of team Scotland (known as the Scottish Saltires), is predominantly blue with a white Saint Andrew's cross. On the flag of Scotland the cross is displayed in the form of an "X" while the cricket uniform displays the patriotic cross on an angle—almost like a badge of honour.

The final team in Group A was the Netherlands (also known as Holland). Considered rank outsiders, it was not surprising that they won only one match —and that was against Scotland. Like Australia, the colours of the national flag are red, white and blue, yet on the cricket field they display a very different colour —orange. Orange is symbolic of the Dutch Royal family and is also displayed in the uniforms of other sporting teams representing the Netherlands.

Group B—Sri Lanka, India, Bangladesh and Bermuda

For the 2007 CWC, Sri Lanka were placed in Group B and eventually made their way to the final against Australia. Sri Lanka made their World Cup debut in 1979 and won the World Cup in 1996. The "Lankan Lions" wear the colours blue and gold on the sporting field and were sponsored by tea manufacturer Dilmah for the 2007 CWC. On the flag of Sri Lanka the ancient golden lion with upright sword is displayed—symbolising authority.

India is regarded by some as "the new cricketing superpower" (Majumdar, 2008: 78). The country's team had once proven their might by winning the 1983 World Cup, but the only team they managed to beat in 2007 was Bermuda. Consequently, India did not make it to the 'Super Eights'. Thus, they disappointed their billion or so fans in a country where cricket is the most popular sport and the players are worshipped like gods. As Bose and Gupta (2004: 176) have argued, cricket "has consumed modern India" with half the population "either engrossed in the game or indirect participants". Sponsored by Sahara Airlines to the tune of 40 million pounds over four years (Gemmell, 2008: xiii), the Indian cricket team wear a light blue uniform featuring a paint-brush style version of the Indian tricolour (saffron, white and green) flag. A central part of the Indian flag and included on the team's uniform is the blue 24-spoke wheel which is symbolic of both the wheel of life and the 24 hour day.

To the delight of their millions of fans and to the surprise of many around the world, Bangladesh managed to win their two matches in Group B (against India and Bermuda) and progress to the Super Eights where they also defeated South Africa. The uniform of the Bangladeshi team (also known as the Tigers) mainly displays the green and red colours of the flag of Bangladesh. The team's main sponsor is the local mobile phone company Grameen.

Bermuda were debutants at the 2007 CWC, and unfortunately did not manage to win any matches against their relatively tough Group B opponents Sri Lanka, India and Bangladesh. Bermuda's red, white and blue uniform largely reflects the colours of the national flag which displays the union flag and a coat of arms on a red ensign.

Group C—New Zealand, England, Kenya and Canada

Placed in Group C, New Zealand (also known as the Black Caps) managed to win their three matches against their opponents in the group. Although yet to win a World Cup, they were considered a strong contender for the 2007 tournament and progressed as far as the semi-finals. The flag of New Zealand is very similar to that of Australia with the main difference being the display of four red stars rather than six white stars. For one day cricket matches, the New Zealand Cricket team wear a black uniform displaying a white fern leaf.

While England played host to the first three World Cups (1975, 1979 and 1983), they have yet to win a tournament. On the one-day cricket field England display the Union Jack colours of red, white and blue in their uniform, although the national flag is simply red and white—a red Saint George Cross on a white background. England is considered the home of cricket but their form in recent years (particularly against test rival Australia) has embarrassed many fans. The team is sponsored by Vodafone.

Kenya was the third team in Group C. Of the three matches they played at the 2007 CWC, they managed a win against Canada. Kenya was part of the inaugural World Cup selection in 1975. Their uniform largely reflects the colour scheme of the national flag where the traditional shield and spears of the Masai warrior are displayed against a background of black, red and green horizontal stripes with white dividing lines symbolising peace.

Against their Group C competitors, Canada—who played their first World Cup match in 1979—was not able to win any matches in the Caribbean. The cricket uniform colours reflect those of the national flag, with the addition of black. The uniform was not unlike that of Zimbabwe. Luckily, by virtue of being in Group D and also performing poorly, the teams did not play each other. The red and white flag of Canada displays a red maple leaf against a white background, with red vertical bars to the left and right.

Group D—Pakistan, West Indies, Zimbabwe and Ireland

Pakistan made their first World Cup appearance in 1975 and won the 1992 CWC. Despite being strong contenders in 2007, Pakistan failed to qualify in the top eight after losing to the West Indies and (to everyone's surprise) Ireland. That night, coach Bob Woolmer died in his hotel room. While a murder investigation was called, it was eventually found (three months later) that Woolmer had died of natural causes. The flag of Pakistan displays a white crescent and star against a dark green background with white vertical band. The Pakistan cricket team sensibly wear a light green uniform with some dark green displayed. The uniform also prominently promotes the logo of sponsor Pepsi.

Having won the first two World Cups in 1975 and 1979, as well as hosting the 2007 tournament, considerable hope and expectation was placed on the shoulders of the West Indies team. Former West Indies captain Clive Lloyd proudly held up the World Cup (then known as the Prudential Cup) at Lords in 1975—an image which was to be repeated four years later. Under Lloyd, the West Indies dominated the game of cricket (Woodward, 1998: 113). The Frank Worrell trophy holds a special place for many Australians as it honours a time (the Summer of 1960–1961) when some thrilling matches were played between Australia and the West Indies before record crowds. For the 2007 CWC, a hopeful team brought back Brian Lara to captain the side. The "Windies" as they are affectionately known, performed well against their group D opponents winning all three matches. The team made it to the Super Eights and managed a respectable but disappointing sixth place overall—behind Australia, Sri Lanka, New Zealand, South Africa and England. The players' uniform incorporates the colours and logo of the West Indies Cricket Board (WICB). Sponsors of the WICB include: Digicel, KFC, Pepsi, Gatorade, Carib and Scotiabank.

Zimbabwe—the third team in Group D—managed to draw in their match against Ireland. The colours of the Zimbabwe flag are green, yellow, red, black and white but the uniforms on the cricket field are predominantly red with green. Due to the unstable political climate in Zimbabwe, the immediate prospects of the national team are looking bleak.

Ireland's first appearance at the World Cup resulted in a tie with Zimbabwe followed by a win against Pakistan—not a bad result for CWC debutants. Many Irish fans and followers celebrated the wins with the traditional stout—Guinness. Luckily for the Irish, Guinness is relatively popular in the Caribbean, though not in the league of the local beers such as Carib, Red Stripe and Piton Lager. As one would expect, the Irish team wear a predominantly green uniform. Green (the colour most associated with the natural beauty of the country) is also displayed in the vertical tricolours of the Irish flag—along with white and orange.

Conclusion

This chapter has examined various mediated images surrounding the biggest sporting event to ever be staged in the Caribbean. The symbolism associated with those staging the mega-events and that of the 16 teams was carefully orchestrated and provided for a colourful and consistent image across the event venues over the six weeks of the tournament. The symbols and images projected played an important role in the way the world's cricket fans, and the global community more generally, perceived the overall event and the countries involved.

The West Indies may have indeed staged "the greatest Cricket World Cup the world has ever seen". While there was much hope that the West Indies might win the World Cup on home soil, careful planning and dedication by the various organizers ensured that a colourful and highly celebrated event which promoted the unity of 'One Caribbean' was successfully presented to the world in 2007.

Chapter 11

A Look at the Watching Friends and Relatives Market Segment at the 2007 Cricket World Cup

Douglas Michelle Turco, Shamir Andrew Ally, Marlene Cox,
Tota Mangar and Cecilia McCalmont

Introduction

Sport tourism is big business and the stakes are high for cities that vie to host international sport events. Millions are wagered to win the rights to host an Olympic Games, Formula One race or World Cup, with the expectation that the event will lure tourists, business development and sponsorship spending. As an indication of what is at stake financially in sport tourism, the budget for the 2012 London Olympics was £9.35 billion in March 2007, nearly four times the £2.4 billion estimate when London's bid succeeded less than two years ago. Similarly, South Africa's government allocated R8.5 billion (US$1.1 billion) for building and renovating ten stadiums ahead of the 2010 FIFA World Cup and another R6.4 billion (US$800 million) for public transport initiatives and supporting infrastructure (BBC, 2006).

Destination marketers and economic developers host sport events with the intention of attracting tourists to benefit local businesses and government coffers. They are interested in high value sport tourists, those who will deliver the greatest net benefit to the economy (Tang and Turco, 2001). It has been suggested that hosting youth sport events is desirable since young athletes will be accompanied by parents and adult chaperones, enlarging the visitor group size and their local spending potential (Turco, 2005). Among event spectators, market segments may include residents, tourists, and those visiting the community for other reasons, termed casuals (Crompton, 1995). It is unclear however which segments of the sport spectator market are most likely to produce the greatest economic benefits (and fewest costs) for the host city. Previous sport tourism event research has failed to identify the spending behaviors of spectators who are friends and/or relatives of the sport participants compared with other spectators. Labeled WFRs (Watching Friends and Relatives), Scott and Turco (2007) found that they tend to stay longer in the host community and spend more money than other tourists. Relatively little is known about the characteristics of sport event tourists in the West Indies as this region has not hosted an international event on the scale of the Cricket World Cup, billed as one of the most popular sport events in the world with over two billion television viewers from 200 countries.

The purpose of this chapter is to profile international sport tourists to the 2007 Cricket World Cup, in particular, the WFR market. Results from a spectator study at the 2007 Cricket World Cup in Guyana are revealed and offer a consumer profile of international sport tourists and the WFR market.

The Watching Friends and Relatives Market

One of the most popular reasons for pleasure travel is to visit friends and relatives (VFR). Sixty-two percent of the overseas travelers visiting the US in 2004 came for leisure purposes and/or to visit friends and relatives (VFR), while the balance came for business and convention purposes (OTTI, 2005). Initially, most researchers treated VFR travelers as one homogeneous market. Morrison, Hsieh, and O'Leary (1995) diverted from conventional wisdom when they segmented VFR Australian travelers by past holiday activity participation. Segments included first-time and repeat travelers, VFR as primary trip purpose and secondary trip purpose. They noted that domestic VFR travelers differ significantly in their socio-demographics, trip characteristics, travel preferences and attitudes.

There are a myriad of reasons why people visit friends and relatives, among the primary motives are attending reunions, celebrations and holidays. One of the under examined reasons for VFR is to witness the sport event participation of a friend or relative. Previous research on VFRs reveals that they typically stay longer and spend less money than other tourists because they often stay at the homes of their hosts and do not pay for lodging or meals. Hu and Morrison (2002) found that US domestic VFR travelers were more likely to be female, and have lower education and household income levels than other pleasure travelers. They also stay longer at their destinations and make greater use of the homes of friends or relatives. Distinctions in the VFR market between domestic and international travelers, accommodation use and travel purposes have also been discovered. Lehto, Morrison and O'Leary (2001) noted that VFR travel has a strong association with repeat travel and recommend that future research examine the difference between VFR repeat travelers and other repeat travelers. Seaton and Tagg (1995) were among the first to suggest that VFRs should be distinguished as those who travel to visit friends (VF) and those who visit relatives (VR). They demonstrated that the majority of relatives (75.6 percent) visiting Northern Ireland had made more than 9 previous trips, compared with less than a third of VFs (30.1 percent).

While considerable VFR research has been conducted of late, most of it centers on the travelers visiting their friends and/or relatives who reside in the destinations. To date, the authors are aware of only (Scott and Turco, 2007) involving the friends and/or relatives of athletes who travel to watch them compete in a sport championship. In studying spectators to the 2005 Little League World Series, Scott and Turco (2007) found the average domestic WFR was in a travel party of

Table 11.1   Characteristics of WFR and other Event Sport Tourists, 2005 Little League World Series

	Domestic WFR Sport Tourist	Domestic Sport Tourist
Travel party	3 persons	4 persons
Sessions attended	6 sessions	4 sessions
Length of stay	7 nights	3 nights
Spending	US$2,337; US$1,215 for travel	US$668; US$175 for travel
	International WFR Sport Tourist	International Sport Tourist
Travel party	4 persons	2 persons
Sessions attended	9 sessions	6 sessions
Length of stay	11 nights	7 nights
Spending	US$4,550; US$1,600 for travel	US$3,200; US$700 for travel

Source: Scott, A.K.S. and Turco, D.M. (2007). VFRs as a Segment of the Sport Event Tourist Market. *Journal of Sport and Tourism*, 12(1), 41–52

three, attended the World Series six times and stayed seven nights (Table 11.1). They spent on average US$2,337 with US$1,215 in travel. The average domestic non-WFR visitor was in a travel party of four, attended the series four times and stayed for three nights. They spent US$175 in travel and US$668 overall. The average international WFR was in a travel party of four, attended the World Series nine times and stayed 11 nights. They spent US$1,600 in travel and US$4,550 overall. The average international non-associated visitor was in a travel party of two, attended the Series six times and stayed seven nights. They spent US$700 in travel and US$3,200 overall. WFRs spent considerably more money than other spectator market segments. Part of this is due to the fact that their length of stay was nearly double that of other travelers. It is also surmised that there is a 'once in a lifetime' effect which induced higher visitor spending. Considering they might not be back to the Little League World Series, visitors may have wanted to experience all the Little League World Series had to offer, including attending most games, purchasing souvenirs, staying the whole time their child/relative/friend played in the World Series, and eating out instead of budget meals. Scott and Turco (2007) conclude that player association does matter with respect to sport tourist behaviors. Relatives and/or friends of Little League World Series participants stayed longer and spent approximately two and a half to three times more money in comparison to other spectator market segments.

2007 Cricket World Cup in Guyana

The International Cricket Council (ICC) World Cup tournament is one of the world's largest sporting events. Cricket World Cup (CWC) matches officially began in 1975 in England, with eight teams; the six Test playing nations (England,

Australia, New Zealand, West Indies, India, Pakistan) along with Sri Lanka and East Africa. The tournament has been taking place every four years since then, participated by major teams all over the world.

Historically, cricket is perhaps the sport played most in the West Indies and the region is noted for this activity among international sporting countries. A conglomerate of cricketers from the English speaking Caribbean Islands was formed in the 1880s as the West Indian Cricket Team, commenced international tours shortly thereafter with a tour to Canada and the United States of America, and played its first official international test match in 1928, after joining the then Imperial Cricket Council (ICC) in 1926. The team (now called the West Indies Cricket Team or The Windies) is administered and selected by the West Indies Cricket Board (WICB, formed in the 1920s with headquarters in Antigua) from cricketers in the Caribbean states of Barbados, Guyana, Jamaica, the Leeward Islands (Anguilla, Antigua, British Virgin Islands, Nevis, Montserrat, St. Kitts, St. Maarten and the United States Virgin Islands), Trinidad and Tobago and the Windward Islands (Dominica, Grenada, St. Lucia and St. Vincent and the Grenadines).

The West Indies was awarded the right to host the 2007 Cricket World Cup by the International Cricket Council (ICC). Through a process of bidding, eight territories (Antigua and Barbuda, Barbados, Grenada, Guyana, Jamaica, St. Kitts and Nevis, St. Lucia and Trinidad and Tobago) were selected to host the main matches.

The competing teams were initially divided into four groups, with the members of each group playing against each other. The two best performers in each group then proceeded to play the "Super Eight" matches (a total of 24 matches), from which the top four teams played the semi finals (a total of two matches) and the winners the final match. The Super Eight was essentially an eight-team round robin competition; these matches were held between 27 March and 21 April in Antigua, Bridgetown in Barbados, Providence in Guyana, and Grenada.

Overall, attendance leading into the semi finals for the 2007 World Cup averaged 8,500 supporters per match (International Cricket Council, 2007) Attendance for the entire 2007 Cricket World Cup averaged 11,176 per match (www.icc-cricket. com). As shown below, attendance at the Super Eight stage matches at the Guyana National Stadium at Providence, East Bank Demerara ranged between 4,800 to 12,208, with an average attendance of 7,310; the sitting capacity was 16,000.

Table 11.2   Match Attendance

Date	Teams	Official Attendance
28 March	Sri Lanka v South Africa	5,220
29 March	England v Ireland	4,800
1 April	Sri Lanka v West Indies	12,208
3 April	Ireland v South Africa	5,673
7 April	Bangladesh v South Africa	9,460
9 April	New Zealand v Ireland	6,500

Source: International Cricket Council (www.icc-cricket.com).

Research Procedures

To facilitate the purpose of the study, visitors were interviewed at the Guyana National Stadium at Providence during selected days on which matches were played in Guyana during the Super Eight stage of the 2007 Cricket World Cup (1, 3 and 7 April) and in the Departure Lounge of the Cheddi Jagan International Airport on 2, 7, 8 and 10 April. Researchers approached adult spectators and invited them to participate in the study. Upon consent, questions were posed to determine the following spectator characteristics.

1. Residency: City, country, postal code
2. Purpose of visit
3. Visitor group size and composition
4. Length of stay in Guyana
5. Spending in Guyana by category: Lodging, food and meals, retail shopping, items at the stadium, transportation, and other
6. Plans to return to Guyana, willingness to recommend Guyana as a tourist destination, and open comments re overall experience in Guyana
7. Gender, age and race of spectator
8. Prior Cricket World Cup and/or international sport event attendance

Survey data were entered and analyzed using the Statistical Package for Social Sciences (SPSS) computer software. Key findings are presented in the following section.

Research Results and Discussion

A total of 394 spectators were interviewed for the study. Spectators resided in the United States (n=201), Trinidad (n=68), Canada (n=33), the United Kingdom (n=30) and Barbados (n=10) (Table 11.3). Visitors from the United States accounted for 50 percent of the total spectator sample, while those from the Caribbean (Trinidad, Barbados, Antigua, Bahamas, St. Lucia) formed 25 percent, followed by Canada with 8.5 percent.

Spectators were asked their primary reason for visiting Guyana. Nearly 80 percent (79.4 percent) were visiting Guyana to attend the Cricket World Cup (Table 11.4). Other primary reasons for visiting Guyana reported by spectators included vacation (9.3 percent), other, including visiting friends and relatives (5.9 percent), and business (4.4 percent).

Cricket World Cup visitors in Guyana averaged three persons in group size and stayed 7.65 nights. By comparison, vacationers were in two person groups and stayed 9.73 nights; visitors for other reasons including visiting friends and relatives were 2.20 persons in size and stayed 10.86 nights; and business travelers in groups of 2.62 persons stayed 7.59 nights in Guyana (Table 11.5).

Table 11.3   Spectator Country of Residence, 2007 Cricket World Cup, Guyana

Country	n	Percent
United States	201	51.8
Trinidad	68	17.5
Canada	33	8.5
United Kingdom	30	7.7
Barbados	10	2.6
Other	46	11.9
Total	388	100.0

Note: "Other" countries represented in the spectator sample included Antigua, Australia, Bahamas, India, South Africa, Spain, Sri Lanka, and St. Lucia. It should be noted that many spectators from India and Pakistan did not attend the Super Eight Games after their home teams were eliminated in the first phase of the competition. Six subjects elected not to respond to this question.

Table 11.4   Primary Reasons for Visiting Guyana

Primary Reason for Visiting Guyana	n	Percent
Business	17	4.4
Cricket World Cup	308	79.4
Vacation	36	9.3
Personal	4	1.0
Other^	23	5.9
Total	388	100.0

Note: Six subjects elected not to respond to this question.

Table 11.5   Primary Reasons for Visiting Guyana by Group Size and Length of Stay, 2007 Cricket World Cup, Guyana

Primary Reason for Visiting Guyana	Visitor Group Size	Nights Stayed in Guyana
Business (n=17)	2.62	7.59
Cricket World Cup (n=308)	3.00	7.65
Vacation (n=36)	2.00	9.73
Personal (n=4)	1.00	8.00
Other (n=23)	2.20	10.86

Note: "Other" includes visiting friends and relatives (VFR).

Spectator visitor groups were comprised of relatives (33.3 percent), friends (30.6 percent), friends and relatives (23.0 percent), business associates (10.6 percent) and other (2.3 percent). Visitors who came to Guyana primarily to witness the 2007

Table 11.6   2007 Cricket World Cup Visitor Group Spending in Guyana

Category	Spending (US$)	% of Sample Spending Money (n)
Food and beverage	934.00	72.7 (n=224)
Retail shopping	439.54	60.7 (n=187)
Items at stadium	248.19	44.1 (n=136)
Lodging	1902.37	62.9 (n=194)
Local transportation	379.49	67.5 (n=208)
Other	475.60	52.1 (n=176)
Air transportation	2548.03	86.4 (n=266)

Table 11.7   Prior Cricket World Cup Attendance—All Apectators

Response	n	Percent
Yes	45	14.1
No	275	85.9
Total	320	100.0

Cricket World Cup and their immediate travel groups spent on average US$1,902 for lodging and US$934 for food and beverage in Guyana (Table 11.6). Additional spending included retail shopping (US$439), stadium purchases (US$248), local transportation (US$379) and other purchases (US$475).

Dividing the average group size (3.0) and length of stay (7.65 nights) by the sum of all average spending by category (excluding air transportation), US$4,379.19, it is estimated that the average visitor spent US$191 per night in Guyana during the 2007 Cricket World Cup.

As revealed in Table 11.7, most spectators (85.9 percent) had not attended a Cricket World Cup prior to 2007. Among the 45 visitors who had previously attended a CWC, most (n=40) were visiting Guyana specifically to attend the 2007 event.

Most spectators (76.9 percent) indicated that they would visit Guyana again, 4 percent would not and 10.1 percent were not sure they would return. A majority (87.8 percent) would recommend visiting Guyana to their friends or relatives, and 12.2 percent would not. Open ended comments from spectators reflected a strong sense of national pride in Guyana as host of the Super Eight matches. Several subjects of Guyanese heritage identified more closely and expressed loyalty to Guyana. Some commented that the Cricket World Cup prompted their visit and presented an opportunity to connect with their place of ancestry.

Interviewers identified the race/ethnicity of survey subjects, reporting 58.5 percent as Indian, 22 percent Black, 14 percent White and 3.6 percent Other (Table 11.8).

Table 11.8   2007 Cricket World Cup Spectator Race/Ethnicity

Race/Ethnicity	Frequency	Percent
Indian	175	58.5
Black	66	22.0
White	42	14.0
Other	11	3.6
Asian	4	1.3
Hispanic	1	0.3
Total	299	100.0

Table 11.9   2007 Cricket World Cup WFR Market Comparison

Relative or Friend Participating in 2007 Cricket World Cup?		
	Yes	*No*
Visitor group size	3.51	2.93
Length of stay	9.55	7.62
Spending (US$):		
– Lodging	4,179	1,626
– Retail shopping	732	380
– Food/beverage	1,846	810
– Local transportation	749	326
– Stadium items	448	226
– Round-trip transportation	5,057	2,311
– Other	597	397

Note: Spending is expressed as mean visitor group spending total by category.

Watching Friends and Relatives

Approximately 13 percent (12.8 percent) of spectators had a friend or relative participating in the 2007 Cricket World Cup. Table 11.9 reveals that spectators with relatives or friends participating in the 2007 Cricket World Cup traveled in larger visitor groups (3.51 to 2.93 visitors) and stayed more nights than other spectatorshr.5 to 7.6 nights). WFRs spent considerable more money in the host economy than other spectators for retail shopping, lodging, transportation and items at the stadium.

Cricket World Cup is one of the world's most viewed sporting events. The 2003 CWC matches in South Africa were attended by 626,845 people, while the 2007 CWC matches were televised in 200 countries to over 2.2 billion television viewers, sold more than 672,000 tickets and recorded the highest ticketing revenue for a CWC tournament (IndiaNews.com, 2007). (Note that the final figure of visitors to the region for CWC is not yet available). The average length of stay of a foreign visitor in CWC 2003 was 16 days, which was slightly longer than for the average non-CWC foreign visitor (12 days). Visitors that came specifically for the CWC 2003 stayed the shortest, while those that had timed their holiday to coincide with the event ended up staying over 22 days—this trend was also evident in the Guyana segment of CWC 2007. Foreigners were generally very satisfied with the event and South Africa. Crime reported was at insignificant levels. Three percent of visitors to CWC 2003 experienced an incident of crime while in the South Africa. Ninety-nine percent of visitors said they would return again and 99 percent said they would recommend a South Africa visit to others. Likewise, visitors to CWC 2007 in Guyana expressed satisfaction with the event and noted low levels of crime. An overwhelming majority (76.9 percent) would visit Guyana again and 87.8 percent would recommend to their friends or relatives that they visit Guyana. It should be noted that comparative data for the other territories in which the CWC 2007 matches were held is unavailable.

Earlier, Tang and Turco (2001) found that spectator spending levels corresponded to their perceptions of the event's prestige. Fans who assigned more prestige to the event spent more than those who perceived the event as less prestigious. Scott and Turco (2007) surmised that the unique and relatively prestigious nature of the Little League World Series negated any differences in spending between repeat and first-time spectators. Future research should continue to examine characteristics of WFRs and the influence of sport event prestige on their consumer behaviors. A better understanding of why sport consumers purchase goods and services would benefit sport and destination marketers (Trail, Fink, and Anderson, 2003).

Watching the wives and girlfriends (WAGs) of sport stars is a popular pastime for some, particularly in the UK and US where tabloid media devote considerable attention to the lifestyles of the rich and famous. Destination marketers welcome WAG-watchers as tourists for FIFA and UEFA championships. As the Cricket World Cup expands in popularity, perhaps more WFRs and WAG-watchers will follow.

Other sporting destinations see value in the WFR market and are implementing innovative strategies to attract them. Lake Placid, New York region produces several youth competitions for winter Olympic sports i.e., hockey, skiing, figure skating, etc. As minors, participants are required to be accompanied by a parent or legal guardian, thereby increasing visitor group size. The events are prestigious, extend several days and often involve international competitors, factors contributing to longer length of stay and increased visitor spending.

Continued spectator profile research is required to firmly establish their characteristics in order to target specific groups in the marketing/promotion strategies of the sport event. In such research consideration should be given to distinguishing WFRs into other groups, along lines similar to those used by Morrison, Hsieh and O'Leary (1995), and Seaton and Tagg (1995). Beyond the "what" of WFR demographics and spending habits, future research should examine their psychographic characteristics including attitudes, opinions, and interests of sport, tourism, spectatorship, etc. to better define and understand this group.

Acknowledgements

The authors thank the following officials from Guyana for their support: Dr Frank Anthony, Minister of Culture, Youth and Sport; Dr James G. Rose CCH, Vice-Chancellor, University of Guyana; Mr Ian Manifold, Head, Survey Department, Bureau of Statistics and Mr Andre Kellman, Operations Manager, Cheddi Jagan International Airport. Special thanks to the following students from the Department of Tourism of the University of Guyana, for administering the survey instrument: Kushana Allen, Trevonna Benn, Aiesha Blair, Marsha Budhu, Candaice Canzius, Donnis Chapman, Kimberly Dutchin, Yasmin Farouk, Davina Linton, Junita Liverpool, Shameeza Mohammed, Candice Morian, Khemattie Rajroop, Rusheena Rogers and Keisha Smith.

PART IV
Conclusion

Chapter 12

Creating a Sports Event Legacy in the Caribbean

Carolyn Hayle, David Truly, Ben Tyson and Leslie-Ann Jordan

Introduction

Legacy is the short and long-term benefits that a country and its people experience as a result of successfully hosting major international events. The concept of legacy encompasses economic, social, cultural, environmental, sporting and political impacts. As Figure 12.1 shows, generally, through the hosting of mega sports events, destinations are striving to create sustainable legacies in sports, recreation, tourism, volunteerism, infrastructure, the environment, accommodation, business activity and regional and economic links, to name a few. However, it is almost impossible for a destination to realize the maximum benefits of a hallmark event without the concerted effort on the part of all major stakeholders to develop a legacy strategy that seeks to harness and leverage the long-term value of the event. In fact, many event organizers have recognized that in order for legacy planning to be effective, it must be included as part of the bidding process (Pellegrino and Hancock 2010). According to Pellegrino and Hancock (2010: 7), "To succeed, a host needs to anchor the realization of benefits before the event takes place, rather than scrambling to pick up the pieces afterwards. Legacy begins from the moment the bid is created, not when the closing ceremony ends". Also, according to Taylor and Edmondson (2007), it is equally critical that the legacy vision, which clearly articulates the legacy benefits, is in place well in advance of the event.

Measuring the true legacy of an event usually takes time because several years must pass, sometimes 10–15 years, before one can make an informed judgment as to whether or not the event has had the anticipated long-term positive impact on the host destination (Schneider 2010). According to Pellegrino and Hancock (2010: 6–7), it is during this phase that the event legacy is most at risk:

> It is this long-term economic legacy that we consider the most challenging to fully realize. After the event—when athletes and entertainers go home, the political spotlight dims, and places that felt secondary to the event location demand their fair share of investment and action—that is when the legacy is most at risk. There is little glory to be had in the ten year slog to deliver all the benefits that were envisioned. Talent can drift away to the next high profile project. Political

Figure 12.1   Event Legacy Benefits
Source: Jordan, 2010.

leadership wearies or changes. And it is all too easy for tumbleweeds to take over the stadiums and parks.

This final chapter offers a brief review of the lessons learned from this collection of writings and offers important insights into one of the most complex Hallmark events ever undertaken.

CWC 2007 Legacy

For those eight countries that participated in this Hallmark event, the anticipated economic benefits were only one of the many reasons for hosting the 2007

Cricket World Cup. Other benefits were thought to include: the generation of new industries and a stimulus for infrastructural development, the creation of new employment opportunities, increased sports and recreation facilities for local communities leading to improved social interaction, and other benefits associated with tourism growth (WICB, 2002; Holder, 2001; Pestano, 2003). The ICC CWC WI 2007 Inc. developed eight objectives for the event: high quality event management, brand legacy, infrastructure improvement, widespread economic opportunity, Caribbean promotion, regional integration, high profitability, and increased popularity of Cricket.

In hindsight, these objectives seem far too idealistic and general in scope, especially considering the numerous challenges that faced the region in organizing and managing the event. The widespread geographical nature of the region and the cultural and political diversity were a significant obstacle.

The reaction of many fans and observers suggests a rather dim view of the legacy of the Cricket World Cup 2007. Journalists have cited the death of Pakistan team coach Bob Woolmer, the "unsatisfactory ending" to the final match, a lack of coordinated organization, ticket prices that excluded local participation, poor local spectatorship throughout the region, and a game schedule that ignored previous concerns over the length of the event. Even the former ICC chief executive Michael Speed admitted that this World Cup was "one of the more disappointing episodes of his seven-year tenure in charge" (CRICINFO 2008). The International Monetary Fund (IMF) reported that expenditure on the event resulted in a debt in excess of 100 percent of GDP at the end of 2006 in the host countries and that tax concessions given to the private sector will prevent any major economic gains to the region (Caribbean Comment Wordpress, 2007). As such, many have stated that the CWC 2007 has left the region with a legacy of debt. For example, the Jamaica Ministry of Finance believes that it is likely that the final bill to the Government of Jamaica from World Cup Cricket 2007 could reach J$1.2 billion because there is debt still to be paid. As such, Jamaica is in a precarious financial position.

Yet, it was also the most financially profitable for the ICC. For many, the major legacy of the CWC 2007 was that the US$53,900,000 profit was greater than any of the previous tournaments. Additionally, although they did not meet the target of US$42 million, ticket sales hit US$31.4 million which is also the highest of all the tournaments. The events organizers have also cited the following legacy benefits:

- Successful management of over 9,000 persons across the region.
- 12 world class cricket stadiums.
- 22 practice facilities for the further development of West Indies cricket.
- Over 4,300 volunteers trained (known as the CWC VIBES volunteers).
- 3,000 event security personnel were trained and deployed.
- A cadre of over 500 West Indians trained and experienced in world games event management.
- Regional solidarity.

- The framework for the creation of a single domestic space (cricketworld. com 2007).

But as Leanne White (Chapter 10) questioned, the West Indies may have indeed staged "the greatest Cricket World Cup the world has ever seen", but at what cost? The event did attract international participants, tourists and media audiences and foreign investments. Guyana's new 16,000-seat stadium was financed in part by the Government of India at a cost of US$25 million to host the Super Eight matches. Chinese and Taiwanese governments made significant investments for stadiums in Barbados and St. Kitts and Nevis and now recognise the potential of the sport and aims to have its own league and a competitive national team by 2020 (Sheringham, 2007). But the question remains, now that the 2007 Cricket World Cup is over, how will these stadiums be used and how will the region build on this event? For instance, in Jamaica, the destination is still wondering what it should do with the Trelawney "Multi-purpose Stadium—for Cricket Only", as some refer to it.

In order to prevent the legacy of "white elephants", some of the host venues attempted to put legacy plans in place before the start of the event. For example, Barbados has scored consistently higher on competitiveness indices than other countries in the Caribbean and recent commentary in the newspapers indicates that Barbados is still benefiting from World Cup Cricket 2007. They are still receiving visitors for sports and from the use of its venue. This can perhaps be attributed to Barbados' development of a legacy vision during the bidding process that clearly articulated how they were going to leverage the CWC 2007 to make "Barbados the number one place to live, work, play and invest" (Legacy Barbados, np). In order to ensure that the momentum generated from hosting the event was maximized beyond 2007, the Legacy Barbados Team developed seven target areas for investment and focus: 1) Export Barbados, 2) Enjoy Barbados, 3) Cricket Barbados, 4) Sports Barbados, 5) Green Barbados, 6) Live Barbados and 7) Think Barbados (Legacy Barbados, np). In Jamaica, the trade and investment facilitation agency (JAMPRO) developed the Jamaica Cricket Legacy Programme Vision 2012. It aimed to build a legacy for Jamaica, with the hope of capitalizing on the economic spin-offs of the event. JAMPRO created a legacy strategy titled Vision 2012 Brand Jamaica, which was designed "to look beyond the closing final match of the event and is directed towards outcomes in 2012, while leveraging immediate opportunities around the time of the event" (Springer, 2006: np). JAMPRO has estimated an increase in exports of US$198 million and US$400 million in foreign direct investment to the period 2012 (Springer, 2006). What is now needed is continuous research to determine to what extent these targets are being achieved.

Organization and Management Issues

Chalip (2004) offers a way of thinking that might help countries planning mega events like the CWC avoid the dilemmas that some Caribbean countries are now facing.

In the case of events, leveraging divides into those activities that need to be undertaken around the event itself, and those which seek to maximize the long-term benefits from events. Immediate event leveraging includes activities designed to maximize visitor spending, utilize local supply chains and build new markets. Long-term leveraging seeks to use events to build the host destination's image in order to enhance the quality of its brand or market position (226).

In the case of the CWC 2007, the sheer number of stakeholders made both the execution of the event and the pursuit of a legacy strategy difficult. These stakeholders can be grouped into essentially four categories: 1) the local community, 2) the local organizing committee (LOC), 3) the government and corporate community, and 4) the ICC. The lack of coordination and communication between local communities, the LOCs, governments and the ICC have been mentioned in several of the previous chapters. Both Sinclair-Maragh (Chapter 2) and McFarlane (Chapter 7) offer insight into how coordination and communication affected socio-economic impacts and legacies of this mega event.

In Jamaica, local citizens and governmental and non-governmental officials in Kingston saw this event as an opportunity to revitalize the downtown area. Although millions of dollars were spent in the Kingston area, the lack of communication and cooperation is particularly evident in McFarlane's assessment of impacts on the impoverished areas of Kingston. The city's staging of the event is now considered "shattered hopes", at least in the eyes of many residents. McFarlane asked: What has the World Cup done for the city's poorest individuals and communities?

Sinclair-Maragh's chapter emphasizes the need for a more empirical approach to the decision to host mega events. The chapter contends that a cost/benefit analysis could have better informed the stakeholders as to the actual impacts of this event. As Shone and Parry (2004) warned, although a sporting event can be seen as a potential for strengthening weak community structures and improving relationships among different ethnic groups, it must not be viewed as a panacea for local social and economic problems.

Issues surrounding how cultural idiosyncrasies affect coordination and communication also emerged as a significant obstacle in this event and manifested itself in many ways. Cumberbatch and Bynoe (Chapter 3) have discussed a basic lack of cultural awareness exhibited by event organizers toward various socioeconomic groups. While the "Bag Your Own Garbage" promoted in Barbados at Kensington Oval was certainly well intentioned, organizers did not anticipate the reaction among some of the area's more affluent spectators. While the general public approved of the effort in theory, in practice many of the elite felt embarrassed to be seen carrying little bags of garbage. Since these elite individuals were the policymakers, it is not surprising that if they refused to participate in this exercise, the larger population would also.

The importance of cultural context becomes even more evident in Rampersad's (Chapter 6) examination of Caribbean cricket fans. A cricket match in the Caribbean may mean "party time", but in other parts of the world it can be a social event equal to an evening at the opera. Evidently in the negotiations for the franchise for this event, negotiators neglected to consider the different cultural values ascribed to this sport and how this may impact the spectator experience. The Caribbean culture is a significant drawing card for any Caribbean destination and ignoring that culture can and did have a negative impact.

In Barbados the main issues confronting the government centered on accommodation issues. A shortage of rooms was forecasted to be a major impediment to hosting the mega-event, so the government devised a plan to address the problem. Jonsson (Chapter 9) discusses the Bed and Breakfast/ Home Accommodation Loan Fund of US$2.5 million that was created by the government to encourage the development of community-based accommodation, alternatively described as Home Accommodation. This Loan Fund was available to property owners in Barbados who wanted to modify portions of their homes to accommodate visitors in a Bed and Breakfast type accommodation. The Government hoped that this plan would address the room stock deficit while offering residents an opportunity to play an active role in the development of CWC. The Home Accommodation Programme (HAP) had to be carefully planned before implementation since it could lead to an oversupply of accommodation after the event. While residents were moderately positive about this program, obstacles centered on concerns about the continuity of the HAP and many were reluctant to take on these loans. Jonnson found that members of the community wanted more involvement in the design and development of the Home Accommodation Programme. However, Hayle et al. (2005) (re. Chapter's 4 and 5 of this book) revealed that in focus groups in Barbados the formal members of the hotels sector were frightened by this programme. They realised that if all the participants came on board as expected by the government, it could result in a dramatic shift in the balance of power in the hotel and lodging industry.

Lopez and Chinnery (Chapter 8) unearthed issues of interest that affected the planners at the local level. Initially, the Sports Agronomy Team (SAT) was set up to provide consultancy services to the CWC 2007 West Indies, Inc. on matters related to pitch and field, and consisted of staff members from the University of the West Indies Sports Agronomy Research Unit, and Department of Biological and Chemical Sciences, Cave Hill Campus, Barbados. A program was set up to ensure that cricket grounds selected for play during Cricket World Cup 2007 met the required standards expected for competition at the highest level of the game. The involvement of a local team involving scientists and cricket experts interacting with overseas consultants was an integral part of creating a legacy of technical skills and research and development infrastructure for sports grounds in the Caribbean. Assessments and advice given on site were supported by appropriate scientific data. Members of the team interviewed venue representatives at summit meetings and made periodic inspection and advisory visits to all countries in which games were scheduled. During the period of venue development, information was provided to grounds staff/management for improvements and to the organizers for evaluation of readiness. Notwithstanding the time and effort necessary to produce international quality cricket venues, some of the practice areas were not prepared on time. Lopez and Chinnery found that lack of attention to pitch and field matters was the main reason for late completion of scheduled work. This was due to communication gaps and unclear management control between the many stakeholders responsible for preparation of the grounds.

Regional Issues

Regional cooperation and coordination has always been an obstacle for the Caribbean region and the staging of World Cup Cricket 2007 highlighted expected problems between agencies, intra-agencies and between the public and private sector across the region. Age old rivalries between countries were evident. Research conducted prior to the event revealed that both Barbados and Jamaica saw the event as an opportunity to showcase their respective destinations. The focus groups in Barbados in particular made no reference to regional issues (Hayle et al., 2005) (re. Chapter's 4 and 5 of this book). In addition, Barbados, itself became the object of much annoyance because it had won the opportunity to host the closing ceremony. It was felt by other nations, and the literature supported the idea, that most sports fans on tour kept their money until the end of the trip before spending. So it was felt that Barbados and islands within easy flying distance would mostly benefit.

The focus groups in Tobago (Hayle et al., 2005) (re. Chapter's 4 and 5 of this book) raised an interesting question that remains to be answered: can these disparate countries really be marketed as one destination? Europe, North and South America trade as economic blocs and establish common trade regimes to increase their economies. Most of the countries that are in the top tier of the GCI are countries that are part of a regional bloc; but does this increase their ability to plan? In a global business environment, regional in-fighting undermines the individual and collective competitive strength. In-fighting and jealousy is the Caribbean's Achilles heel. These issues have hindered regionalism. These types of problems surrounding World Cup Cricket 2007 began at the inception of the initial negotiating process.

Managing the Impacts

As part of implementing an event's legacy strategy, the host destination should conduct a thorough pre and post event assessment. The Global Tourism Competitiveness report, which examines 14 components of tourism across several disciplines and sectors, can be utilized as a tool for such an analysis. This report suggests that tourism is a composite of many different socio-economic factors all of which when combined and managed effectively attract people to a destination. Boxill, Ramjeesingh and Segree (2004) indicate that tourism by itself does not contribute to economic development. This point is central to the management of tourism, especially in developing countries. So what might have been done to better manage the impact that the Cricket World Cup had on tourism in the region? Perhaps the 14 components of the Global Tourism Competitiveness report could provide a guide:

1. **Policy rules and regulations**
   What economic targets did each government wish to achieve? What regional economic rules and regulations needed to be advanced to help governments achieve these goals? What type of tourism products do countries need to develop individually and collectively to better attract visitors? What type of structures and systems are/were needed to make all of this happen?

2. **Environmental sustainability**
   What is the likely environmental impact of so many people coming to the country? Does the country have an impact study completed? Does the study tell the country how to plan its social, environmental and economic responses to accommodate the proposed influx of visitors?

3. **Safety and security**
   Will crime in the country increase? Will terrorism in the country and within the region increase? Can the citizens and visitors be protected against potential criminals?

4. **Health and hygiene**
   Does the country have adequate infrastructure and services to guard against all likely health threats?

5. **Prioritization of travel and tourism**
   How does the country receive the maximum benefit possible from this event? What systems have to be in place to ensure that tourism receives priority attention so that it can maximize its pull with visitors?

6. **Air transport infrastructure**
   Does the country have adequate airlift from the feeder markets? Does the region have adequate regional airlift? Do they have adequate baggage handling facilities?

7. **Ground transport infrastructure**
   Does the country have adequate ground transport systems for tourists and for locals? What about a ferry system? What systems are in place to receive visitors from cruise ships?

8. **Tourism infrastructure**
   Does the country have sufficient inter-ministerial/inter-agency collaboration needed to create a world-class tourism product and respond in a coordinated, efficient and effective manner?

9. **ICT infrastructure**
   Does the country have state of the art telecommunication systems to ensure that businesses and tourists are continuously connected?

10. **Price competitiveness in the travel and tourism industry**
Does the country have a price competitiveness study and know the desired price points and link with its tourism product by market segment?

11. **Human resources**
Does the country have sufficient human resources to deliver the type of products and services necessary to meet and exceed the visitors' expectations?

12. **Affinity for Travel and Tourism**
Does the country (its people and businesses) have an affinity for travel and tourism? How is this exhibited? Can it be improved?

13. **Natural resources**
Are the country's natural resources being managed, preserved and conserved in an effective manner? Are they being used to effectively brand the destination? Are they being used to create unique tourism products?

14. **Cultural resources**
Are the country's cultural resources being managed, preserved and conserved in an effective manner? Are they being used to effectively brand the destination? Are they being used to create unique tourism products?

Conclusion

The Caribbean region's ability to learn from the errors that were made in hosting the CWC and profit from this experience may be best categorized using the critical success factors presented by Jordan (Chapter 1).

- **Executive Management** – Management of the event was hindered by the unusually large number of stakeholders involved in staging the event. This was exacerbated by the wide regional and cultural diversity of the region and the broad socioeconomic disparity found amongst its citizens. Importantly, the excessive power wielded by the ICC and the governments proved to be an impediment to local interests and planning.
- **Collaboration and Communication** – As explained throughout this final chapter, issues negatively affecting collaboration and communication and the lack of regional cooperation that has plagued this region for centuries posed significant obstacles to staging CWC 2007.
- **Community Participation and Involvement** – There appears to have been little gained from CWC 2007 at the grass roots/community development level. The unilateral power wielded by the ICC and the national governments proved to be an impediment to local interests and planning.
- **Best Practices**
  - Efforts need to be made to reduce barriers facing both local and foreign entrepreneurs who wish to develop tourism enterprises (e.g., lower taxes, ease import restrictions/duties, provide incentives for food

production (especially to youth), set performance standards, provide low interest loans for new businesses, facilitate financing for renovating existing businesses).

- Efforts need to be made to develop a crop production plan that puts idle lands to use.
- Efforts need to be made to institute a poverty alleviation plan in rural areas that creates employment opportunities and minimizes harassment of visiting tourists.
- Efforts need to be made to organize and coordinate the planning, development and marketing of tourism activities across the various sectors (e.g., accommodations, attractions, transportation, food services). There is no doubt that the Watching Friends and Relatives market segment identified by Turco et al. (Chapter 11) offers future marketing opportunities.
- Efforts need to be made to develop a communications strategy that links all organizations and stakeholders at all levels.
- Efforts need to be made to link poor rural areas to resort areas through agriculture and micro-enterprise opportunities.

Bibliography

Adams, W.A. and Gibbs, R.J. 1994. *Natural Turf for Sport and Amenity: Science and Practice*. Wallingford: CAB International, 404.

Aderhold, P. 1997. *The European Holiday Markets for Developing Countries 1997–99*. Copenhagen: Institute for Tourism Research.

Amir, Y. 1998. Contact Hypothesis in Ethnic Relations, in *The Handbook of Interethnic Coexistence*, edited by E. Weiner. New York: The Continuing Publishing Company, 162–81.

Anderson, B. 1991. *Imagined Communities: Reflections on the Origins and Spread of Nationalism*. 2nd Edition. London: Verso.

Andranovish, G., Burbank, M. and Heying, C. 2001. Olympic Cities: Lessons Learned from Mega-event Politics. *Journal of Urban Affairs*, 23(2).

Arthur, O. 2007. A Job Well Done for CWC 2007. [Online, May 4]. Available at: http://www.labourparty.wordpress.com.

Atwell, C. 2006a. SSA Complete Clean-up. *Daily Nation*, August 9, A4.

Atwell, C. 2006b. 90-tonnes of Festival Thrash. *Daily Nation*, August 10, A3.

Austin-Boos, D. 1995. Gay Nights and Kingston Town: Representations of Kingston, Jamaica, in *Postmodern Cities and Spaces*, edited by S. Watson and K. Gibson. Oxford: Blackwell Publishers, 149–64.

AVERT. 2008. World AIDS Day. [Online, June 2]. Available at: http://www.avert.org.

Babbie, E. 2004. *The Practice of Social Research*. 10th Edition. Surrey: Wadsworth.

Bacchus, R. 2005. Laws for Illegal Dumping. *Weekend Nation*, April 22, 22.

Barbados Advocate. 2007. St. Lucia Declares That it is Ready to Host Matches in ICC CWC 2007. [Online, January 10]. Available at: http://www.caribbeanbusinessclub.com.

Barbados Democrats. 2007. Will Caribbean Governments Show Balls. [Online, April 2]. Available at: http://dipbarbados.wordpress.com.

Barbados Nation Newspaper. 2004. Going for the Greatest World Cup 2007. *Barbados Nation Newspaper*, May 16. Available at: http://windiescricket.com/article [accessed: June 15, 2005].

Barbados Ministry of Tourism. 2003. Annual Tourism Statistical Digest 2003. [Online]. Available at: http://www.barmot.gov.bb/reports/Statistical%20Digest2003_4.pdf [accessed: November 16, 2008].

Barbados Tourism Authority. 2007. Long Stay Visitor Arrivals 1960–2005. [Online]. Available at: http://www.visitbarbados.org/pressroom/statistics.aspx [accessed: June 10, 2008].

Baron, R. and Byrne, D. 2003. *Social Psychology*. 10th Edition. Boston, MA: Allyn and Bacon.

Baron, R. and Byrne, D. 2000. *Social Psychology*. 9th Edition. London: Allyn and Bacon.

Beard, J.B. 2005. *Beard's Turfgrass Encyclopedia for Golf Courses Grounds Lawns and Sports Fields*. East Lansing, MI: Michigan State University Press, 513.

Beckles, H. McD. 2006. *The First West Indies Cricket Tour: Canada and the US in 1886*. Kingston, Jamaica: Canoe Press.

Beckles, H. McD. 1998. *The Development of West Indies Cricket: Vol. 2 The Age of Globalization*. Kingston, Jamaica: The University of the West Indies Press, 190.

Bennett-Templer, S., Lyn, M. and Whatley, S. 2006. JAMPRO Announces Partnership with CricketWorld.com. *Jamaica Gleaner*. [Online]. Available at: www.investjamica.com/news/articles/jamproCricketWorldcom.php.

Berelson, B. 1952. *Content Analysis in Communication Research*. New York: Free Press.

Berridge, G. 2007. *Events Design and Experience*. Oxford: Butterworth-Heinemann.

Bertrand, I. 2001. *Airlift to, and Within, the Caribbean*. Speech to Heads of Government at Tourism Summit, Nassau, Bahamas.

Bianchi, R.V. 2002. Towards a New Political Economy of Global Tourism, in *Tourism and Development: Concepts and Issues*, edited by R. Sharpley and D. Telfer. Clevedon, Bristol: Channel View Publications.

Bond, M.E. and Ladman, J.R. 1993. International Tourism: An Instrument for Third World Development, in *Dialectics of Third World Development*, edited by I. Vogeler and A. De Sousa. Lanham, MD: Rowman & Littlefield.

Bose, S. and Gupta, S. 2004. Money Tames Cricket, in *Cricketing Cultures in Conflict: World Cup 2003*, edited by B. Majumdar and J.A. Mangan. London: Routledge, 176–97.

Bossellman, F., Peterson, C. and McCarthy, C. 1999. *Managing Tourism Growth: Issues and Applications*. Washington, DC: Island Press.

Bourdieu, P. 1988. Program for a Sociology of Sport. *Sociology of Sport Journal*, 5(2), 153–61.

Bourdieu, P. 1978. Sport and Social Class. *Social Science Information*, 17(6), 819–40.

Bowdin, G., Allen, A., O'Toole, W., Harris, R. and McDonnell, I. 2006. *Events Management*. 2nd Edition. Oxford: Butterworth-Heinemann.

Boxill, I., RamjeeSingh, D. and Segree, M.D. 2004. Caribbean Tourism and the FTAA, in *The Caribbean Economies in an Era of Free Trade*, edited by N. Karagiannis and M. Witter. Aldershot; Burlington, VT: Ashgate.

Boyd, S.W. and Singh, S. 2003. Destination Communities: Structures, Resources and Types, in *Tourism in Destination Communities*, edited by S. Singh, D.J. Timothy and R.K. Dowling. Wallingford: CABI International.

Boyle, R. and Haynes, R. 2000. *Power Play: Sport, the Media and Popular Culture*. Harlow: Longman.

Bramwell, B. 1997. Strategic Planning Before and After a Mega-Event. *Tourism Management*, 18(3), 167–76.

Bull, C. and Lovell, J. 2007. The Impact of Hosting Major Sporting Events on Local Residents: An Analysis of the Views and Perceptions of Canterbury Residents in Relation to the Tour de France 2007. *Journal of Sport and Tourism*, 12(3), 229–48.

Burbank, M., Andranovish, G. and Heying, C. 2002. Mega-events, Urban Development, and Public Policy. *Review of Policy Research*, 19(3), 179–202.

Burgan, B. and Mules, T. 2000. Event Analysis – Understanding the Divide Between Cost Benefit and Economic Impact Analysis, in *Events Beyond 2000: Setting the Agenda, Australian Centre for Event Management*, edited by J. Allen, R. Harris, L. Jago and A. Veal. Sydney: University of Technology.

Burton, R. 1995. Cricket, Carnival and Street Culture in the Caribbean, in *Liberation Cricket: West Indies Cricket Culture*, edited by H. Beckles and B. Stoddard. Manchester: Manchester University Press.

Butler, R. 1980. The Concept of a Tourist Area Cycle of Evolution: Implications for Management of Resources. *Canadian Geographer*, 24, 5–12.

Campbell, J. 2005. World Cup 2007 Challenging for Lockerbie. *Sunday Trinidad Express*, 29 May, 59.

Caribbean Airlines News Articles. 2007. Caribbean Airlines Offers 100 Extra Flights for Cricket World Cup. [Online]. Available at: http://www.caribbean-airlines.com.

Caribbean Business Club. 2006b. Do Developing Countries Benefit from Hosting Major Events. [Online]. Available at: http://www.caribbeanbusinessclub.com/forums/news.

Caribbean Comment Wordpress. 2007. IMF Assess Economic Impact of CWC: Don't Expect Much From it. [Online]. Available at: http://www.caribbeancomment.wordpress.com [accessed: April 14, 2007].

CaribbeanCricket.com. 2004. No threat to Guyana WC Stadium. [Online, 29 July]. Available at: http://www.caribbeancricket.com [accessed: August 1, 2004].

CaribbeanCricket.com. 2004. B'dos gets WC Finals; J'ca gets W.I. [Online]. Available at: http://www.caribbeancricket.com [accessed: April 6, 2005].

Caribbean Development Bank. 2006. *CDB Annual Economic Review of St. Vincent and the Grenadines 2006*. [Online]. Available at: http://www.caribank.org/AnReport.net.

Caribbean Media Corporation. 2008. T&T Board Unclear Over World Cup Monies, Trinidad.

Caribbean Net News. 2007. St. Lucia Executive Promises Best Cricket World Cup. [Online, January 25]. Available at: http://www.caribbeannetsnews.com.

Caribbean Net News. 2006a. Antigua and Barbuda Launches Homestay Programme for CWC. [Online]. Available at: http://www.caribbeannetsnews.com [accessed: September 8, 2006].

Caribbean Net News. 2006b. Antigua and Barbuda Receives US$7.5m from Venezuela for Airport Upgrade. [Online]. Available at: http://www. caribbeannetnews.com [accessed: November 4, 2006].

Caribbean Press Releases. 2008. CWC 2007 Inc. Nets US$53.9 Million Surplus. [Online]. Available at: http:// www.caribbeanpressreleases.com/articles/2955.

Caribbean Tourism Organization. 2008. *Latest 2007 Tourism Statistics Tables.* [Online, February 20]. Available at: http://www.onecaribbean.org/information/ documentview.php?rowid=4476 [accessed: February 28, 2008].

Caribbean Tourism Organization. 2006. *Latest Statistics, 2004.* [Online] Available at: http://www.onecaribbean.org [accessed: September 18, 2007].

Caribbean Tourism Organization. 2006. Barbados Tourism Statistics Tables. [Online]. Available at: http://www.onecaribbean.org/statistics/countrystats/ [accessed: February 28, 2008].

Caribbean Tourism Organization. 2005. Cricket World Cup and the Caribbean Hotel Sector: Preparing to Perform. *Caribbean Alliance for Sustainable Tourism*, 17(1). Available at: http://www.cha-cast.com/Publications.htm [accessed: May 10, 2005].

Caribbean Tourism Organization. 2001. *Caribbean Tourism Statistical Report 2000–2001.* St. Michael, Barbados: Caribbean Tourism Organization.

Caribbean Tourism Organization. 1999. *A Guide to Tourism Careers, Education and Training in the Caribbean.* St. Michael, Barbados: Caribbean Tourism Organization.

CARICOM Secretariat. 2008a. *The West Indies Federation.* [Online]. Available at: http://www.caricom.org/jsp/community/west_indies_federation.jsp?menu= community.

CARICOM Secretariat. 2008b. *The CARICOM Single Market and Economy.* [Online]. Available at: http://www.caricom.org/jsp/single_market/index.

CARICOM Secretariat. 2008c. *The Caribbean Court of Justice.* [Online]. Available at: http://www.caribbeancourtofjustice.org.

Carlsen, J. 2004. The Economics and Evaluation of Festivals and Events, in *Festival and Events Management an International Arts and Culture Perspective*, edited by I. Yeoman, M. Robertson, J. Ali-Knight, S. Drummond and U. McMahon-Beattie. Oxford: Elsevier Butterworth-Heinemann.

Cashman, R. 2001. Introduction, in *Sport, Federation, Nation*, edited by R. Cashman, J. O'Hara and A. Honey. Petersham: Walla Walla Press (in conjunction with the Centre for Olympic Studies), University of New South Wales, 1–13.

Central Bank of Barbados. 2005. *In BTI – Barbados Tourism Investment Inc.* [Online]. Available at: http://www.barbadostourisminvestment.com.

Chalip, L. 2004. Beyond Impact: A General Model for Sport Event Leverage, in *Sports Tourism: Interrelationships Impact and Issues*, edited by B.W. Ritchie and D. Adair. Clevedon, Bristol: Channel View Publications.

Chambers, R. 2002. *Participatory Workshops: A Sourcebook of 21 Sets of Ideas and Activities.* London: Earthscan.

Chambers, R. 1997. *Whose Reality Counts? Putting the First Last*. London: ITDG Publishing.

Chambers, R. 1983. *Rural Development: Putting the Last First*. London: Longman.

Charles, F. 2007. *Barbados Small Island, Big Dreams – Chronicle of the World Cup Barbados Journey*. Barbados: World Cup Barbados Inc., 78.

Cho, M. 2004. Assessing Accommodation Readiness for the 2002 World Cup: The Role of Korean-Style Inns. *Event Management*, 8, 177–84.

Ciupak, Z. 1973. Sport Spectators – An Attempt at a Sociological Analysis. *International Review for the Sociology of Sport*, 89–102.

Clarke, C. and Howard, D. 2006. Contradictory Socio-Economic Consequences of Structural Adjustment in Kingston, Jamaica. *The Geographical Journal*, 172(2), 106–29.

Clayton, A., Duncan, N. and Hayle, C. (forthcoming). *Impact of Trade Liberalization on Tourism and Environment*.

Cleaver, F. 2001. Institutions, Agency and the Limitations of Participatory Approaches to Development, in *Participation: The New Tyranny?*, edited by B. Cooke and U. Kothari. London: Zed Books Limited, 37–55.

Coakley, J. 2004. *Sports in Society: Issues and Controversies*. New York: McGraw Hill.

Coleman, J. 2000. Social Capital in the Creation of Human Capital, in *Social Capital: A Multifaceted Perspective*, edited by P. Dasgupta and I. Serageldin. Washington, DC: World Bank Publications, 13–39.

Collis, R.H. 2006. *The Importance of Cricket World Cup 2007 in Antigua and Barbuda (With the Focus on the Socio-Economic Benefits to Communities)*. [Online]. Available at: http://www.onecaribbean.org/information/document download.php.

Commonwealth Secretariat. 2002. *Master Plan for Sustainable Tourism Development*. London: New Image Ltd.

Cooper, C., Fletcher, J., Gilbert, D. and Wanhill, S. 1998. *Tourism Principles and Practices*. 2nd Edition. London: Prentice Hall.

Cornell University Center for Hospitality Research. 2005. [Online]. Available at: http://www.hotelschool.cornell.edu/alumni/chs/specialevent.html [accessed: November 3, 2005].

Cosier, G. 2008. Discussion on the Home Accommodation Programme (Personal communication) February 29 and August 28, 2008.

Cozier, T. 2007. The Caribbean's Big Stage, in *ICC Cricket World Cup 2007 Official Souvenir Guide*, edited by R. Gibbs. St. Michael, Barbados: The Nation Publishing Co. Ltd, 14–18.

Cozier, T. 2006. World Cup 2007, in *Wisden History of the Cricket World Cup*, edited by T. Cozier. Hampshire: John Wisden and Co. Ltd, 194–7.

Cozier, T. 2004. Caribbean Facing Crisis Over World Cup 2007. *Stabroek News*, January 29. [Online]. Available at: http://www.landofsixpeoples.com/gynewsjs.htm [accessed April 12, 2005].

Crawford, G. 2001. Characteristics of a British Ice Hockey Audience: Major Findings of the 1998 and 1999 Manchester Storm Ice Hockey Club Supporter Surveys. *International Review for the Sociology of Sport*, 36(1), 71–81.

Cricinfo.com. 2008. Speed Regrets World Cup Failure. [Online, December 5, CTO]. Available at: http://www.cricinfo.com/ci/content/story/380886.html?CMP=OTC-RSS.

Cricinfo.com. 2007. Ticket Sales Double of Previous World Cup – Dehring, April 16. [Online]. Available at: http://www.cricinfo.com.

Cricketworld.com. 2007. Profits From World Cup Will Eliminate WICB Deficit. [Online]. Available at: http://www.cricketworld.com/archive_series/2007/world_cup_2007/article/?aid=12255.

Cricketworldcup.com. 2006. Anti-Infringement Programme (2006). [Online]. Available at: http://www. cricketworldcup.com/anti-infringement-programme. html.

Crompton, J., Lee, S. and Shuster, T. 2001. A Guide for Undertaking Economic Impact Studies: The Springfest Festival. *Journal of Travel Research*, 40(1), 78–87.

Crompton, J.L. 1995. Economic Impact Analysis of Sports Facilities and Events: Eleven Sources of Misapplication. *Journal of Sport Management*, 9(1), 14–35.

Dann, G.M.S. 1996. Socio-cultural Issues in St Lucian Tourism, in *Sustainable Tourism in Islands and Small States: Case Studies*, edited by L. Brigulio, B. Davies, D. Harrison and W.L. Filho. New York: Pinter Press.

Davidson, O. 2002. WICB to Earn Hefty Sum. *Stabroek News*, August 4. [Online]. Available at: http://www.landofsixpeoples.com/gynewsjs.htm [accessed: May 21, 2005].

Davidson, R. 1994. European Business and Travel and Tourism, in *Tourism the State of the Art*, edited by C.L. Jenkins, R.C. Wood, P.U.C. Dieke, M.M. Bennett, L.R. MacLellan and R. Smith. Chichester: John Wiley & Sons.

Davis, D., Allen, J. and Cosenza, R.M. 1988. Segmenting Local Residents by Their Attitudes, Interests and Opinions Toward Tourism. *Journal of Travel Research*, 27(2), 2–8.

Deccio, C. and Baloglu, S. 2002. Nonhost Community Resident Reactions to the 2002 Winter Olympics: The Spillover Impacts. *Journal of Travel Research*, 41(1), 46–56.

Dehring, C. 2007a. Beaming Dehring in Seventh Heaven. *Sunday Gleaner*, February 25.

Dehring, C. 2007b. World Cup Reviving Caribbean Unity. *Jamaica Observer.* [Online]. Available at: http://www.caribbeanbusinessclub.com [accessed: January 26, 2007].

De Kadt, E. 1979. *Tourism: Passport to Development*. Oxford: Oxford University Press.

Derriman, P. 2006. Landmarks, in *Long Shadows: 100 Years of Australian Cricket*, edited by M. Ray. Milsons Point, NSW: Random House, 116–41.

Devers, S. 2003. Hall Bowls Bouncer at Regional Tourism Industry. *Stabroek News*, June 8. [Online]. Available at: http://www.landofsixpeoples.com/gynewsjs.htm [accessed: December 10, 2004].

Dodman, D. 2006. Post-independence Optimism and the Legacy of Waterfront Redevelopment in Kingston, Jamaica. *Cities*, 24(4), 273–84.

Doxey, G.V. 1975. A Causation Theory of Visitor Related Irritants: Methods and Research Inferences, in *The Impact of Tourism: Sixth Annual Conference Proceedings*. Salt Lake City, UT: Travel and Tourism Research Association, 195–8.

Dunn, L.D. 1999. *Tourism Attractions: A Critical Analysis*. Jamaica: University Press.

Ecorecycle. 2005. Waste Wise Events Bin Placement and Maintenance Guidelines. Waste Wise Events Toolkit. [Online]. Available at: http://www.ecorecycle.sustainability.vic.gov.au/www/html/900-waste-wise-events-toolkit.asp?intSiteID=1 [accessed: July 19, 2006].

EIU Travel and Tourism Analyst. 1993. *The Market of Cultural Tourism in Europe*. No. 6. The Economist Intelligence Unit Limited.

Ejimofor, P. 2004. Crop of Litter Bugs. *Sunday Sun*, August 8, A5.

Ejimofor, P. 2003. Call to Restart Litter Patrol. *Daily Nation*, October 10, 7.

Ejimofor, P. 2002. Dirty ABC Highway. *Sunday Sun*, February 2, 46.

Emery, P.R. 2002. Bidding to Host a Major Sports Event: The Local Organizing Committee Perspective. *The International Journal of Public Sector Management*, 15(4), 316–35.

Erikson, D.P. and Wander, P. 2007. China: Cricket 'Champion'. *Inter-American Dialogue*. [Online]. Available at: www.thedialogue.org/page.cfm?pageID=32&pubID=274 [accessed: April 28, 2007].

Ernst & Young. 2004. *Focus on Barbados Budget 2004*. [Online]. Available at: http://www.ey.com/global/download.nsf/Caribbean/bb_budget_04-05_-_focus_on_barbados_budget/$file/BBBudget04-Document%20new.pdf [accessed: September 20, 2007].

Etter, D. 2007. Situational Conditions of Attitude Change within Tourism Settings: Understanding the Mechanics of Peace through Tourism. *IIPT Occasional Paper, 11*. Global Educators' Network of the International Institute for Peace through Tourism (GENIIPT). [Online]. Available at: http://www.iipt.org/educators/OccassionalPapers.htm [accessed: January 2, 2008].

Ferguson, J. 2006. *World Class: An Illustrated History of Caribbean Football*. Oxford: Macmillan Caribbean.

Few, R. 2003. Participation or Containment? Insights from the Planning of Protected Areas in Belize, in *Participatory Planning in the Caribbean: Lessons from Practice*, edited by J. Pugh and R. Potter. Aldershot: Ashgate Publishing Limited, 23–44.

FIFA. 2006. FIFA Quality Concept: Handbook of Test Methods for Football Turf. March 2006 Edition. Switzerland, FIFA, 54.

Forgas, J. and Williams, K. 2001. *Social Influence: Direct and Indirect Processes.* Philadelphia, PA: Psychology Press.

Fredline, E. and Faulkner, B. 2002. Variations in Residents' Reactions to Major Motorsport Events: Why Residents Perceive the Impacts of Events Differently. *Event Management*, 7, 115–25.

Fredline, E. and Faulkner, B. 2000. Host Community Reactions – A Cluster Analysis. *Annals of Tourism Research*, 27(3), 763–84.

Gemmell, J. 2008. Introduction: Cricket, Race and the 2007 World Cup, in *Cricket, Race and the 2007 World Cup*, edited by J. Gemmell and B. Majumdar. London: Routledge, x–xix.

Getz, D. 1997. *Event Management and Event Tourism*. New York: Cognizant Communication Corporation.

Getz, D. 1993. Festivals and Special Events, in *Encyclopaedia of Hospitality and Tourism*, edited by M.A. Khan, M.D. Olsen and T. Var. New York, NY: Van Nostrand Reinhold, 789–810.

Giulianotti, R. 2005. The Socialibility of Sport: Scotland Football Supporters as Interpreted through the Sociology of Georg Simmel. *International Review for the Sociology of Sport*, 40(3), 289–306.

Giulianotti, R. 2005. Sport Spectators and the Social Consequences of Commodification: Critical Perspectives from Scottish Football. *International Review for the Sociology of Sport*, 29(4), 386–410.

Gordon, K. 2008. CWC 2007 Inc. Nets US$53.9 Million Surplus. [Online]. Available at: http://www.caribbeanpressreleases.com/articles/2955.

Gordon, K. 2007. WICB to Eliminate Debt Through CWC Profits: West Indies Cricket Board. [Online]. Available at: http://www.windiescricket.com [accessed: July 18, 2007].

Gordon, K. 2006. Region to Win from Cricket World Cup. [Online]. Available at: http://www.caribbeanbusinessclub.com/forums/news [accessed: November 24, 2006].

Government of Barbados. 2004. *Cricket World Cup Environmental Plan Barbados*. Unpublished manuscript.

Gray, O. 2004. *Demeaned but Empowered: The Social Power of the Urban Poor in Jamaica*. Kingston, Jamaica: The University of the West Indies Press.

Gursoy, D. and Jurowski, C. 2004. Distance Effects on Resident Attitudes toward Tourism. *Annals of Tourism Research*, 31(2), 296–312.

Gursoy, D. and Rutherford, D. 2004. Host Attitudes towards Tourism: An Improved Structural Model. *Annals of Tourism Research*, 31(3), 495–516.

Gursoy, D., Jurowski, C. and Uysal, M. 2001. Resident Attitudes: A Structural Modelling Approach. *Annals of Tourism Research*, 29(1), 79–105.

Guyana Chronicle. 2004a. PM Anthony Urges Better Distribution of Profits. *Guyana Chronicle*, April 29. [Online]. Available at: http://www.landofsixpeoples.com/gynewsjs.htm [accessed: December 11, 2004].

Guyana Chronicle. 2004b. Hosting World Cup Cricket Could be Tourism Watershed. *Guyana Chronicle*, July 16. [Online]. Available at: http://www.landofsixpeoples.com/gynewsjs.htm [accessed: December 11, 2004].

Guyana Chronicle. 2003a. Leading Hospitality Players Look at Tourism Opportunities in CWC 2007. *Guyana Chronicle*, November 23. [Online] Available at: http://www.landofsixpeoples.com/gynewsjs.htm [accessed: December 10, 2004].

Guyana Chronicle. 2003b. CWC 2007 is a Big Responsibility. *Guyana Chronicle*, December 3. [Online]. Available at: http://www.landofsixpeoples.com/gynewsjs.htm [accessed: December 11, 2004].

Hall, C.M. 1992. *Hallmark Tourist Events: Impacts, Management and Planning*. London: Belhaven Press.

Hansmann, R. and Scholz, R. 2003. A Two-step Informational Strategy for Reducing Littering Behaviour in a Cinema. *Environment and Behavior*, 35(6), 752–62.

Harambolas, M. and Holborn, M. 2004. *Sociology Themes and Perspectives*. 6th Edition. London: Harper Collins Publishers Limited.

Harill, R. and Potts, D. 2003. Tourism Planning in Historic Districts: Attitudes Towards Tourism Development. *Journal of American Planning Association*, 18(3), 251–66.

Harrison, L., Jayawardena, C. and Clayton, A. 2003. Sustainable Tourism Development in the Caribbean: Practical Challenges. *International Journal of Contemporary Hospitality Management*, 15(4/5), 294–315.

Harrison, D. 1992. *Tourism and the Less Developed Countries*. London: Belhaven.

Hawkes, C. 2007. *Cricket World Cup 07 Guide*. Sydney: Australian Broadcasting Corporation.

Hayle, C., Jordan, L., Thame, M., Truly, D. and Tyson, B. 2005. *Potential World Cup Cricket Impacts on Community Tourism Development in Barbados, Jamaica, and Trinidad and Tobago*. Research Report for Association Liaison Office (ALO) for University Cooperation in Development and the American Council on Education (USAID) and The University of the West Indies Institute for Hospitality and Tourism School for Graduate Studies and Research.

Haynes, C. 2006. Hilton Rooms Booked for CWC. *The Nation Newspaper*, July 30. [Online]. Available at: http://www.caribbeanbusinessclub.com/forums/newsDetails.php?try=50 [accessed: July 30, 2006].

Herek, G.M. and Capitanio, J.P. 1995. Black Heterosexuals' Attitudes towards Lesbian and Gay Men in United States. *The Journal of Sex Research*, 32(2), 95–105.

Hernandez, A., Cohen, J. and Garcia, L.H. 1996. Residents' Attitudes towards an Instant Resort Enclave. *Annals of Tourism Research*, 23(4), 755–79.

Hines, H. 2004. Region Could Earn $36b from Cricket World Cup. *Jamaica Observer*, July 26. [Online]. Available at http://jamaicaobserver.com [accessed: July 28, 2004].

Hobsbawm, E. 1990. *Nations and Nationalism Since 1780: Programme, Myth, Reality*. New York: Cambridge University Press.

Holder, J. 2003. What is at Stake for the Caribbean in Hosting the Cricket World Cup 2007 Event – An Address to the CTO Teachers Forum. [Online]. Available at: http://www.onecaribbean.org [accessed: February 23, 2005].

Holder, J. 2001. Meeting the Challenge of Change. Speech to Heads of Government at Tourism Summit, Nassau, Bahamas.

Horak, R., Waddington, I. and Malcom, D. 1998. The Social Composition of Football Crowds in Western Europe: A Comparative Study. *International Review for the Sociology of Sport*, 33(2), 155–69.

Horne, J. and Manzenreiter, W. 2006a. *Sports Mega-Events: Social Scientific Analyses of a Global Phenomenon*. Malden, MA: Blackwell Publishing.

Horne, J. and Manzenreiter, W. 2006b. An Introduction to the Sociology of Sports Mega-events. *The Editorial Board of the Sociological Review*, 1–24. Oxford: Blackwell Publishing.

Horne, D. 1981. National Identity in the Period of the New Nationalism. *Nationalism and Class in Australia: 1920 – 1980*. Australian Studies Centre, University of Queensland, Brisbane.

Hosein, A. 2005. Region's Hosting of World Cup 2007…Trouble Ahead! *Trinidad Express Sports*, April 15, 18–20.

Howard, D. 2005. *Kingston: A Cultural and Literary History*. Oxford: Signal Books Limited.

Huang, R. and Sarigollu, E. 2007. Benefit Segmentation of Tourists to the Caribbean. *Journal of Consumer Marketing*, 2(2), 67–83.

Humphreys, J.M. and Plummer, M.K. 1995. *The Economic Impact on the State of Georgia of Hosting the 1996 Summer Olympics*. [Online]. Available at: www.selig.uga.edu/forecast/olympics/OLYMTEXT.HTxx.

Hutchings, C. 1996. Trouble in Paradise. *Geographical Journal*, 68(1).

Hutchinson, G. 2002. *True Blue*. Camberwell: Viking.

ICC Cricket World Cup West Indies. 2007. Ticket Brochure. Jamaica Information Service. 2006.

International Cricket Council (ICC). 2007. Event Symbol and Event Mascot. [Online]. Available at http://cricket2007.com/worldcup/WorldCup2007_Mascot.asp [accessed: January 17, 2008].

International Cricket Council (ICC). 2005a. Senior Police Representatives Arrive from Across the Region for Cricket World Cup Planning Meetings, ICC. [Online]. Available at: http://www.icc-cricket.com [accessed: June 15, 2005].

International Cricket Council (ICC). 2005b. Cricket World Cup Calls for a Team Effort, ICC. [Online]. Available at: http://www.icc-cricket.com [accessed: March 10, 2005].

International Cricket Council (ICC). (n.d.) ICC CWC 2007 Venue Summary, ICC. [Online]. Available at: http://www.icc-cricket.com [accessed: April 8, 2005].

International Olympic Committee (IOC). 2008. HIV & AIDS Prevention Through Sport. Switzerland. [Online]. Available at: www.multimedia.olympic.org. [accessed: March 2008].

Jago, L. and Shaw, R. 1998. Special Events: A Conceptual and Definitional Framework. *Festival Management and Event Tourism*, 5(1/2), 21–32.

Jamaica Gleaner. 2007a. Bed and Breakfast Programme Gaining Momentum. [Online]. Available at: http://www.jamaicagleaner.com.

Jamaica Gleaner. 2007b. Kingston Hotels Ready for Cricket World Cup. [Online]. Available at: http://www.jamaicagleaner.com [accessed: January 9, 2007].

Jamaica Information Service. 2007. *'One Love' Village To Be Set Up In New Kingston During CWC* 2007. [Online]. Available at: http://www.jis.gov.jm/officepm.

Jamaica Observer. 2007a. *Profits from ICC CWC 2007 Will Eliminate WICB Deficit*, July 13.

Jamaica Observer. 2007b. *CWC Local Sponsors Happy Despite Small Number of Visitors*, March 28.

James, C.L.R. 1963. *Beyond a Boundary*. London: Hutchinson.

James, D.M. 2004. *Understanding the Playing Performance of Cricket Pitches*. Ph.D. Thesis, The University of Sheffield, UK, 202.

JAMPRO. 2006. Caribbean Businesses Drive New Mechanism to Strengthen Relations. [Online]. Available at: http://www.investjamaica.com/news/articles/cbos.php.

John, A. 2004. Global Games: Culture, Political Economy and Sport in the Globalised World of the 21st Century. *Third World Quarterly*, 25(7), 1325–37.

Jordan, L. 2003. *Institutional Arrangements for Tourism in small Twin-Island States of the Caribbean: The Role of the Internal Core-periphery Model*. Doctoral thesis. University of Otago, New Zealand.

Jordan, L. 2006. Staging the Cricket World Cup 2007 in the Caribbean: Issues and Challenges for Small Island Developing States, in *Sporting Events and Event Tourism: Impacts, Plans and Opportunities*, edited by M. Robertson. Eastbourne: Leisure Studies Association, 17–42.

Jordan, R. 2002. Costly Crop Over clean-up. *Daily Nation*, June 12, A5.

Kaieteur News. 2004. Regional Govts. Set Up Committee for World Cup 2007. *Kaieteur News*, July 10. [Online] Available at: http://www.landofsixpeoples.com/gynewsjs.htm [accessed: March 10, 2005].

Katzel, C.T. 2007. *Event Greening: Is This Concept Providing a Serious Platform for Sustainability Best Practice*. A thesis submitted in partial fulfilment for the degree of Master of Philosophy Development Planning Sustainable Development at the University of Stellenbosch.

Kearney, A.T. 2005. *Building a Legacy: Sports Mega-Events Should Last a Lifetime*. Chicago, IL: AT Kearney Inc.

Keogh, B. 1990. Public Participation in Community Tourism Planning. *Annals of Tourism Research*, 17(3), 449–65.

Kessler, R. 2005. Sustainable Development: Empowering Indigenous Peoples. *Environmental Health Perspectives*, 113(9), A588–A588.

Kim, H.J., Gursoy, D. and Lee, S.B. 2006. The Impact of the 2000 World Cup on South Korea: Comparisons of Pre and Post Games. *Tourism Management*, 27(1), 86–96.

Kim, S.S. and Petrick, J.F. 2005. Residents' Perceptions on Impacts of the FIFA 2002 World Cup: The Case of Seoul as a Host City. *Tourism Management*, 26, 25–38.

King, T. and Laurie, P. 2004. *The Glory Days: 25 Great West Indian Cricketers*. Oxford: Macmillan Caribbean.

Kotas, R., Teare, R., Logie, J. and Jayawardena, B.J. 2001. *Hotel and Catering International Management Association Silver Anniversary Textbook.* Cassell, UK: The International Hospital Business.

Kotler, P., Bowen, J.T. and Makens, J.C. 1996. *Marketing for Hospitality and Tourism*. 1st Edition. Upper Saddle River, NJ: Prentice-Hall.

Lamon-Famaey, A. 1981. Some Social Aspects of Spectators of Sports Events. *International Review for the Sociology of Sport*, 87–96.

Lankford, S.V. 1994. Attitudes and Perceptions toward Tourism and Rural Regional Development. *Journal of Travel Research*, 33(4), 35–43.

Legacy Barbados (n.d.) *Legacy Barbados: The Legacy Vision for Barbados*. [Online]. Available at: http://www.totallybarbados.com/barbados/Barbados_News/Legacy_Vision_for_Barbados/ [accessed: December 20, 2008].

Lehto, X.Y., Morrison, A.M. and O'Leary, J.T. 2001. Does the Visiting Friends and Relatives' Typology Make a Difference? A Study of the International VFR Market to the US. *Journal of Travel Research*, 40(2), 201–12.

L.H. Consulting Limited and Associates. 2005. *Solid Waste Characterization Study Draft Final Report*. Sewerage and Solid Waste Project Unit, Ministry of Health, Barbados. Unpublished report.

Lindberg, K. and Johnson, R. 1997. Modelling Residents Attitudes toward Tourism. *Annals of Tourism Research*, 24(2), 402–24.

Liu, Z.H. 1994. Tourism Development—A Systems Analysis, in *Tourism State of the Art*, edited by C.L. Jenkins, R.C. Wood, P.U.C. Dieke, M.M. Bennett, L.R. MacLellan and R. Smith. Chichester: John Wiley & Sons Ltd.

Lloyd, C. 2006. Foreword, in *Wisden History of the Cricket World Cup*, edited by T. Cozier. Hampshire: John Wisden and Co. Ltd, 4–6.

Loveridge, A. 2008. Discussion on the Home Accommodation Programme. Personal communication, February 28, 2008.

Lush, W.M. 1985. Objective Assessment of Turf Cricket Pitches Using an Impact Hammer. *Journal of the Sports Turf Institute*, 61, 71–9.

Lynch-Foster, A. 2005. No Way to Nab Dirty Culprits. *Weekend Nation*, April 29, 7.

Madrigal, R. 1993. A Tale of Tourism in Two Cities. *Annals of Tourism Research*, 20, 336–53.

Majumdar, B. 2008. Nationalist Romance and Postcolonial Sport: Cricket in 2006 India, in *Cricket, Race and the 2007 World Cup*, edited by J. Gemmell and B. Majumdar. London: Routledge, 78–90.

Mallen, C. and Adams, L.J. 2008. *Sport, Recreation and Tourism Event Management: Theoretical and Practical Dimensions*. Oxford: Butterworth-Heinemann.

Manley, M. 1995. *A History of West Indies Cricket*. London: Andre Deutsch.

Marcelle, G. 2004. Mobilizing for Development: An E-Vision for ICC Cricket World Cup as a Lever. [Online]. Available at: http://www.caribank.org/events. nsf/ICCWorldCup?OpenPage.

Mason, P. 2003. *Tourism Impacts, Planning and Management*. Oxford: Elsevier Butterworth-Heinemann.

Masterman, G. 2004. *Strategic Sports Event Management*. Oxford: Elsevier Butterworth-Heinemann.

Matheson, V. and Baade, R. 2003. Mega-Sporting Events in Developing Nations: Playing the Way to Prosperity. [Online]. Available at: http://www.williams. edu/Economics/wp/mathesonprosperity.pdf. [accessed: September 10, 2008]. Unpublished paper presented at the 2002 Northeast Universities Development Consortium Conference.

McClean-Trotman, L. and Dabney, R. 2007. ICC Cricket World Cup 2007 Hits a Six for Children Affected by AIDS. [Online]. Available at: http://www.unicef. org/sport/index_39504.html.

McCree, R. 1995. *Professionalism and the Development of Club Football in Trinidad*. M.Sc. Thesis, University of the West Indies.

McElroy, J. 2004. Global Perspectives of Caribbean Tourism, in *Tourism in the Caribbean: Trends, Development and Prospect*, edited by D. Dual. London: Routledge, 39–58.

McIntyre, K. and McIntyre, D. 2001. *Cricket Wickets: Science v Fiction*. Australia: Horticultural Engineering Consultancy, 282.

McKercher, B. and Ho, P. 2006. Assessing the Tourism Potential of Smaller Cultural and Heritage Attractions. *Journal of Sustainable Tourism*, 14(5), 473–88.

McMahon-Beattie, U. and Yeoman, I. 2004. *Sport and Leisure Operations Management*. London: Thompson Learning, ix

Mihalik, B.J. and Simonetta, L. 1998. Resident Perceptions of the 1996 Summer Olympic Games–Year II. *Festival management and Event Tourism*, 5(1), 9–19.

Mohammed, F. 2005. Wake-up Call for Windies World Cup. *Trinidad Express*, July 8, 53.

Morrison, A.M., Hsieh, S. and O'Leary, J.T. 1995. Segmenting the Visiting Friends and Relatives Market by Holiday Activity Participation. *Journal of Tourism Studies*, 6(1), 48–63.

Mosse, D. 2001. People's Knowledge, Participation and Patronage: Operations and Representations in Rural Development, in *Participation: The New*

Tyranny?, edited by B. Cooke and U. Kothari. London: Zed Books Ltd, 16–35.

Mules, T. and Faulkner, B. 1996. An Economic Perspective on Special Events. *Tourism Economics*, 2(2), 107–17.

Murgatroyd, B. 2007. Cricket World Cup Set to Deliver 239m Profit in the Caribbean. [Online]. Available at: http://www.sportbusiness.com.

Murphy, P. 1985. *Tourism: A Community Approach*. London: Methuen.

Nation News 2007. Hugh CWC Benefits in Ten Years. [Online]. Available at: http://www.nationnews.com/story.

Nation Newspaper (2006) *Ambassador Wants Cricket on the Menu.*

Neuman, W.L. 2003. *Social Research Methods: Qualitative and Quantitative Approaches*. 5th Edition. Boston, MA: Allyn and Bacon.

Niaah, S.S. 2006. Kingston's Dancehall Spaces. *Jamaica Journal*, 29(3), 14–21.

Nikolai, T.A. 2005. *The Superintendent's Guide to Controlling Putting Green Speed*. Honoken, NJ: John Wiley & Sons, Inc., 148.

Noel, J. 2008. *Faith and Sports Tourism: Way Forward for Grenada*. [Online]. Available at: http://www.positivetourism.com/content/view.

Office of Travel and Tourism Industries. 2005. [Online]. Available at: http://tinet. ita.doc.gov.

O'Sullivan, T., Hartley, J., Saunders, D., Montgomery, M. and Fiske, J. 1994. *Key Concepts in Communication and Cultural Studies*. 2nd Edition. London: Routledge.

Order of Business of the Senate of Jamaica. 2009. Presentation of Bills: Private Members Motion. [Online]. Available at: http://www.japarliamenr.gov.jm [accessed: October 2, 2009].

Pal, A. 2006. Scope for Bottom-Up Planning in Kolkata: Rhetoric vs. Reality. *Environment and Urbanization*, 18(2), 501–21.

Patterson, O. 1995. The Ritual of Cricket, in *Liberation Cricket: West Indies Cricket Culture*, edited by H. Beckles and B. Stoddard. Manchester: Manchester University Press.

Pawson, M. and Buisseret, D. 2000. *Port Royal, Jamaica*. Kingston, Jamaica: University of the West Indies Press.

Pearce, D.G. and Butler, R. 1993. *Tourism Research: Critiques and Challenges*. London: Routledge.

Pearce, P.L., Moscardo, G. and Ross, G.F. 1996. *Tourism Community Relationships*. Oxford: Pergamon.

Pellegrino, G. and Hancock, H. 2010. *A Lasting Legacy: How Major Sporting Events can Drive Positive Change for Host Communities and Economies*. Deloitte Touche. [Online]. Available at: http://www.deloitte.com/assets/Dcom-Brazil/Local%20Assets/Documents/DeloitteOlympicsMajorEventsReport. pdf [accessed: January 2, 2010].

Pestano, C. 2003. Huge Economic Benefits for Hosts of World Cup 2007 Matches. *Stabroek News*, June 13. [Online]. Available at: http://www.landofsixpeoples. com/news304/ns3112310.htm [accessed: December 10, 2004].

Pires, B.C. 2007. Interview with ICC CEO Malcolm Speed. *Sunday Express*, 5.

Pizam, A. and Pokela, J. 1985. The Perceived Impacts of Casino Gambling on a Community. *Annals of Tourism Research*, 12(2), 147–65.

Planning Institute of Jamaica. 2007. *Economic and Social Survey Jamaica 2006*. Kingston, Jamaica: Planning Institute of Jamaica.

Potter, R., Binns, T., Elliot, J. and Smith, D. 2004. *Geographies of Development*. 2nd Edition. Harlow: Pearson Education Ltd.

Pretes, M. 2003. Tourism and Nationalism. *Annals of Tourism Research*, 30(1), 125–42.

Pugh, J. and Potter, R. 2003. *Participatory Planning in the Caribbean: Lessons from Practice*. Aldershot: Ashgate Publishing Limited.

Reece, T. 2005. Ambush Marketing…and the World Cup Cricket 2007. *Trinidad Express Business*, March 23, 13–14.

Reno, R., Cialdini, R. and Kallgren, C. 1993. The Transsituational Influence of Social Norms. *Journal of Personality and Social Psychology*, 64(1), 104–12.

Ritchie, J.R.B. 1984. Assessing the Impact of Hallmark Events: Conceptual and Research Issues. *Journal of Travel Research*, 22(1), 2–11.

Ritchie, B. and Adair, D. (eds) 2004. *Sport Tourism: Interrelationships, Impacts and Issues*. Clevedon and New York: Multilingual Matters Ltd.

Ritchie, B. 1988. Assessing the Impact of Hallmark Events: Conceptual and Research Issues. *Journal of Travel Research*, 23(1), 2–11.

Ritchie, J.R.B. and Lyons, M.M. 1987. Olympics III/Olympuse IV: A mid-term Report on Resident Attitudes Concerning the XV Olympic Winter Games. *Journal of Travel Research*, 26(1), 18–26.

Ritchie, J.R.B. and Aitken, C.E. 1984. Assessing the Impacts of the 1988 Olympic Winter Games: The Research Program and Initial Results. *Journal of Travel Research*, 22(3), 17–25.

Ritzer, G. (ed.) 2002. *McDonaldization: The Reader*. Thousand Oaks, CA: Pine Forge Press.

Rivenburgh, N., Louw, E., Loo, E. and Mersham, G. 2004. *The Sydney Olympics and Foreign Attitudes Towards Australia*. Gold Coast, Australia: Cooperative Research Centre for Sustainable Tourism.

Roberts, K. 2004. *The Leisure Industries*. London: Palgrave.

Roche, M. 1994. Mega-events and Urban Policy. *Annals of Tourism Research*, 21(1), 1–19.

Rogerson, C.M. 2004. Transforming the South African Tourism Industry: The Emerging Black-owned Bed and Breakfast Economy. *GeoJournal*, 60(3), 273–81.

Rohler, G. 1994. Music, Literature, and West Indies Cricket Values, in *An Area of Conquest: Popular Democracy and West Indies Cricket Supremacy*, edited by H. Beckles. Kingston, Jamaica: Ian Randle Publishers.

Roper, T. 2006. Producing Environmentally Sustainable Olympic Games and 'Greening' Major Public Events. *Global Urban Development Magazine*, 2(1).

Rousseau, P. 2007. Beaming Dehring in Seventh Heaven. *Sunday Gleaner*, February 25.

Ryan, C. 1994. Leisure and Tourism—The Application of Leisure Concepts to Tourist Behaviour—A Proposed Model, in *Tourism the State of the Art*, edited by C.L. Jenkins, R.C. Wood, P.U.C. Dieke, M.M. Bennett, L.R. MacLellan and R. Smith. Chichester: John Wiley & Sons.

Ryan, C. and Montgomery, D. 1994. The Attitudes of Bakewell Residents to Tourism and Issues in Community Responsive Tourism. *Tourism Management*, 15(5), 358–69.

Sandiford, K. 2004. Apocalypse? The Rise and Fall of the West Indies, in *Cricketing Cultures in Conflict: World Cup 2003*, edited by B. Majumdar and J.A. Mangan. London: Routledge, 82–98.

Schneider, T. 2010. The Legacy of Hosting Sporting Events. *Sports Travel Magazine*, February 2010. [Online]. Available at: http://www.schneiderpublishing.com/blog/category/publishers-updates/ [accessed: April 1, 2010].

Schnelle, J., McNees, P., Thomas, M., Gendrich, J. and Beagle, G. 1980. Prompting Behaviour Change in the Community: Use of Mass Media Techniques. *Environment and Behavior*, 12(2), 157–66.

Scholl, R. 2002. *Attitudes and Attitude Change*. [Online]. Available at: http://www.cba.uri.edu/scholl [accessed: February 23, 2007].

Scott, A.K.S. and Turco, D.M. 2007. VFRs as a Segment of the Sport Event Tourist Market. *Journal of Sport and Tourism*, 12(1), 41–52.

Scotia Economic Reports. 2007. *Cricket World Cup Delivering an 'All Rounder' to West Indies Economies says Scotia Economics*. [Online April 20, Toronto: CNW]. Available at: http://www. newswire.ca/en/releases/archive/April 2007.

Scotiabank. 2007. *Report: Cricket and Economics*. [Online, Scotiabank]. Available at: http://www.scotiacapital.com/English/bns_econ/special0420.pdf [accessed: January 28, 2008].

Seaton, A.V. and Tagg, S. 1995. Disaggregating Friends and Relatives in VFR Tourism Research: The Northern Ireland Evidence 1991–1993. *Journal of Tourism Studies*, 6(1), 6–18.

Seaton, A.V. 1994. Are Relatives Friends? Reassessing the VFR Category in Segmenting Tourism Markets, in *Tourism the State of the Art*, edited by C.L. Jenkins, R.C. Wood, P.U.C. Dieke, M.M. Bennett, L.R. MacLellan and R. Smith. Chichester: John Wiley & Sons.

Seton-Watson, H. 1982. The History of Nations. *Times Literary Supplement*, August 27.

Sewerage and Solid Waste Project Unit. 2000. *The Solid Waste Management Programme*. Sewerage and Solid Waste Project Unit, Ministry of Health, Barbados.

Shekhawat, B. 2006a. India Should Step up Investment in the Caribbean. *Caribbean Business Club*. [Online]. Available at: http://www.caribbeanbusinessclub.com [accessed: November 14, 2006].

Sheringham, S. 2007. Chinese Invade the Caribbean in an Attempt to Isolate Taiwan. *Taipei Times*, March 11, 9. Available at: http://www.taipeitimes.com/ News/editorials/archives/2007/03/11/2003351858.

Shone, A. and Parry, B. 2004. *Successful Event Management*. 2nd Edition. London: Thomson.

aechnology.com 2004, *Case Study: Canadian Technology Utilized to Attract Sports Events*.

Soutar, G. and McLeod, P.B. 1993. Residents' Perceptions on Impact of the America's Cup. *Annals of Tourism Research*, 20, 571–82.

Spooner, P. 2003. $40 million Asia Hit for Windies. *Guyana Chronicle*, July 4. [Online]. Available at: http://www.landofsixpeoples.com/gynewsjs.htm [accessed: December 11, 2004].

Springer, B. 2006. CWC 2007 and Return on Investment. *Caribbean Business Enterprise Trust Inc*, May 21. [Online]. Available at: http://www.cbetmodel. org/business-articles-details.cfm?pluginState=Details&newsID=105 [accessed: April 12, 2010].

St. Pierre, M. 1995. West Indian Cricket, Part II: An Aspect of Creolization, in *Liberation Cricket: West Indies Cricket Culture*, edited by H. Beckles and B. Stoddard. Manchester: Manchester University Press.

Stabroek News. 2008. CWC 2007 Nets an Overall Profit of US$53.9M. [Online]. Available at: http://www.stabroeknews.com.

Stabroek News. 2004. Regional Intelligence Network Highest Priority – CARICOM Crime Meeting, March 6. [Online]. Available at: http://www. landofsixpeoples.com/gynewsjs.htm [accessed: April 5, 2005].

Stabroek News. 2003. Banks Urged to Help Caribbean Businesses Benefit from ICC CWC 2007, December 4. [Online]. Available at: http://www. landofsixpeoples.com/gynewsjs.htm [accessed: June 5, 2005].

Stabroek News. 2002. 2007 World Cup Cricket to Test Single Market – Carrington, July19. [Online]. Available at http://www.landofsixpeoples. com/gynewsjs.htm [accessed: 5 June 5, 2005].

Statistical Institute of Jamaica (STATIN). 2003. *Population Census 2001, Jamaica Volume 1: Country Report*. Kingston, Jamaica: STATIN.

Stewart, V.I. and Adams, W.A. 1968. County Cricket Wickets. *Journal of the Sports Turf Institute*, 44, 49–60.

Street, C. 2005. A Closer Look at World Cup 2007. *Trinidad Express Business*, July 27, 4–5.

Sunday Gleaner. 2007a. CWC Was No Help to Tourism Figures, November 4.

Sunday Gleaner. 2007b. Cricket World Cup Legacy: Investments Coming, November 4.

Tainton, N. and Klug, J. 2002. *The Cricket Pitch and its Outfield*. South Africa: University of Natal Press, 175.

Tang, Q. and Turco, D.M. 2001. A Profile of High-value Event Tourists. *Journal of Convention and Exhibition Management*, 3(2), 33–40.

Taylor, M. and Edmondson, I. 2007. Major Sporting Events: Planning for Legacy. *Proceedings of the Institution of Civil Engineers: Municipal Engineer*, 160(4), 171–76.

Thomas, K. 2008. For Many Olympic Families, the Dream is Proving Costly. *The New York Times*, May 21. [Online]. Available at: http://www.nytimes.com.

Thrane, C. 2001. Sport Spectatorship in Scandinavia: A Class Phenomenon? *International Review for the Sociology of Sport*, 36(2), 149–63.

Timothy, D. 2002. Tourism and Community Development, in *Tourism and Development: Concepts and Issues*, edited by R. Sharpley and D.J. Telfer. Clevedon, Bristol: Channel View Publication.

Timothy, D. 1999. Participatory Planning: A View of Tourism in Indonesia. *Annals of Tourism Research*, 26(2), 371–91.

Tomlinson, A. 2004. Pierre Bourdieu and the Sociological Study of Sport, in *Sport and Modern Social Theorist*, edited by R. Giulianotti. New York: Palgrave Macmillan.

Tosun, C. 2004. Stages in the Emergence of a Participatory Tourism Development Approach in the Developing World. *Geoforum*, 36, 333–52.

Tosun, C. 2000. Limits to Community Participation in he Tourism Development Process in Developing Countries. *Tourism Management*, 21, 613–33.

Totallybarbados.com. 2007. Barbados Island Guide.

Trail, G.T., Fink, J.S. and Anderson, D.F. 2003. Sport Spectator Consumption Behavior. *Sport Marketing Quarterly*, 12(1), 8–17.

Trinidad Express. 2004. Caribbean Leaders Pleased with ICC Decision on World Cup Venues, *Trinidad Express*, July 7, 76.

Trinidad News Chronicles. 2007. ICC Cricket World Cup 2007: Opening New Market. *Trinidad News Chronicles*, April 10.

Turco, D., Shamir, A. and Cox, M. 2007. Globalization, Sport and Tourism: The Case of the 2007 Cricket World Cup in Guyana. *Proceedings of the Globalization and Performance in the European Tourism Industry Conference.* Burcharest: Romanian American University.

Turco, D.M. 2005. *Sport Tourism as a Strategy for Sustainable Development: Issues, Impacts, and Implications.* Presented at the Globalization and Sustainable Development International Scientific Conference, October 22, 2005, Gyor, Hungary.

Turco, D.M., Riley, R. and Swart, K. 2002. *Sport Tourism.* Warrington, WV. Fitness Information Technology, Inc.

Tyson, B., Hayle, C., Truly, D., Jordan, L.A. and Thame, M. 2005. West Indies Cup Cricket: Hallmark Events as Catalysts for Community Tourism Development. *Journal of Sport and Tourism*, 10(4), 323–34.

UN News Centre. 2008. *UN Group Meets to Promote Sports for Peace and Development.* [Online]. Available at: http://www.un.org.

United Nations Code of Ethics for Tourism. [Online]. Available at: http://www.tourism.it/nsv/engl/Codigo_tico_Ing.pdf.

United Nations Economic and Social Council. 1998. *Promoting Social Integration and Participation of all People, including Disadvantaged and Vulnerable Groups and Persons*. [Online]. Available at: http://www.un.org/esa/socdev/docs/csd36e2.pdf [accessed: April 8, 2008].

United Nations, Millennium Development Goals. [Online]. Available at: http://www.un.org/milleniuum.

Urry, J. 2003. The Sociology of Tourism, in *Aspects of Tourism: Classic Reviews in Tourism*, edited by C. Cooper. Clevedon, Bristol: Channel View Publication.

US Department of Commerce, ITA, Office of Travel and Tourism Industries (OTTI), Bureau of Economic Analysis, and Travel Industry Association of America (TIA), June 2005. [Online]. Available at: http://www.tinet.ita.doc.gov.

UWI. 2006. *Chillings*. Oct/Nov 2006.

UWI. 2003. Departmental Reports 2002–2003. The University of the West Indies, Cave Hill, Barbados, 392.

Valayer, D. 1999. The Human Dimension of an Expanding Sector. *The Courier*, 175, 47.

Van Vugt, M. 1998. The Conflicts in Modern Society. *The Psychologist*, 11, 289–92.

Vice, T. 2005. Much Talk, Little Action as 2007 World Cup Looms. *Trinidad Sunday Express*, May 8, 65.

Vincent, M., Milne, S. and Sarigollu, E. 1998. Changing Tourist Profiles for Grenada: Evidence from 1988 and 1992. *Journal of International Consumer Marketing*, 10(3), 63–83.

Waitt, G. 2003. Social Impacts of the Sydney Olympics. *Annals of Tourism Research*, 30(1), 194–215.

Waters, A. 2003. Heritage Tourism Development and Unofficial History in Port Royal, Jamaica. *Social and Economic Studies*, 52(2)1, 27.

Waters, A. 2006. *Planning the Past: Heritage Tourism and Post-Colonial Politics at Port Royal*. Oxford: Rowan and Littlefield Publishers.

Weaver, D. 2001. Mass Tourism and Alternative Tourism in the Caribbean, in *Tourism and the Less Developed World: Issues and Case studies*, edited by D. Harrison. Wallingford: CABI International, 161–87.

Weaver, D.B. and Lawton, L.J. 2001. Resident Perceptions in the Urban-Rural Fringe. *Annals of Tourism Research*, 28(2), 439–58.

Williams, J. and Lawson, R. 2001. Community Issues and Resident Opinion of Tourism. *Annals of Tourism Research*, 28(2), 269–90.

Weed, M. 2006. Sports Tourism, in *The Business of Tourism Management*, edited by J. Beech and S. Chadwick. Harlow: Pearson Education Limited, 305–20.

Weed and Bull 1999 cited by Dean and Callannan 2004. Sports Tourism in the UK: Policy and Practice. Sports Tourism, in *Interrelationships Impact and Issues*, edited by B.W. Ritchie and D. Adair. Clevedon, Bristol: Channel View Publication.

West Indies Cricket Board (WICB). 2007. Government Receive Interim Payment of CWC 2007 Profits. [Online]. Available at: www.windiescricket.com. [accessed: July 18, 2007].

West Indies Cricket Board (WICB). 2005a. ICC Cricket World Cup West Indies 2007 Inc. to Short-list Tour, Travel and Hospitality Bidders. April 6. [Online]. Available at: http://windiescricket.com/article [accessed: June 16, 2005].

West Indies Cricket Board (WICB). 2005b. ICC Cricket World Cup Official Tour Operator Selected. June 21. [Online]. Available at: http://windiescricket.com/article [accessed: June 25, 2005].

West Indies Cricket Board (WICB). 2005c. US$100 Million Insurance Coverage for 2007 World Cup. May 7. [Online]. Available at: http://windiescricket.com/article [accessed: June 23, 2005].

West Indies Cricket Board (WICB). 2005d. Q and A with Chris Dehring on Venues for ICC Cricket World Cup 2007. March 21. [Online]. Available at: http://windiescricket.com/article [accessed: June 16, 2005].

West Indies Cricket Board (WICB). 2004a. WICB President Predicts 2007 will be Best Ever World Cup. June 6. [Online]. Available at: http://windiescricket.com/article [accessed: June 15, 2005].

West Indies Cricket Board (WICB). 2004b. Cricket World Cup Bid opens February 19, WICB, 16 February. [Online]. Available at: http://windiescricket.com/article [accessed: June 15, 2005].

West Indies Cricket Board (WICB). 2004c. ICC World Cup Windies 2007 Bid Books Delivered. February 21. [Online]. Available at: http://windiescricket.com/article [accessed: June 15, 2005].

West Indies Cricket Board (WICB). 2004d. St. Kitts/Nevis Submit Letter of Intent for 2007 World Cup. March 10. [Online]. Available at: http://windiescricket.com/article [accessed: June 15, 2005].

West Indies Cricket Board (WICB). 2004e. Separate Groups for Windies, Aussie, Indians, English at 2007 World Cup. February 21. [Online]. Available at: http://windiescricket.com/article [accessed: June 15, 2005].

West Indies Cricket Board (WICB). 2004f. Report on 2007 World Cup Accommodation, Transportation by August. March 30. [Online]. Available at: http://windiescricket.com/article [accessed: June 15, 2005].

West Indies Cricket Board (WICB) 2004g. It's Barbados!! ICC World Cup West Indies 2007. [Online]. Available at: http://windiescricket.com/article [accessed: June 16, 2005].

West Indies Cricket Board (WICB) 2003a. T&T Airport Expresses Regret Over Australian Gear Theft. June 6. [Online]. Available at: http://windiescricket.com/article [accessed: June 30, 2005].

West Indies Cricket Board (WICB) 2003b. Barbados Confirms Kensington for World Cup Bid. January 4. [Online]. Available at: http://windiescricket.com/article [accessed: November 23, 2004].

West Indies Cricket Board (WICB). 2002a. World Cup 2007: Business Opportunities for the Private Sector – Part III. December 1. [Online]. Available at: http://windiescricket.com/article [accessed: November 23, 2004].

West Indies Cricket Board (WICB). 2002b. World Cup 2007: Business Opportunities for the Private Sector – Part I. December 1. [Online]. Available at: http://windiescricket.com/article [accessed: November 23, 2004].

West Indies Cricket Board (WICB). 2002c. World Cup 2007: Business Opportunities for the Private Sector – Part II. December 8. [Online]. Available at: http://windiescricket.com/article [accessed: November 23, 2004].

West Indies Cricket Board (WICB). 2002. World Cup 2007: Business Opportunities for the Private Sector – Part III. December 1. [Online] Available at: http://windiescricket.com/article [accessed: November 23, 2004].

White, P. and Wilson, B. 1999. Distinction in the Stands: An Investigation of Bourdieu's "Habitus", Socioeconomic Status and Sport Spectatorship in Canada. *International Review for the Sociology of Sport*, 34(3), 254–64.

Wickham, M. 2006. Party's Over, but East Coast Still a Mess. *Daily Nation*, August 3, A4

Wilkinson, B. 2004. Caribbean Governments Bail out Airline Again. *New York Amsterdam News*, July 22, 95(30). [Online]. Available at: http://web11.epnet.com [accessed: February 3, 2005].

Wilkinson, P.F. 1997. *Tourism Policy and Planning: Case Studies from the Commonwealth Caribbean.* New York: Cognizant Communication Corporation, 162.

Williams, C. 2004. T&T to spend $140m on World Cup. *Trinidad Express*, July 9, 86.

Williams, J. and Lawson, R. 2001. Community Issues and Resident Opinion of Tourism. *Annals of Tourism Research*, 28(2), 269–90.

Woods, B. 2007. *Social Issues in Sport.* Champaign: Human Kinetics.

Woodward, I. 1998. *Aussies versus Windies: A History of Australia-West Indies Cricket.* Petersham, NSW: Walla Walla Press.

World Cup St. Lucia (WCSL). 2004. The Saint Lucia Bid for Cricket World Cup West Indies – 2007. [Online]. Available at: http://windiescricket.com [accessed: May 10, 2005].

Xavier, F. 2002. *Standards for Sustainable Tourism for the Purpose of Multilateral Trade Negotiations.* Leeds Metropolitan University, United Kingdom. [Online]. Available at: http://www.rainforest-alliance.org/programs/sv/stcs-gats-standards.pdf.

Yelvington, K. 1995. Ethnicity "Not Out": The Indian Cricket Tour of the West Indies and the 1976 Elections in Trinidad and Tobago, in *Liberation Cricket: West Indies Cricket Culture*, edited by H. Beckles. Manchester: Manchester University Press.

Yew, W. 1996. *The Olympic Image: The First 100 Years.* Alberta: Quon Editions.

Index

For Product Safety Concerns and Information please contact our
EU representative GPSR@taylorandfrancis.com Taylor & Francis
Verlag GmbH, Kaufingerstraße 24, 80331 München, Germany